Trinity and Monotheism
A historical and theological review of the origins and substance of the doctrine

A. Keith Thompson

Modotti Press

Published in 2019 by Connor Court Publishing Pty Ltd under the Modotti Press Imprint.

Copyright © A. Keith Thompson 2019

All rights reserved. No part of this book may be reproduced or transmitted in any form or by any means, electronic or mechanical, including photocopying, recording or by any information storage and retrieval system, without prior permission in writing from the publisher.

Connor Court Publishing Pty Ltd
PO Box 7257
Redland Bay QLD 4165
sales@connorcourt.com
Web: www.connorcourtpublishing.com.au

ISBN 9781925826630

Printed in Australia

Cover Picture: The Doubting Thomas by Carl Heinrich Bloch, Wikipedia Commons

TABLE OF CONTENTS

Foreword – Professor Gary Doxey   1
Personal Introduction   7

1	**Where did the 'one God' idea come from?**	13
	Introduction	13
	Israelite theology	15
	Part One – Israel's God is a man	15
	Sommer's scriptural evidence for God's body	20
	Part Two – The Divine Council in Hebrew theology	23
	Conclusion – Traditional Jewish history and theology	26
2	**When and why did the Jews become monotheists?**	29
	Introduction	29
	Part One – The Demise of Divine Council Theology	30
	Aniconism	30
	The religious policies of the superpowers in the late first millennium	33
	The Persians – inclusive monotheism	33
	The Greeks and Romans – cultural toleration and homogenisation	35
	Summary of this review of the history of Jewish Theology	37
	Part Two - Jewish theology at the time of Christ	37
	Talmudic evidence	39
	Rebuttal of the dualism of God in the Jerusalem Talmud	40
	Conclusion	42
3	**Christians as Jewish heretics**	
	– the origins of the idea of Trinity	43
	Introduction	43
	Part One – Early conflict between Christians and Jews	45
	Theological battle lines	47
	Part Two – Development of the idea of Trinity	50
	Justin Martyr	50
	To the Romans	51
	To the Jews	52
	Theophilus	55
	Clement of Alexandria	57
	Part Three – Tertullian and Origen	61
	Tertullian	61
	Tertullian's Trinitarianism	63

	Origen	71
	Part Four - Other Ante-Nicene theologians	75
	Conclusion	80

4	**Why the Nicene Council and what did it decide?**	**83**
	Introduction	83
	Part One – The history and politics surrounding Nicaea	85
	Part Two – Constantine's unity agenda	86
	The Council of Nicaea – attendance	90
	Part Three – The Council of Nicaea – methodology	92
	The deliberation concerning Christology	94
	Part Four – The *homoousios* idea	96
	Part Five – Consensus?	100
	Conclusion	102

5	**What the Nicene Creed says and what it means**	**105**
	Introduction	105
	Part One – The Nicene theological argument in its fourth century context	106
	The key theological question at Nicaea	106
	Part Two – The Nicene Creed	110
	Part Three – What did those attending mean by the words they used?	115
	Conclusion	115

6	**How the idea of Trinity was developed in Western Christian theology after Nicaea until the Reformation**	**117**
	Introduction	117
	Part One – The immediate aftermath of the Nicene Creed	118
	Part Two – The Nicene theology after the Council	119
	Part Three – The Trinity doctrine from the Council of Serdica (342 A.D.) to the Protestant Reformation	121
	The Athanasian Creed	129
	The filioque clause and the schism between East and West	131
	Conclusion	133

7	**How Protestant Christianity contributed to the theology of the Trinity**	**135**
	Introduction	135
	Part One - The Protestant Reformation in England	136
	The Nicene Creed – Original 325 A.D. version	140
	The Nicene Creed – Constantinople 381 A.D. version	140
	The Athanasian Creed	141
	The Apostle's Creed	143

Part Two - Michael Servetus		145
Servetus on the Trinity		147
Conclusion		151
8	**Non-Trinitarian Christians in the twenty-first century?**	**153**
	Introduction	153
	Part One – Modern criticisms of Nicene theology	155
	The Unitarian view of Christ	158
	Part Two – The Latter-day Saint view of Christ	159
	Part Three – The Jehovah's Witness view of Christ	163
	Conclusion	167
9	**What can Constantine's encompassing theological vision teach modern Christianity?**	**171**
	Introduction	171
	Part One – Monotheism and Judaism	173
	Part Two – Jewish doctrinal criticism of Christianity and the Christian response	175
	Part Three - Trinitarian theology after Nicaea, the 'schism' and modern challenges to Trinitarian 'orthodoxy'	177
	Part Four – Constantine's unity agenda	179
	Part Five – Religious 'otherness'	181
	Conclusion	183

Appendix - Constantine's letter to Alexander, Bishop of Alexandria and Arius, one of his presbyters	185
Bibliography	**191**
Index	**203**

FOREWORD

It is difficult to imagine anything more universally significant than the quest to understand the true nature of God. This book offers a perspective relevant to that quest; but to be precise, it does not pretend to answer the main question—a subject obviously beyond the scope of scholarly inquiry. Rather, author Keith Thompson urges greater respect and inclusiveness among followers of the various faith traditions rooted in the Christian bible. He concludes in the end that their respective views about the nature of God have been unnecessarily divisive and actually share more in common than previously supposed.

This unusual and engaging book invites reflection. It is not really a philosophical piece or even exactly a theological one. True to his professional experience as a lawyer and law professor, Thompson has written a book more in the style of an extended legal brief. It has clearly outlined and well-organized arguments, with documented "evidence" to accompany them. Rather than tendentiously seeking to prove a point as one might in a legal brief, however, Thompson illustrates and explains. The tone is far removed from arrogance and insistence. From the author's "personal introduction" through the final chapter and conclusion, Keith Thompson's sincerity and good will are overflowing. His points are well-thought-out and carefully researched; his insights are original and thought-provoking; and his perspectives are respectful and unabashedly personal.

The unlikely premise for Thompson's plea for greater understanding among believers is found in the historical evolution of the doctrine of the Holy Trinity announced at the seminal Council of Nicaea in 325. To casual observers interpreting the events by modern lights, the Council of Nicaea and the other "ecumenical" councils of Late Antiquity may seem ironically labelled. Many could say that instead of unifying the Church, Nicaea and subsequent councils, by their insistence on a single declared belief, actually contributed to discord and division.

Broad agreement on the true nature of God is certainly not our present-day reality. Even anciently, agreement remained elusive after the dust settled at Nicaea. Constantine had convoked the council in an effort to reconcile differing views, but it fell short of that goal. Participants retained their disparate views well after the council's conclusion, and the winning faction declared anathema upon the losers. Further, western Christendom was barely cognizant of the doctrines from Nicaea until quite a bit later. Predominant majority support for the position announced in the Nicene Creed developed only over an extended period and through influences that had at least as much to do with political power as they did with theology.

Such is a common interpretation of the events from a present-day perspective. With great originality, Keith Thompson gives a different interpretation. Setting forth numerous arguments, he suggests that the Nicene Creed is, in point of fact, rightly considered a symbol of unity—and not because everyone was (or is) in agreement. It was intended to represent, and was written in terms consistent with, a broadly accommodating understanding of the Trinity, one that was meant to leave room for unresolved questions and differing opinions among Christian believers. It was not intended as a litmus test for identifying and flushing nonconforming believers to the fringes, much less separating them from the Church.

Constantine's overriding agenda at the Council of Nicaea was unity—unity for the empire and all Christendom. To this agenda, according to Thompson, the resulting formula of the Nicene Creed was made to bend. "Constantine saw to it that the resulting creed was ambiguous—abstracted to a level of generality that would allow agreement by all...."[1] Constantine sought to obtain unity by glossing over technicalities on which the attendees could not agree, and which he thought were, in any case, probably beyond human capacity to ascertain fully.

Thompson sees the creed as an example of Constantine's statesmanship and respect for a degree of pluralism among Christian believers in the name of unity of the whole. This is a unique and optimistic proposition. It is a far cry from the image modern critics have of Roman Caesaropapism:

---

[1] Above 182.

heavy-handed imperial intervention in religion in order to enforce the ideological loyalty of subjects and quash rivals. Thompson's perspective is more in keeping with an earlier Roman attitude rosily described by Gibbon as "the mild spirit of antiquity," a time when "nations were less attentive to the difference than to the resemblance of their religious worship."[2]

To make his point, Thompson outlines a long history of Judeo-Christian belief about God. Among other things, he traces how early Hebrew religion was not strictly monotheistic in the modern sense. The Israelite God appears in early times to have been anthropomorphic, a being who presided over a Divine Council of divine anthropomorphic beings. Emphasis on the One God, with consequent sublimation of the Divine Council and related beliefs, was a defensive response to the cultural ascendency of Greek and Roman overlords—a way to distinguish and protect Jewish belief in a Supreme Being from sliding toward syncretistic confusion with the Greek and Roman pantheon.

According to Thompson, early Christian theological attempts to explain the divinity of Jesus Christ as the Son of God in the face of Jewish criticism led eventually to the elaboration of the doctrine of the Holy Trinity. Jews criticized Christians as blasphemous polytheists because they worshipped the Father *and* Jesus Christ. At some length, Thompson elucidates a succession of textual formulae developed by theological commentators in antiquity. These statements belie some degree of early uncertainty about the true nature of and exact relationship between Father and Son. In time, the prevailing formula is that of the Nicene Creed. Thompson argues that in its historical context, this creed was broad enough to encompass competing views in the eastern Church. It took time for western Christendom to recognize the creed and subsequent iterations as authoritative.

In the centuries following Nicaea, two significant accretions found their way into the doctrine of the Trinity, as it is followed in the West. Each has contributed to division among Christian denominations. The first was the addition of *filioque* ("and the Son") to the creedal formula under the influence of Augustine. This is the idea that the Holy Spirit

---

[2] Edward Gibbon, *The Decline and Fall of the Roman Empire*, Vol. 1, Ch. 2. (1776).

emanates from the Father "and the Son." Eastern Christians, in contrast, insisted on the earlier formula stating that the Holy Ghost emanates from the Father, a point that eventually sealed the divide between East and West in the Great Schism of 1054. The second accretion is the Anglican doctrine propounded during the Reformation by Archbishop of Canterbury Thomas Cranmer that God is "without body, parts, or passions." This statement was eventually incorporated into the Westminster Confession of Faith of 1646 and became the basis not only for Anglican but for Baptist, Congregationalist, and Methodist theology. Other protestant groups accepted the incorporeality of God but rejected the idea that God is without passion.

Despite these two western additions to the doctrine of the Trinity, almost the whole of Christendom has accepted the basic formula declared at Nicaea. But what of the outliers, those who believe firmly in Father, Son, and Holy Ghost but who do not describe God entirely in harmony with the creedal view of the Trinity?

The arc of Thompson's analysis flows naturally toward this question, which he answers with characteristic humanity. Thompson considers three principal groups of self-described Christians who have been variously criticized, excluded, and even persecuted by other Christians because of differences in belief about the Trinity: classical Unitarians, members of The Church of Jesus Christ of Latter-day Saints, and Jehovah's Witnesses.[3] The upshot is that the original and unmodified Nicene Creed, when understood in context, is more accommodating of these groups' views than many may have thought—even if not entirely so. Thompson makes no claim to be able to reconcile such differences as exist in Trinitarian and non-Trinitarian Christian views of God, but he calls for us to finally recognize the silliness of stumbling over whether a self-described Christian is or is not a Christian based on an unwarrantedly narrow reading of the Nicene Creed.

The way in which believers in the Judeo-Christian traditions have described the nature of God has evolved over time, which says something about the imprecision of the exercise. Ultimate clarity on this subject is a matter of revelation and not theological argument. In the spirit

---

[3] Thompson concedes that modern Unitarians, as opposed to classical Unitarians, are not prone to consider themselves Christians in the traditional sense.

of Constantine's goal of inclusion and unity at the Council of Nicaea, Thompson asks us to rise to a higher level of respect and inclusion. "Our human tendency," he notes, "to characterize those we do not know as 'others,' can be separated from the truth claims we make about each other's beliefs."[4] Important differences in doctrine exist, but "religious liberty, tolerance, and respect coupled with the history [Thompson has] outlined provide the framework from which greater unity among Christians can be found."[5]

Regardless of where one stands on the doctrine of the Holy Trinity, its evolution, and context, the increase in mutual understanding and respect that Keith Thompson encourages is something we all should seek.

-- Gary Doxey, PhD, JD, International Center for Law and Religion Studies, Brigham Young University

---

[4] Above 183.
[5] Ibid.

PERSONAL INTRODUCTION

This book rejects the idea that human beings can only know anything by their five physical senses. This book is written for people who either know or believe in God and who also know or believe that Jesus Christ is his Son and was sent to earth as a child born of Mary to redeem the world. I do not mind if non-believers read it. I do not mind if they criticise it for perceived irrationality. But it is written for those who either know or believe in Jesus Christ.

My friend Paul Morris peer reviewed an early draft of this book for me. Paul is a practising Jew who has been the Programme Director for Religious Studies at Victoria University Wellington New Zealand, for more than 20 years.

One of Paul's recommendations was that I need to state from the outset why I have written it. He said that I need to be transparent if I am to achieve my personal objective. My friend Michael Quinlan, who is also my Dean in the Law School at The University of Notre Dame Australia's Sydney Law School, has made a similar recommendation. Michael has suggested I should set out some of the contemporary conflicts that exist within contemporary Christianity because of the Trinity doctrine. He has suggested that as "a mysterious community demonstrative of how God's perfect love" should be lived, many mainstream Christians do not perceive any tension in underlying Trinity theology.

I recognise their wisdom. In particular I recognise that no one can write anything that is truly unbiased. That is because we are all the autobiographical products of our life experiences. To answer Paul's recommendation, I must record some of mine.

I am a practising member of The Church of Jesus Christ of Latter-day Saint (LDS), and have served in that Church in many lay offices including as a Bishop, a Stake President and as a Mission President. I also worked as a paid LDS Church employee for twenty years. During that term I served as International Legal Counsel for the Church in the Pacific and then through the African continent. Because of a personal interest, at the time of this writing, I have been serving as the LDS Church's lay Australian Interfaith Director for six years. But that is not the entire story of my personal faith journey nor of my reason for writing this book. For context, I must add that I was born an Anglican and was christened in St Paul's Church at the Octagon in Dunedin, New Zealand. My parents joined the LDS Church when I was six years old and I had a personal conversion experience of my own when I was sixteen before breaking my legal studies at the age of eighteen to serve a full-time, two year volunteer LDS mission. I have also worked for The University of Notre Dame Australia's Sydney School of Law as a teacher and Associate Dean since 2012 – seven years as of this writing.

My current LDS volunteer work as Australian Interfaith Director has enabled me to follow my passion and build bridges of understanding with many other people of faith in Australia and internationally. In particular, I serve as the Secretary of SEIROS, an interfaith research think tank based in Sydney, Australia which has a brief to Study the Economic Impact of Religion on (Australian) Society. That service has given me the opportunity to develop my interfaith friendships well beyond the confines of traditional Christianity. I work closely with fellow Board members from Judaism, the Buddhist tradition, the Baha'i faith and Islam as well as representatives of the Catholic, Anglican, Methodist, Uniting, Hillsong, Seventh Day Adventist and Baptist churches from Christianity.

Many spiritual experiences have informed my faith, two deserve special mention in the current context.

First, when I was eleven years old and living in Invercargill, New Zealand, I was excused for two years from attendance at a compulsory religious education class at my Intermediate School because I disagreed with the Anglican minister who taught that class about the Trinity. I acknowledge that my understanding of the doctrine was not well formed at that time, but it was clear that our disagreement was not going to help either of us.

Secondly, in 2012, I was invited by John Cleary of the Australian Broadcasting Corporation, to answer questions on his Evenings Show about Mitt Romney's LDS faith during the US presidential election campaign that year. John Dickson of the Centre for Public Christianity was also invited to join the program. Despite my suggestion that LDS Christianity had much commonality with John Dickson's Protestant Christian faith, he was emphatic and unoriginal in repeating the refrain that Mormons were not Christians because they did not subscribe to the Nicene creed. I have since agreed with my friend Mariusz Biliniewicz in the School of Philosophy and Theology at Notre Dame in Sydney, that the Christianity label must involve some doctrinal content. I agree with that general proposition since I would not consider myself a Christian if I lived my life according to Christian ethics even though I did not accept Jesus Christ as God's son and the redeemer of the world. But I do not accept John Dickson's view that Tertullian would disagree with my personal theology of God.

My purpose in writing this monograph is to actively build bridges of understanding. I know that what I have written will not please everybody. While 'pleasing everybody' is not my purpose, I do not wish to fight with anyone who disagrees with me. What I seek again is to build bridges of understanding. I have sought and still seek to better understand God and Christ in this process. I have recorded what I have learned, and some of what I feel, in the sincere hope that everyone who reads will understand Christian theologies better or will be led by reading what I have written to further study that will help them understand those theologies better. I hope that genuine points of difference and similarity will be recognised even though they cannot all be right. But I have a further hope when the disagreements are recognised.

I believe in freedom of conscience. I think that ideal is well expressed in Article 18 of the *International Covenant on Civil and Political Rights* (ICCPR). There the idea is that conscience itself is non-derogable - that no government or person should seek to identify what an individual human being believes so as to coerce that person in any way. I believe that such coercion is evil – *malum in se*. But I believe it is legitimate for human governments to regulate manifestations of religious belief (free exercise as it is incompletely expressed in the *Australian Constitution*) where they do so by law and where there is no other way (the *ICCPR* word is 'necessary', not 'reasonable') "to protect public safety, order, health, morals or the fundamental rights and freedoms of others".

Because of my belief in freedom of conscience, I do not believe it is good for any physical consequence (coercion) to follow the clarified understanding of Christian theologies which I seek for all. What I am conducting here in legal terms, is an 'examination for discovery'. In 'discovery', lawyers identify their clients' areas of disagreement so that they can refine the issues they have to debate. But as Christians, we leave to God and Christ to resolve those outstanding matters when they choose to do so.

Now a word about their choices in these matters. I believe that God and Christ are fully competent as we might again say in lawyer parlance, but they are not compellable. They retain their own free will. They can and do answer prayers, but they are free to answer prayers in the negative or to keep the supplicants waiting or guessing. If they choose to answer no, or not to answer, they have reasons for actively deciding to answer no, or not to answer at all. And that recognition of their conscience and agency infers for me that they have reasons for not resolving our theological disputes including our disputes about their nature. They could resolve our disputes about their nature, but I infer because I know they exist, that they have chosen not to answer. That insight leads to the further question of why they would not answer questions about their nature in an absolute and incontrovertible way that would undo all the friction that has flowed because of their failure to answer. Again, I infer that they have good reasons and I speculate just a little on what one of those reasons might be.

They want us to learn to live together in uncertainty. For if we can live together in uncertainty in peace, then when we are resurrected by Christ to live with him in some form of glory, we will still know how to live together in peace. The inference continues and requires that we then strive for peace despite uncertainty; that we try and build bridges of understanding.

Thank you, Paul Morris and Michael Quinlan. That is why I have written this book.

Now some words about theology. In this book, I have tried to avoid reference to religious tradition. I believe that tradition plays a large part in all religious faith. Catholic theologians maintain that the scriptures cannot be understood without the tradition of the fathers. Some Protestant faiths have made a point of avoiding tradition in their theology by insisting that they rely solely on biblical scripture for theological understanding. And I acknowledge that some traditions have misguided correct theological understanding. Because I think reliance on agreed scriptural accounts are more likely to enable understanding, I have therefore relied on those scriptures and historical sources that I currently trust for the discussion and analysis that follows. That is not to say I subscribe to the view that history and even scriptural sources are inerrantly correct. I believe all are as fallible, and in the case of history, as provisional, as the understanding of their human authors.

Theological introduction

When Christ appeared to his disciples in the Upper Room in the weeks following his resurrection,[1] he continued the establishment of faith in those He had appointed as the leaders of His church. Thomas's initial uncertainty shows the variable quality of human faith.[2] To strengthen Thomas's faith, Christ insisted that Thomas stretch forth his hand and feel the prints of the nails in His hands and feet and the gash made by the spear in His side.[3] Peter had earlier been admonished about the quality of his faith and instructed that when he was truly converted, he was to strengthen his brethren.[4] The instructions of the risen Christ to Thomas about his faith are preserved as:

> Thomas, because thou hast seen me, thou hast believed: blessed are they that have not seen, and yet have believed.[5]

John's record does not explain the nature of the blessing for belief without seeing, but it is explained in other scripture. For example, the Apostle Paul taught that it was impossible to please God without faith[6] which suggests that the development of faith in men is one of God's primary purposes in creating the earth. But the kind of faith which the risen Christ recommended to Thomas, is clearly not the simple faith that gets someone out of bed in the morning; the kind of faith which Christ recommended to Thomas and which Paul also commended, is the faith that we will also be resurrected.

Belief in the physical resurrection of Christ attested by the eleven apostles in that Upper Room in Jerusalem in the first century AD, is

---

[1] Luke 24:33-51; John 20: 19-29.
[2] John 20:24-25.
[3] John 20:27.
[4] Luke 22: 31-34.
[5] John 20:29.
[6] Hebrews 11:6.

the foundation of the faith of most Christians. It justifies their lives of obedience to the great commandments that He gave; that they love God with all their hearts, might, mind and strength, and that they love their neighbours as themselves.[7]

But the idea that Christian salvation includes bodily resurrection from the dead is not something shared by all the branches of Christianity. If the Christian God does not have a body, then why did Christ present himself to the disciples in that Upper Room and insist that they become witnesses of his bodily resurrection?

Thomas was not alone in learning by sight and touch that Jesus Christ was resurrected with a body. The previous week, He had also shown the other ten disciples His hands, feet and side[8] and asked for food and eaten it in front of them[9] to put his corporeality beyond any doubt.[10] How does this fact-based faith in the bodily resurrection of Jesus Christ as the resurrected Redeemer of all mankind, co-exist with the Christian teaching that "God is a Spirit"?[11] And how does Christ's corporeal resurrection synch with the Trinitarian idea that Father, Son and Holy Ghost exist eternally as an intangible spiritual unity? And what is the significance to Paul's qualification of one of his visions with the words "whether in the body or out of the body, I cannot tell."[12]

These are the questions I explore in this book. This study includes a review of ancient Hebrew beliefs in their Egyptian and Mesopotamian context long before the advent of Christianity. But it also unpicks the nature of Christian and Jewish interaction during the first two centuries of the Christian era when the Jews persecuted the Christians because they believed in two Gods – the Jewish Yahweh or Father God, and His Only Begotten Son, Jesus Christ.

---

[7] Luke 10:25-37.
[8] Luke 24:39-40; John 20:20.
[9] Luke 24:41-43.
[10] Note that the meaning of Christ's resurrected corporeality is theologically challenging since it is a different form of corporeality than applies to mortals. That is, during both of these upper room visits, Christ appeared corporeally, when the doors were shut where the disciples were assembled meaning that his corporeal body can do things that ours cannot (John 20:19, 26).
[11] John 4:24.
[12] 2 Corinthians 12:2-3. That is, when Christ appears but is not touched as in Thomas' case, does he appear only in the mind of the receiver, does he appear as a holograph a la Star Wars, or does he always appear in his resurrected bodily form?

1

WHERE DID THE 'ONE GOD' IDEA COME FROM?

Introduction

The 'one God' idea that Christianity inherited from Judaism is not modern monotheism because the term 'monotheism', was not coined until the 17th century A.D.[13] And the simple idea that monotheism involves the worship of only one God, must be distinguished from many related ideas including henotheism where a believer worships one God without denying that others exist, and monolatry, where a believer recognizes the existence of many gods, but worships only one. Monotheism in modern Christianity holds that there is only one God and that no others exist. But modern Christianity has long had a problem explaining its assertion that it worships only one God, since it holds that its one God comprises three persons – the Father, the Son and the Holy Ghost.

It is not the purpose of this book or this chapter to explain Christianity's mysterious One God. This book discusses Christian theological attempts to understand and explain the God of Christianity, but that task is not begun in this chapter. The more modest task of this

---

[13] The term monotheism was first used by Henry More in his 1660 book, *An Explanation of the Grand Mystery of Godliness* (Flesher and Morden, London, 62).

chapter is to trace the origin of the 'one God' idea in human history and to identify when it was received by the Hebrews so that the Christians could receive it from their predecessors, the Jews. I approach this lesser task in two parts. In Part One, I set to one side the assumptions that modern conceptions of God bring to this historical search. The modern Jewish historian of religion, Benjamin Sommer, is my principal source in the first part, but I also rely on Jon Levenson. Sommer and Levenson have helped many students set aside their modern assumptions as they have approached the study of ancient religion. One of the paradigms that Sommer insists be set aside as we reach back into Israelite religious history, is the idea that Israel's God is a spirit being. Sommer is emphatic. Israel's God was anthropomorphic. Though Sommer acknowledges there was some fluidity in the ancient Hebrew traditions since 'God' sometimes sent a *mal'akh* or messenger to represent Him, behind the heavenly bureaucracy, God Himself was understood by the ancient Hebrews to be a glorious and exalted man, and so were some of the beings who worked with him on his Divine Council. I therefore begin with Sommer's survey of the literature about the corporeality of Israel's God, before I introduce the Divine Council.

In Part Two I explain that Israel's corporeal God did not work alone. He was the Chairman of a Board. That Board is most simply understood as a Divine Council so that it is not confused with the god pantheons of some of the empires that later ruled the Israelites after the demise of the empire set up by David and Solomon. Below the Divine Council in the Israelite heavenly hierarchy was an Assembly comprised of four levels of beings – simply, God, his Sons, Angels and Men. But Israelite religion is always 'monotheistic' for Sommer at least, because God is always supreme over all the other beings in heaven and on earth.

I conclude this chapter with a summary and an affirmation. My summary restates Israel's Divine Council theological history but acknowledges the beginnings of rabbinical monotheism by the 5th century B.C. even though that theology did not crystallize into code until much later. But I note that the rabbinical Jews of that half millennium also wrestled with explaining the dualism of their historical God – El, or Elohim and Yahweh.

Israelite theology

Part One – Israel's God is a man

Benjamin Sommer begins his 2009 book entitled *The Bodies of God and the World of Ancient Israel* with the provocative statement that "[t]he God of the Hebrew Bible has a body".[14] He says that opening statement is necessary since "so many people, including Protestant Old Testament scholars, assume otherwise".[15] Sommer then documents the assumption that the Hebrew God does not have a body in scholarship and catalogues some of the consequences that flow from this assumed but incorrect understanding. In some ways, Sommer's may be compared with Jon Levenson's introduction of his book about resurrection theology in ancient Israel. He says the doctrine of resurrection is not "a Christian innovation"[16] and is a "weight-bearing beam in the edifice of rabbinic Judaism".[17] While many recent scholars have spiritualized away resurrection theology, the fact remains that the Hebrew Bible assumes and rests upon this idea though it is not set out plainly in that scripture. "[I]t drew, most centrally, on the long-standing conviction that God would yet again prove faithful to his promises of life for his people".[18]

Sommer says that Erhard Gerstenberger studied the way Israelites understood divinity at various times.[19] Sommer says Gerstenberger also understood Israel's "strong connections to Canaanite and Mesopotamian religions"[20] so that one might have thought he would have been

> open to acknowledging the anthropomorphisms ever present in biblical conceptions of God. But Gerstenberger never mentions the embodied nature of Yhwh. The closest he comes…is a passing reference to Yhwh as 'the invisible God' who nonetheless can smell the sacrifices. The repeated references to God's visibility…go unnoticed.[21]

---

[14] Sommer BD, *The Bodies of God and the World of Ancient Israel*, (Cambridge University Press), 2009, 1.
[15] Ibid
[16] Levenson Jon D, *Resurrection and the Restoration of Israel: The Ultimate Victory of the God of Life*, (Yale University Press, 2006), ix.
[17] Ibid x.
[18] Ibid xiv.
[19] Sommer, (above n14), 4 citing Gerstenberger E, *Theologies of the Old Testament*, (T & T Clark, 2002).
[20] Ibid.
[21] Ibid.

Sommer says that Elaine Scarry "devotes a third of [her] book to analyzing notions of the body, human and divine, in biblical texts from both Old and New Testament"[22] but maintains that

> [t]hroughout the Old Testament God's power and authority are.... extreme and continual amplifications of the fact that people have bodies and He has no body.[23]

Sommer continues that "Scarry seems genuinely unaware of the fact that the Hebrew Bible contains not a single verse denying that God has a body".[24] Sommer's overall point is to show that the ancient Hebrews always thought of God as a man like themselves, and finds it difficult to understand when serious scholars seem to miss that basic premise of their understanding.

Though Walter Eichrodt admits the presence of anthropomorphism in Israelite theology, Sommer says he downplays biblical belief that God could dwell in a Temple as evidence of foreign ideas planted "into the true religion of Israel"[25] and suggests the Israelites were always striving for "a doctrine of God as spirit in the philosophical sense" though they never found that "in the pages of the Old Testament".[26] Sommer says Eichrodt's claim that "God's non-physicality is 'left veiled'…is but a clever way of importing into the Hebrew scriptures a notion they lack".[27]

Sommer continues that despite the focus on "the varied testimonies of God's works and God's nature"[28] in Walter Brueggerman's 1997 *Theology of the Old Testament*, he similarly ignores the Hebrew Bible's "testimony that God is a physical being".[29] When testimony of God's physicality comes up in his discussion, Brueggerman quickly translates the biblical witness "into a more abstract idea".[30] For Brueggerman,

---

[22] Ibid, referring to Scarry E, *The Body in Pain*, (Oxford University Press, 1985).
[23] Sommer, ibid 4-5 quoting Scarry, (above n22), 210.
[24] Sommer, ibid 5.
[25] Ibid 6.
[26] Ibid, referring to Eichrodt W, *Theology of the Old Testament*, 6th ed., (The Westminster Press, Philadelphia, 1959), 1:211.
[27] Ibid.
[28] Ibid.
[29] Ibid.
[30] Ibid.

God's "aura...power, authority and sovereignty" are what theologians should focus on with the result that he personally cannot find a "notion of a truly embodied God" in the Old Testament because the doctrine of incarnation was preserved to be revealed in the New Testament.[31]

Sommer's criticism of Christian Old Testament scholars (he admits that he is a "committed Jew...hop[ing] to contribute something to the ongoing development of Torah"[32]), might seem like simple sectarian rivalry, except that he continues and finds the same blinkered judgments expressed by Christian Hebrew scholars.

Menahem Haran studiously refuses to acknowledge "the unabashed anthropomorphism of the Hebrew Bible..[i]n his oft-cited book, *Temples and Temple Service in Ancient Israel*".[33] Even though Haran repeatedly demonstrates "the ways...the ancient Israelite priests approached their God as tangibly and dangerously present behind the curtain separating their section of the sanctuary (the holy place...) from God's (the holy of holies...)",[34] yet he "chooses to regard all the evidence... as metaphorical".[35] Rimon Kasher does the same thing. Though he shows "that the conception of God throughout the Book of Ezekiel is thoroughly anthropomorphic", [36] yet Kasher explains that Ezekiel chose that language because his audience was primitive and would only understand if he spoke in anthropomorphic terms.[37]

Sommer says that the need to explain away the embodied nature of God in the Hebrew scriptures can be traced to the time when "Jewish and Christian thinkers began to believe that God [wa]s not a physical being".[38] In Jewish philosophy, Sommer says the metaphorical interpretations can be traced back to Maimonides' *Guide of the Perplexed* in the twelfth century A.D.[39] Maimonides believed that "the denial of

---

[31] Ibid 7.
[32] Ibid 125.
[33] Ibid 7 referring to Haram M, *Temples and Temple Service in Ancient Israel*, Eisenbrauns, (Winona Lake, Indiana, 1985).
[34] Ibid.
[35] Ibid.
[36] Ibid referring to "Anthropomorphism, Holiness, and Cult: A New Look at Ezekiel 40-48", *BM*, 1995, 359.
[37] Ibid 8.
[38] Ibid.
[39] Ibid.

God's corporeality"[40] was crucial to the validity of monotheistic belief and accordingly he sought "to sublimate the Hebrew Bible's physical God".[41] Sommer does not similarly identify a date or author responsible for 'incorrect' Christian ideas about God's incorporeality, but he is unrepentant in his statement that these ideas cannot be justified from the Hebrew Bible.

For Sommer, all this avoidance of the obvious by Jewish theologians was the simple result of embarrassment – the sacred scriptures speak of a corporeal God, but all these authors thought that must be metaphorical since they each believed that God was a spiritual being and does not have a body.[42]

But theologians are not the only modern scholars who have difficulty in understanding the way their more ancient forebears thought. Modern lawyers also have difficulties understanding past institutions and practice because they assume an "anachronistic viewpoint".[43] They ask "unreal questions…[that are] preoccupied with today's details"[44] – for example, details that would have had no meaning in the mind of either a medieval English lay-person, or a medieval English lawyer.[45]

Human beings living in the twenty and twenty-first centuries have different patterns of thinking. It is very difficult for modern lawyers to understand that church and state were not legally separate in medieval times. In those times, church and state together constituted the governing influence in life. They presided at birth and marriage, and

---

[40] Ibid.
[41] Ibid. Note that Levenson also finds that Maimonides wanted to spiritualize away bodily realities in the world to come in his "bold reinterpretation of the Jewish doctrine of the hereafter" (Levenson, (above n16), 18-20 (19)).
[42] Ibid.
[43] Milsom SFC, *Historical Foundations of the Common Law*, (Butterworths, London, 1969), xii; Helmholz RH, *Canon Law and the Law of England*, (Hambledon Press, London, 1987), 101.
[44] Milsom, ibid.
[45] While Paul Brand traces the origin of the English legal profession to the twelfth century AD (*The Origins of the English Legal Profession*, (Oxford, UK and Cambridge, USA, Blackwell, 1992)), he is not convinced that such lawyers as there were could be described as anything more than "narrators" (ibid 85) in that century. It is not until the later thirteenth century in the reign of Edward I, when he finds "controls on practice" (ibid 115) and "the education of professional attorneys" (ibid 119) that he is satisfied with the use of the term, "the legal profession".

they pronounced upon the disposal of goods following death.[46] The English legal historian, Theodore Plucknett, explained these conceptual difficulties with a theological analogy when he said that the idea of any separation between church and state "introduces a sort of polytheism utterly repugnant to medieval thought".[47] It requires a change in thinking if twenty-first century lawyers are to understand the role of the church in medieval England. The idea that ecclesiastical courts had final legal jurisdiction in questions of marriage, bigamy, divorce and adultery, estate administration, crime and contract,[48] is unfamiliar to contemporary Western lawyers. Pollock and Maitland explained this involvement of the church in what are now deemed 'secular matters' when they wrote

> Every layman, unless he were a Jew, was subject to ecclesiastical law. It regulated many affairs of his life, marriages, divorces, testaments, intestate succession; it would try and punish him for various offences, for adultery, fornication, defamation; it would constrain him to pay tithes and similar dues; in the last resort it could excommunicate him and then the state would come to its aid. Even the Jews...were... within the sphere of ecclesiastical legislation and subject to some of the processes of the spiritual courts.[49]

Sommer might thus have said that the Christian and Jewish theologians he criticized had not sufficiently distanced themselves from their own spiritual beliefs when they tried to understand the nature of God from an ancient Israelite perspective. That Sommer does better is demonstrated in his admission that though he is a committed Jew,[50] he can still see that the whole of the Hebrew Bible is written from the ancient theological premise that the God of Israel had a body.[51]

---

[46] Pollock Sir F & Maitland FM, *The History of English Law*, 2nd ed., (Cambridge University Press, 1968), Vol 1, 614-632.
[47] *A Concise History of the Common Law*, 5th ed., (Butterworths, London, 1956), 40.
[48] Holdsworth says that the church "claimed criminal jurisdiction in all cases in which a[n ecclesiastical] clerk was the accused"; contractual jurisdiction where its justification was the need "to enforce all promises made with oath or pledge of faith"; and "jurisdiction over matrimonial and testamentary causes" were not removed from the church until 1857 when Probate and Divorce Courts in England were established by the Statute 20, 21 Victoria c 77 and c 85 respectively (*A History of English Law*, 2nd ed., Little Brown and Co., Boston, 1923, Vol 1, 614-632).
[49] Pollock & Maitland, (above n46), Vol 1, 439.
[50] Sommer, (above n14), 125. See also above n32 and supporting text.
[51] Sommer, (above n14) and supporting text.

Sommer's scriptural evidence for God's body

Sommer does not set out to make a catalogue of scriptural evidence for his simple statement. But as he points out implicitly, the authors of the Hebrew scriptures did not include a justification for their anthropomorphic theology because they did not perceive a need to justify it against later criticism. They simply believed that God was an exalted glorified human being – indeed, Sommer points out several times that the Hebrew God (whether named Yhwh or Elohim), was blazingly bright.[52] However, Sommer's text does identify scriptural passages in Genesis, Exodus, the Psalms, Isaiah and Ezekiel that spell out the biblical anthropomorphism he claims.

Sommer's favourite Genesis evidence[53] concerns the visit of the three messengers to Abraham while "amidst the trees of Mamre [he] was sitting at the entrance of his tent, at the heat of the day".[54] For Sommer, the text suggests at first that "Yhwh appears in the form of three men, or at least in the form of one of the three men".[55] At the beginning of the visit, Abraham does not realize that his visitors are human,[56] but his attention is drawn to one of the three men who addresses him personally. "All three...subsequently speak",[57] announce that Abraham will have a son, and then Sommer says "the narrator stops being coy and simply refers to one of the visitors as Yhwh".[58] When the other two leave, Yhwh stays behind and continues to speak with Abraham personally. For Sommer, the account is written as it is, so that, like Abraham, those who read it find their knowledge growing as the account proceeds. That is because the narrator wants the reader to realize that Abraham did not realize the identity of the chief among his visitors at first.[59] "The other two beings are subsequently referred to

---

[52] Sommer, (above n14), 60 and 69.
[53] Ibid 40 where he describes this reference as "one of the most revealing cases".
[54] Ibid.
[55] Ibid. I have used the abbreviation "Yhwh" when citing or discussing the writings of Jewish authors out of respect for their wish not to use the full name of deity. When discussing the writing of other authors who have not followed that Jewish protocol, I have included the vowels.
[56] Ibid.
[57] Ibid.
[58] Ibid.
[59] Ibid 40-41.

as angels".[60] Sommer concludes that "[i]t is clear that Yhwh appears in bodily form to Abraham in this passage" though it is not clear whether all three bodies somehow pertained to Yhwh "or whether the other two were merely servants (perhaps human, perhaps divine)"[61] who were simply accompanying Yhwh.[62] After Yhwh has been identified, he personally discusses with Abraham, his plan "to 'come down' from heaven to observe Sodom and Gomorrah".[63] However, Sommer does qualify the nature of this personal visit when he suggests that the person who met and conversed in this account with Abraham, may simply have been an avatar or *mal'akh* of Yhwh[64] - meaning a "temporary manifestation of the deity"[65] who is nonetheless, an embodied corporeal being wherever he is physically located in person. Though the Hebrews may have believed that Yhwh had the capacity to manifest himself at different places at the same time, Sommer is clear that Yhwh is an embodied individual.[66]

Following the chronology of the biblical record, Sommer then notes that Jacob physically wrestled with a personal being at Peniel – a being whom he first thought was a *mal'akh* but later identified as Yhwh.[67] Sommer says that Moses first thought that he had encountered a *mal'akh* on Mount Sinai, but recognized as the experience continued, that he was in conversation with Yhwh himself.[68] According to Sommer, Gideon had a similar experience when he thought he was interacting with "the angel of the Lord", but came to realize as his experience unfolded, that he was dealing with either Yhwh himself or with his *mal'akh*.[69] Sommer says that God had intended to accompany the children of

---

[60] Ibid citing Genesis 19:1.
[61] Ibid 40.
[62] Ibid.
[63] Ibid 41.
[64] Ibid.
[65] Ibid.
[66] Ibid. Sommer goes to great lengths, particularly between pages 60 and 69 to try and nail down what he calls this belief in Yhwh's 'fluidity', but it does not take away from Yhwh's corporeal identity. For example at page 62 he says that even though there are scriptural verses "that point in all…directions [,p]riestly and deuteronomic traditions…reject both the notion of fluid divine selfhood and the concept of multiple divine embodiment". "[H]uman beings have the same form as God and other heavenly beings" (ibid 69).
[67] Sommer, (above n14), 41 referring to Genesis 32.
[68] Ibid referring to Exodus 3-4.
[69] Ibid 42-43 referring to Judges 6.

Israel personally on their journey in the wilderness but after the golden calf episode, instead sent "[h]is *mal'akh*",[70] and that God's body is in the same form as the human body.[71] Sommer acknowledges that each of these prophetic biblical figures was initially confused about the identity of his heavenly visitor because Yhwh "acts with a humility unbecoming a deity".[72] But neither that humility nor issues of fluidity which he cannot fully pin down,[73] diminish Sommer's certainty that the God of the children of Israel in the Hebrew Bible is a corporeal individual who deals with them on a personal basis.[74]

Sommer is not content to simply assert that the God of the Hebrews was a personal and anthropomorphic being. He explains that even though the ancient Hebrews believed that there was more than one God or *Elohim*, the ancient Hebrews were not polytheists according to the modern meaning of that term.[75] Sommer says that twenty-first century confusion about the nature of Hebrew belief in heavenly beings has two sources. The first is that ancient Hebrews used the term *elohim* in two different ways. It was a plural noun which can be reasonably translated to mean 'divine beings',[76] and as a singular noun to refer to one of that plurality, as for example in the Hebrew name title Yhwh. Jacob said that he came to identify the being with whom he wrestled, not only as an *elohim*, but as the *Elohim* his fathers had worshipped as the God Yhwh.[77]

---

[70] Ibid referring to Exodus 23 and 33.
[71] Ibid 70 referring to Genesis 1 and 5. Also note that Sommers says that Ezekiel says that Yhwh's divine *kabod* closely resembles "a typical human body" (ibid 70).
[72] Ibid 40-41.
[73] See above n66.
[74] Sommer, (above n14).
[75] Ibid 41. Note that Sommer's text includes a 29 page appendix entitled "Monotheism and Polytheism in Ancient Israel" which will be discussed in more detail below.
[76] Ibid 41.
[77] Ibid.

Part Two - The Divine Council in Hebrew theology

Michael S. Heiser[78] has written that "[i]t is generally accepted that Israelite religion 'was much closer to Canaanite religion' than to the religion the Hebrew Bible advocates".[79] He draws attention to the similarity of beliefs about deity that existed in ancient Palestine and Mesopotamia but says that the Israelite religion "was distinct in important ways".[80] Because the "Israelite religion grew out of a polytheistic Canaanite background", one must understand both systems of worship to understand their differences. Though Sommer might agree with Heiser's assertion that the Hebrew Bible is polytheistic since Sommer acknowledges that the Hebrew Bible refers to many gods who were worshipped by a variety of people, both scholars maintain that the Israelite religion was or became monotheistic despite the Hebrew Bible's reference to a plurality of heavenly beings including gods. That is because the Israelites believed in a 'Divine Council'.[81] But the

---

[78] Michael S. Heiser is a biblical scholar who works as Academic Editor for Logos Bible Software. His PhD dissertation at the University of Wisconsin-Madison in 2004 was entitled "The Divine Council in Late Canonical and Non-Canonical Second Temple Literature" (ibid) and he has published a number of articles on related subject material both on and offline – for example; "Yahweh and his Asherah? Epigraphic Evidence for Religious Pluralism in Old Testament Times", in *One God, One Lord in a World of Religious Pluralism,* Clarke AD & Winter BW, Tyndale House, Cambridge, 1991; "Deuteronomy 32:8 and the Sons of God", *BibSac* 158, (2001); "Israel's Divine Council, Mormonism and Evangelism: Clarifying the Issues and Directions for Future Study", *The FARMS Review* 19/1, 2007; "You've seen on Elohim, You've seen them all? A Critique of Mormonism's Use of Psalm 82", *The FARMS review,* 19/1, 2007.

[79] At <http://lehislibrary.files.wordpress.com/2009/08/divinecouncil-1.pdf > 1 citing *The Social Roots of Yahwism,* Cook SL, Brill, 2005, 7.

[80] Heiser, 1.

[81] Johannes C. De Moor observes that "the biblicists hold…that the concept of God in Israel was monotheistic from the beginning", but he suggests a gradual evolution from polytheism to monotheism citing Albright and Lang (De Moor JC, *The Rise of Yahwism, The Roots of Israelite Monotheism,* 2nd ed., (Leuven University Press, 1997), 2-3). He traces the idea of monotheism to Amenophis IV in Egypt who reigned briefly in Egypt between c. 1358BC and c. 1338 BC when Tutankhamun succeeded him and restored the former polytheism (ibid 41-45). Diana V. Edelman, Philip Davies and Thomas Thompson also believe that monotheism was of later origin than the biblicists suggest and imply that belief in early origins for monotheism are "colored by personal religious beliefs" (*The Triumph of Elohim, From Yahwishm to Judaisms,* Edelman DK ed., (William B. Eerdmans Publishing Company, Grand Rapids, Michigan, 1996), 15-16 summarizing later chapters in the book by Davies and Thompson). She suggests that what she calls "inclusive monotheism…g[ave] way to forms of exclusive monotheism" during the Hellenistic period, though the exact time "cannot be pinpointed" (ibid 23). Lowell K. Handy in Edelman's book also agrees that the early Israelites were not monotheists (ibid 27-30).

Israelite Divine Council was quite different than the later Greek and Roman 'pantheon of Gods'.

Heiser says the Hebrew Bible has an assembly of Heavenly beings in four tiers.[82] "In Psalms 89 there is mention of the congregation and the assembly of the holy ones",[83] and there are references to the "Sons of God" in Genesis and Job.[84] These same titles occur in independent contemporary and archaeological evidence.[85] For Sommer, the biblical references to what modern Bible readers call polytheism, are included as a contrast to Israel's enduring and orthodox belief in one true god. The Hebrew Bible's acknowledgment of the contemporary 'polytheism', exists to criticize false belief and to demonstrate Israel's enduring contrary belief in one supreme God to whom all other heavenly beings including other gods, are subject.[86] For Heiser, Israelite religion developed from Canaanite religion and became monotheistic in process of time.[87] Both scholars agree that Israel believed in a Divine Council, but they interpret its meaning differently. For Heiser, there are many divine beings in the Hebrew Bible – the warrior patriarch El, his seventy sons by Asherah,[88] including Yahweh who usurped El's role as

---

[82] Heiser. See also Handy in Edelman, n81, 32-33. Handy says that "[t]he Bible reflects a knowledge of this four-tiered system" (ibid 39).

[83] Heiser. Heiser's reference is to Psalms 89:5-7 where he translates "the congregation of the saints" from the Hebrew to mean "the council of the holy ones" (see also Heiser, Michael S, *Angels: What the Bible Really Says About God's Heavenly Host*, (Lexham Press, 2018), Chapter 1).

[84] Ibid.

[85] Ibid.

[86] Sommer, (above n14), 149, 172.

[87] Heiser, <http://www.thedivinecouncil.com/DivineCouncilLBD.pdf>.

[88] Edelman says that the "divine couple, Yahweh and Asherah" headed an Israelite "national pantheon" "from ca. 960-586BCE (Edelman, (above n81), 19), but Johannes C. De Moor denies that YHWH ever had a consort despite frequent attempts by commentators to provide him with one (De Moor, (above n81), 168). Handy also says that El and Asherah were the divine couple at the top of the four-tiered Ugarit pantheon to which the Israelites originally subscribed (in Edelman, above n81, 32-33). Niehr says that Asherah was YHWH's "paredra" or consort (in Edelman, (above n81), 59). Though Daniel C Peterson acknowledges that "the developing [Israelite] conception of Yahweh…[may] have absorbed [Asherah's] functions and epithets much as it had earlier absorbed those of Yahweh's father, El" which saw her "eliminated from the history of Israel and subsequent Judaism", he prefers André Lemaire's view that "Asherah may have been the consort of El, but not [of] Yahweh" ("Nephi and His Asherah", *Journal of Book of Mormon Studies*, 9/2 (2000) 16, 18 citing André Lemaire in "Who or What was Yahweh's Asherah", *Biblical Archaeology Review* 10/6 (1984): 46).

head of the pantheon, the congregation, and the accuser, Satan.[89] For Sommer, the Israelite religion was always monotheistic because their one God was always supreme over all the others – it is the Israelite understanding of the relationship between divine beings that sets their monotheistic belief apart from those who believed in a pantheon.[90]

But Sommer does not explore the connection between the divine beings which make up the Divine Council in the same detail as Heiser. Heiser says the earliest Israelite beliefs follow their Canaanite and Ugaritic origins in holding that El was the supreme God who administered all nations on the earth. But Heiser says Israel developed the belief that one of his sons, Yahweh, an elohim in his own right, was asked (by El?) to "judge the earth" and "to inherit all nations".[91] There is an early distinction between El and Yahweh in Heiser's analysis, but eventually references to El fall away and Yahweh assumes control of the Divine Council.[92] Sommer and Heiser agree that Yahweh became or was the one God of Israel. But neither scholar is clear whether that is because El ceased to exist, handed over the reigns of control of the Earth or Israel to Yahweh,[93] or because El and Yahweh were really always just two different names for the same one God. Neither scholar is sure of the nature of the connection between El and Yahweh because there is no adequate biblical or archaeological evidence to enable clear answers. What is clear from both writers is that Israel believed in a Divine Council, and that one God, whether identified as El or Yahweh

---

[89] Heiser. Johannes C. De Moor says more matter of factly, that "the majority of Israelites worshipped YHWH whom they also called El", (above n81), 10 citing a variety of authorities.

[90] Sommer, (above n14), 147.

[91] Heiser.

[92] Handy says bluntly that El and Yahweh "were understood by the Judahites, or at least the biblical heirs to the Judahites, to be the same god" (in Edelman, n81, 38). Herbert Niehr in Edelman's book says more carefully suggest that although "some scholars believe that YHWH was identified with El", YHWH likely "reached his status as supreme god by taking over the traits from the gods El and Baal as they were depicted in Ugaritic mythology" (in Edelman, n81, 45).

[93] Sommer does not deal with the separate identities of El and Yahweh and one is left with the impression from his work that he prefers to see them as different names for the same pre-eminent God. Heiser is much more detailed. He notes this identity, but also acknowledges other views that hold Yahweh was one of El's seventy sons to whom he assigned Israel as his particular responsibility (n82, 2 citing Mark S. Smith and Patrick D. Miller's discussion of Deuteronomy 32:8,9 in *The Early History of God: Yahweh and the Other Deities in Ancient Israel*, (William. B. Eerdmans Publishing, 2002), 32).

was always pre-eminent and subject to no other. This is the distinctive feature of Israelite theology and it does seem to justify Sommer's assertion that orthodox biblical Israel was never polytheistic in the same way as were other nations that believed in a pantheon of gods.

Daniel Peterson, citing Frank Moore Cross Jr, notes that the Canaanites and the Israelites shared a theology which held that El, the "lord of eternity" and "the Ancient One" was the pre-eminent God,[94] but saw him give way to Baal in northern Syria by the fourteenth century B.C.[95] But the Israelite conception of El held that He "had a divine son named Jehovah or Yahweh"[96] who gradually "absorbed" His Father's functions and was fully identified with Him (El) by the end of the tenth century B.C.[97]

Conclusion

Traditional Jewish history and theology

Sommer says from his very first chapter, that the Hebrew Bible manifests the physicality of God.[98] He cites scripture from Genesis, Exodus, Judges, 1 Kings, Isaiah, Jeremiah, Psalms, Daniel, Hosea, Amos and Micah to demonstrate. While there are some verses which "point toward a nonmaterial anthropomorphism"[99] - "God's body, at least at times, has the same shape and the same sort of substance as a human body."[100] De Moor generalises. He refers to 'the book of Job' in his discussion of the nature of monotheism in ancient Israel,[101] but says that many see Moses and the Exodus as nothing more than legend.[102] From Joshua to David, the idea of a "kingdom of priests" is

---

[94] "Nephi and His Asherah", *Journal of Book of Mormon Studies*, 9/2 (2000) 16, 18 citing Frank Moore Cross Jr. in "Yahweh and the God of the Patriarchs", *Harvard Theological Review* 55 (1962): 240
[95] Ibid.
[96] Ibid 19.
[97] Ibid.
[98] Sommer, (above n14), 1-2.
[99] Ibid 2.
[100] Ibid.
[101] De Moor, (above n81), 142-143. Note that De Moor says that the book of Job only "seems...monotheistic" but that Job "is not a 'monotheist' in the strict sense of the word".
[102] Ibid 209 though noting "the possibility that real historical experiences are at the basis of the Exodus narrative".

politically unifying,¹⁰³ though in Abraham's day, "men are supposedly able to detain gods to wrest a blessing from them."¹⁰⁴ There is similar skeptical objectivity in the work of Handy, Niehr, Schmidt, Davies and Thompson that Diana Edelman has collected in her book.¹⁰⁵ The Hebrew scriptures are only referenced to demonstrate what the Jews redactively said they believed about their gods,¹⁰⁶ not to confirm what they really believed. Edelman's authors set the Hebrew scriptures to one side so that scientific sources can objectively confirm the reality.

However Sommer says Jewish and Christian scholars read the Hebrew scriptures through the lens of their own beliefs – and they find a god without a body because that is what they have been taught to believe. Scholars who set aside the Hebrew scriptures and seek to work out what the ancient Israelites believed from what the archaeological remains say, tell the story of a polytheistic people who worshipped idols. In their study, they ignore the insight that a believing minority within a dominant idolatrous culture, would not leave many archaeological remains behind to tell their part of a more complete story. But even if the Old Testament Hebrew scriptures must be set aside to satisfy the objective requirements of physical scientists, it is more difficult to ignore Talmudic writings since the provenance of both the Jerusalem (or Palestinian) and Babylonian versions are seldom questioned and thus present as ancient artifacts in their own right.

With this understanding of the nature of Israel's God and the Divine Council, we are now prepared to ask the question why the concept of the Divine Council subsided and disappeared from Israelite theology in the second half of the first millennium B.C.

---

[103] Ibid 273.
[104] Ibid 319.
[105] Edelman, (above n81).
[106] For example, when explaining aniconism (the ban of anthropomorphic images in ritual performance), Schmidt provides his own translation of Exodus 20: 3-6 and Deuteronomy 5: 7-10 so that he can develop his proposition that the existence of aniconism does not prove the ancient Jews were monotheistic. He provides his own translation of both passages because of the likelihood that the Exodus version had been redacted by the Deuteronomists so that it conformed to their later orthodoxy ("The Aniconic Tradition on Reading Images and Views Texts" in Edelman DK, 77, 78-79).

2

WHEN AND WHY DID THE JEWS BECOME MONOTHEISTS?

Introduction

In this chapter I explain why an anthropomorphic understanding of God and his Divine Council subsided and disappeared from Israelite theology after the demise of the kingdoms of David and Solomon. While the gods of most nations gave way to the gods of their conquerors, Israel would not relinquish her worship of the Supreme God but developed different strategies to avoid offending her overlords. While Israel's spiritual leaders believed that their strategies of careful subservience enabled the preservation of their traditional theology, they had lost their anthropomorphic God and his Divine Council before the advent of Christianity. I discuss the reasons for the demise of the Divine Council in three parts.

In Part One, I identify the command that Israel should have no other gods before Yahweh as one reason why the descendants of the Israelites ceased referring to their Supreme God's sovereignty over other heavenly beings. The point was not that their recognition of the Divine Council had ever offended that commandment, but that it was legitimate to cease referring to other beings in heaven to more fully respect the Supreme God.

In Part Two, I discuss how Israel's theology responded to the worship policies of her overlords. I discuss the Persian one God policy that did not accept any god greater than Ahura Mazda, and the more accommodating Greek and Roman approach which allowed conquered nations to retain their gods, so long as they remembered their place in the multi-god pantheon.

I conclude this chapter with a summary and an affirmation. My summary restates Israel's Divine Council theological history but acknowledges the beginnings of rabbinical monotheism by the fifth century B.C. But I note that the rabbinical Jews of that period also wrestled with explaining the dualism of their historical God – El, or Elohim and Yahweh.

Part One – The demise of Divine Council theology

Aniconism

Neither Sommer nor Heiser suggest an answer to why or how the Divine Council disappeared from Israelite theology. But an explanation may have originated in the first two commandments given to Moses at Sinai, and Israel's need to distinguish its beliefs from those of other nations. Brian B. Schmidt says the term 'aniconism' "refers to the imposition of a ban against the use of anthropomorphic, theriomorphic, or physiomorphic images to represent or house the deity as an object of worship in ritual performance"[107] and may well have originated in the first and second commandments given to Moses on Sinai. But he denies that these commandments were aniconic at the beginning.

It will be remembered that those commandments prevented the Israelites under Moses from

> hav[ing] other gods before me[108] [Yahweh]
>
> or of
>
> mak[ing] any graven image or any likeness of any thing that is in heaven above, or that is in the earth beneath, or that is in the water under the earth[109]
>
> or of

---

[107] Schmidt in Edelman, (above n81), 77.
[108] Holy Bible, King James Version, Exodus 20:3.
[109] Ibid Exodus 20:4.

> bow[ing] down...to them,...or serv[ing] them[110]
> because their God
> was a jealous God.[111]

Perhaps because Schmidt subscribes to the view that the early Israelites under Moses were still polytheists, he says that one must read these commandments from a monotheistic or aniconic frame of reference to find monotheism or aniconism in them.[112] But Schmidt's reasoning is unhelpfully circular since the converse is also true. That is, if one is determined to interpret these commandments from the perspective that the early Israelites were still polytheists under Moses, then they are not inconsistent with polytheism. From Schmidt's perspective, these commandments did not ban images of Yahweh, but only images of his competitors or perhaps, Yahweh's anthropomorphic form.[113] Schmidt cites the existence of "the bronze serpent...as YHWH's image"[114] in Solomon's temple for several centuries until king Hezekiah removed it, as proof of his argument.[115] Schmidt concedes that the deuteronomizers denied that the bronze serpent was a representation of Yahweh,[116] but the deuteronomic interpretation of the meaning of the bronze serpent is not the only interpretation available.[117]

Whether Schmidt's suggestion about the original meaning of these commandments is correct or not, the deuternomizers did not reintroduce the brazen serpent sculpture back into the temple under Josiah, and Edelman observes with empirical evidence in the 3rd century B.C., that these first two commandments were observed as prohibiting

---

[110] Ibid Exodus 20:5.
[111] Ibid.
[112] Schmidt, (above n106), 80.
[113] Ibid 86.
[114] Ibid.
[115] Ibid.
[116] Ibid.
[117] For example, it may have simply served to remind Israel that they need only look to their God Yahweh to live, which is another credible interpretation of the events recounted in Numbers 21 and resonates with Christ's later interpretation of Israel's daily manna in the wilderness. Christ said, repeating thought attributed to Moses, that "Man shall not live by bread alone, but by every word that proceedeth out of the mouth of God" (Matthew 4:4; Deuteronomy 8:3).

any images of Yahweh whatever.[118] So since even Schmidt would have to concede that these two commandments came to proscribe all manner of polytheistic practice, it is reasonable to infer that the earlier Israelite belief in the existence of a Divine Council, was a casualty of this developing theology.

As noted above and contrary to Sommer, De Moor did not accept that Israel was monotheistic from Moses as biblicists assert and traces the idea of monotheism from Egypt,[119] and increasing as Joshua and Gideon looked to secure God's favour as they engaged in perilous military undertakings.[120] But De Moor does not explain why either of those leaders should culturally or theologically have believed that such undivided loyalty to Yahweh should have secured his favour. That leaves the now orthodox interpretation of those first two commandments in the biblical texts as the best explanation.[121] After much discussion, Edelman and her colleagues seem to settle upon the idea that Israelite polytheism evolved into exclusive monotheism much later during the Hellenistic period,[122] but they are not clear on exactly why that was.

And so we have an unresolved academic disagreement. In this writer's view, Heiser and Sommer are convincing in their thesis that Israelite monotheism has origins in or before the second millennium B.C., and they are supported by other traditional Hebrew and Christian scholars whom De Moor discounts with the somewhat condescending

---

[118] "Tracking Observance of the Aniconic Tradition Through Numismatics", Edelman DV in *The Triumph of Elohim, From Yahwishm to Judaisms*, Edelman DK ed., (William B. Eerdmans Publishing Company, Grand Rapids, Michigan, 1996), 185.

[119] De Moor (above n81), 2-3, 40-45.

[120] Ibid 290 and 295.

[121] Joshua 24:14-15; Judges 6.

[122] Edelman, (above n81), 23. In the same book, Thomas L. Thompson says that Israelite theology was reinterpreted into monotheism and eventually exclusive monotheism as a response to crises when their old polytheistic gods did not meet their human needs (ibid 114-115). For Thompson, Xerxes is the author of exclusive Israelite monotheism because he demonstrated the strength that came from a consolidation of government control over religious ideology (ibid 122). Bolin notes the religious tolerance of the Persian kings Cyrus and Darius who repaired the temples of their foreign peoples. But Bolin says that their successor Xerxes, destroyed the foreign temples of evil gods in conquered territories to impose exclusive monotheism in favour of the Persian god Ahura Mazda as part of his program of political expediency. For Bolin, this policy which began with inclusive monotheism under Cyrus, is the seed of the idea of monotheism which was picked up and developed in Judaism (ibid 127-142).

'biblicist' label. But other twentieth century revisionists assert that Israelite monotheism was a reaction to Persian and Greek religious policy somewhere between the third and fifth centuries B.C. This book is not the place to finally settle that academic argument, but it does seem reasonable to conclude this summary of the debate with the observation that even De Moor can find origins for the idea of exclusive monotheism in Egypt long before the Persians and Greeks began their vacillating exploration of religious tolerance late in the first millennium B.C.

Both views of the origin of the idea of exclusive monotheism can also accept that the Israelite Divine Council subsided in theological importance when Israelite theology came into contact and contest with the religious policies of the late first millennium B.C. superpowers – Babylon, Persia, Greece and then Rome. For rather than assert Israel's detailed four tiered Heavenly assembly with one ascendant God who ruled all others, Israelite theology retreated to the safer, simpler and yet still accurate foundational idea that Yahweh was Israel's one God. This idea was safer because 'one God worship' was familiar to the various temporal overlords who came and went, and it did not require the constant assertion of Yahweh's sovereignty in a pantheon which Israel did not accept anyway.

But what were the religious policies of the superpowers in the late first millennium B.C?

The religious policies of the superpowers in the late first millennium

The Persians – inclusive monotheism

Diana Edelman and Thomas Thompson call the religious policy of the Persians, 'inclusive monotheism'.[123] The Persians first simply demoted the Gods of conquered lands to lesser status within their pantheons,[124] but as their policy grew more sophisticated, they identified the pre-eminent Gods of their conquests with "the new empire God,

---

[123] Edelman, (above n81), 22; Thompson, ibid 116.
[124] Edelman, (above n81), 20.

Ahura Mazda".[125] Thompson says that giving the one divine "life-giving spirit"[126] a name is, for the Persians, a human and regional need and "reflects a world-view that distinguishes"[127] local religious and political perceptions from an "ultimate reality that is beyond human expression, perception and understanding".[128] "Religious traditions of a specific" geographical past within their empire, are merged into an 'inclusive monotheism' which can re-interpret and accommodate them all.[129] While "the Greek historians, philosophers and playwrights" chose to reject the traditions of other cultures, "the intellectuals of Asia chose…to affirm the traditions of the past as expressions of true reality that previously had only been perceived darkly".[130] That the Jews as descendants of the Israelites accepted this benign interpretation of their traditions is manifest for Thompson in the Cyrus decree that they could go back and rebuild their temple. Cyrus is charged by "the ancient god of the state of Israel, to reestablish his people by building a temple dedicated"[131] to him at Jerusalem. The Jews within his empire, are "legitimate successors of the neglected and forgotten Yahweh traditions of ancient Israel"[132] which are also traditions about the one divine life-giving spirit. Because Cyrus' decree accorded with the Israelite practical wish to rebuild their temple, they did not fuss the underlying theology. They had learned to live within the accommodating Persian religious worldview.[133]

---

[125] Ibid 22.
[126] Thompson, ibid 115.
[127] Ibid.
[128] Ibid.
[129] Ibid 115-116.
[130] Ibid.
[131] Ibid 116.
[132] Ibid.
[133] James Barr rejects the idea that the Jews in Persia assimilated very much from their overlords. He considers the idea that Jewish resurrection theology originates in Zoroastrianism or that there was any theological influence at all "has not been answered." He prefers the view that Jews either ignored and did not try and understand Zoroastrianism, or that they acknowledged common elements in a limited quest for mutual understanding without any assimilation ("The Question of Religious Influence: The Case of Zoroastrianism, Judaism and Christianity", *Journal of the American Academy of Religion*, Vol. 53, No. 2 (June 1985) 201-235 (223-230)).

The Greeks and Romans – cultural toleration and homogenisation

Mark S. Smith has confirmed with Edelman and Thompson that the monotheistic worldviews in the ancient world were not all intolerant and violent.[134] But the Greeks and Romans chose a different approach towards religious diversity and accommodation.[135] They interpreted the mythology and religion of other cultures using their own religious concepts and practices as comparative analogues which assisted understanding and enabled homogenisation.[136]

Smith quotes and critiques Jan Assmann's concept of "intercultural translation".[137] Smith says Assmann believed that all the polytheistic peoples of the Near East worshipped the same God under a different name – Assmann was convinced "that God or the gods [we]re international".[138] The *interpretatio Latina* translated Greek gods so that Romans could understand them as the *interpretatio Graeca* had translated Eygptian gods for the Greeks.[139] But Smith says the process was not one of simple translation. The gods were re-interpreted as well. Assmann's concept of translation was as much about politics as it was about religion.[140] The Greeks and Romans made comparisons of the names and character traits of the gods of the various cultures which they conquered or with whom they interacted, so that they could understand them, perhaps accommodate them, but certainly govern them.[141] Tacitus used the phrase *interpretatio Romana* to explain to Romans how the people of Germania worshipped the same gods the Romans called Castor and Pollux in a sacred grove in Nahanarvali under a priest dressed as a woman.[142] Tacitus also wrote that the principal German god of that age was really Mercury.[143] But Mark Smith says that it is misleading and

---

[134] Smith, Mark S., *God in Translation: Deities in Cross-Cultural Discourse in the Biblical World*, (William. B. Eerdmans, Grand Rapids, Michigan, 2010), 26-27.
[135] Ibid 255.
[136] Ibid 325.
[137] Ibid 38.
[138] Ibid quoting Assmann J, *Moses the Egyptian, The Memory of Egypt in Western Monotheism*, (Harvard University Press, Cambridge Massachusetts and London, 1997), 45.
[139] Ibid 39 quoting Assmann, 45.
[140] Ibid 17.
[141] Ibid 243-244.
[142] Tacitus, *Germania*, 43.
[143] Ibid 9, probably referring to Odin.

simplistic to suggest as Assmann does,[144] that this translation process was only about accommodation and understanding.[145] It was really about empire[146] and translation was often a defensive strategy adopted by a vassal state which wished to retain its own cultural and religious identity against the unifying drive of the empire.[147] For vassals, knowledge of the empire pantheon was an essential diplomatic tool.[148] But such nations often had one religious posture for external consumption and another that they lived domestically.[149]

Smith concedes that there is some truth in Assmann's idea that the Jews were different;[150] that the Jewish 'Mosaic distinction' set them apart from other nations from the beginning of their relationship with the various Bronze and Iron Age superpowers.[151] But Smith says Assmann was critical of Jewish resistance to the homogenizing press of the empires because that resistance led to violence.[152] Smith maintains that the move to one-god monotheism came much later[153] when it had been seeded by similar ideas from Assyria and Babylon[154] and that it was not inherently violent. But even after the exile when Smith acknowledges that monotheism was well established in Judaism,[155] there is still translation by the Jews themselves for pragmatic reasons as when educated men like Philo sought to explain Jewish theology for Greek philosophers[156] and when Aristeas sought the release of Jewish prisoners by explaining that Jews really worshipped the same universal god.[157]

---

[144] Smith, n134, 324.
[145] Ibid 78, 327-329.
[146] Ibid 89, 329.
[147] Ibid 37, 52, 108, 272.
[148] Ibid 81.
[149] Ibid 184.
[150] Ibid 282-283.
[151] Ibid 183.
[152] Ibid 21-25.
[153] Ibid 19,
[154] Ibid 157-166.
[155] Ibid 10, 19-20
[156] Ibid 239, 293, 296-299.
[157] Ibid 301-302.

Summary of this review of the history of Jewish theology

This review of the scholarship concerning Jewish theology from perhaps the third millennium B.C., to the Greek and Roman empires, is a composite. That is, the scholarship shows the efforts of its authors to be objective. But it does not achieve that goal because, for the most part, it excludes reference to the Hebrew scriptures themselves. No writing can ever be completely objective. All written and spoken words include the experience of their authors. Though we try to set our experience, beliefs and even our hopes to one side as we write, those parts of our character remain subliminally present even in those sincere efforts towards balance.

Some of the experience and expectation of these authors is manifest in their exclusion of what the Hebrew scriptures themselves say about deity. In other cases, the authors' reach toward the elusive goal of objectivity, can be seen in the inclusion of a reference to some of those scriptures because it has seemed unreasonable to ignore material with ancient contextual genealogy even if it was redacted and edited to conform to changing orthodoxies.

Sommer is one scholar who has tried to factor the Hebrew scriptures into his explanation of Israelite theology.

Part Two - Jewish theology at the time of Christ

In his introduction to his edited translation of the Babylonian Talmud, Leo Auerbach has written that

> [T]he Talmud is a record of about a thousand years of accumulated Jewish learning and wisdom in all fields of endeavor: Law, religion, ethics, history, science and folklore.[158]

But the Talmud is called "Oral Lore, in contra-distinction to the

---

[158] *The Babylonian Talmud*, Leo Auerbach ed., (Philosophical Library, New York, 1944) (hereafter "*Babylonian Talmud*"), 7. Michael L. Rodkinson (*The Babylonian Talmud*, 1918 Translation) takes the origin of the 'Mishnayoth' behind the Talmud back to "the students of Jewish academies which existed since the days of Jehosphat, King of Judah [II Chron, xvii,9]" and says the Mishnayoth was sourced in earlier customs and traditions (ibid, xv).

Bible"¹⁵⁹ which was the Written Law or "Torah".¹⁶⁰ The Oral Lore of Talmud is a record of the exposition and interpretation of the Torah which was handed down from one generation of Jews to the next. Its genesis probably lies with the scribes who flourished from about 500B.C. after the dispersion of the nation of Judah when the Written Law became the only way the Jewish people could hold on to their faith after the exile and the destruction of their Temple at Jerusalem.¹⁶¹

It has come to cover all Jewish "fields of endeavor",¹⁶² because interpretation and exposition by experts enabled the Jewish people to have the spiritual guidance of the Torah in every part of their lives when that guidance was not plainly obvious to lay Jews from the face of the Torah. Because the scope of the Talmud reaches into every area of Jewish life, it enables close insight into what Jews between 500B.C. and 500A.D. believed about God, a period which encompasses the advent of Christianity.

There are two Talmuds, the Jerusalem or Palestinian and the Babylonian. The Babylonian Talmud is larger and has had more influence on Jewish life,¹⁶³ probably because the Jewish seat in Babylon was more constant, established and larger than that in Jerusalem during the formative period. One reason for that stability and endurance was the absence of Rome and its ultimate policy of Jewish suppression. While both seats existed, there were "cordial relations and frequent interchange of teachers…so that the names of the same teachers appear in both *Talmuds*".¹⁶⁴ But neither text presents as a code. Many of the entries are little more than notes of agreement following dialogue and even debate. Auerbach frankly concedes that the recorded discussions "sometimes seem lengthy and pointless…[even] hairsplitting"¹⁶⁵ and to follow no logical sequence. But "the *Talmud* served as a storehouse of

---

[159] Auberach, ibid.
[160] Ibid 7-8.
[161] Ibid 8-11.
[162] Ibid 7.
[163] Ibid 17.
[164] Ibid.
[165] Ibid 18. Rodkinson is more respectful. He says that although the Talmud has remained stationary through all the vicissitudes of the Jews, yet it remains as a "vast storehouse of Jewish knowledge" and is only attacked by those who have not read it right through (above n158, ix-x).

folklore, history, ancient custom, and wisdom"[166] and the two are ideal for our purpose in seeking understanding of everyday orthodox Jewish belief about God during and after the Roman era and again, during the advent of Christianity.

Talmudic evidence

The overriding impression one is left from versions of both Talmuds, is that the Rabbis whose interpretations have been compiled in these two books were strict monotheists. The need to express that strict monotheism is not so emphatic in the Babylonian record, perhaps because there was no need to rebut or expunge any sense of God's dualism as appears in the Jerusalem Talmud (discussed below), but both records are clear that God is one. Perhaps the most elementary example that is clear in both, is the affirmation that man was made in God's image. In some Christian commentaries on that simple Genesis 1 statement, there is considerable effort to explain how a God without a body could nevertheless have made corporeal men and women in his own image. But there is none of that in either Talmud. In the Babylonian, Rabbi Akiba "would"[167] simply say that man is "Blessed...because he was born in the image of the Lord... [and they] were called children of the Lord"[168] with references to Genesis 9:6 and Deuteronomy 14:1.[169] In the Jerusalem Talmud, the reference is more oblique and comes as various Rabbis discuss the custom of overturning their house furniture on Saturday evening.[170] Consensus holds that this is to make men uncomfortable as they mourn their separation from God,[171] but Bar-Kapara adds that is also because "God...has given [them] a form to His own likeness" and the discomfort of reclining without furniture is to remind them that punishment for sin should make men

---

[166] Ibid.
[167] Ibid 34.
[168] Ibid.
[169] Ibid.
[170] *The Talmud of Jerusalem*, Moses Schwab, Translator, (Williams and Norgate, Covent Garden, England 1886) (reprinted by the University of California Libraries using various digital technologies) (hereafter "*Jerusalem Talmud*"), 56-57.
[171] Ibid.

uncomfortable.[172] There is a further oblique reference to the Genesis 1:26 statement – "Let us make man in our image, after our likeness" to make sense of the dualism implicit in the word "us" appearing in all orthodox translations of the original manuscripts,[173] but again, that is discussed in more detail below.

In both Talmuds, God is the solitary Lord or King of the Universe,[174] the Father of mankind in heaven,[175] the Most High,[176] the Living God,[177] the Author of Creation,[178] the Rock of the World,[179] the Eternal God of Truth,[180] the Creator[181] and the Almighty.[182] When He is not referred to by one of His names or name titles, He is always referred to using the third person singular pronoun – "He". Save for the extended discussion of the need to expunge dualist interpretation of references to God in scripture at Jerusalem, there is no suggestion of a Divine Council, no reference to God's having a consort, nor any progeny. Messiah will simply be a King called David whether he resides among the living or the dead.[183]

Rebuttal of the dualism of God in the Jerusalem Talmud

The issue of the possible dualism of God is introduced in the Jerusalem Talmud by a question put to the Rabbi Samlai[184] by "some bad men".[185] His interlocutor asks – 'How many Gods created the

---

[172] Ibid, 57.
[173] Ibid, 151.
[174] *Babylonian Talmud*, 94, 121, 140; *Jerusalem Talmud*, 21. See also for example at <http://www.aish.com/atr/Let-Us-Make-Man.html> where the Aish Rabbi says there is only one God in Genesis 1:26, 27. When the pronoun us is used in Genesis 1:26, God is simply explaining what he is doing to the angels.
[175] *Babylonian Talmud* 129.
[176] *Jerusalem Talmud* 10.
[177] Ibid 21.
[178] Ibid 23.
[179] Ibid.
[180] Ibid 34.
[181] Ibid 116.
[182] Ibid 50.
[183] *Jerusalem Talmud*, 44.
[184] Ibid 150.
[185] The identity of the 'bad men' is not revealed, but the footnote suggests the question is a response to criticism from contemporary Christian apologists.

universe?"[186] which the context confirms is a reference to the use of the plural "us" in the standard translation of Genesis 1:26 into English as – "Let *us* make man in our image, after our likeness",[187] and to Joshua 22:22 where God is referred to as "The Lord God of gods".

Rabbi Samlaï responds with references to Deuteronomy 4:32 and Genesis 1:1 though with clarifications from the questioners' references and some others. His answers are avowedly monotheistic. The references to God in Genesis 1:1 and Deuteronomy 4:32 to God as creator are both in the singular and the verb used confirms the fact. Similarly, he explains that in Genesis 1:26 the fact that God is singular is confirmed in the following verse 27 where the creation of man by God in the singular is confirmed by the use of the personal pronouns "He" and "His" when the plan or creation is carried into effect. The same answer is given in relation to Joshua 22:22 – the verb used in the original language text denotes God in the singular and the Rabbi Samlaï puts the matter to bed by saying the confusion has arisen because God has multiple names, just as their emperor had three names – "Caesar, Augustus or Emperor".[188] The discussion in the Jerusalem Talmud continues with the Rabbi Isaac explaining that the confusing plural had been used "to show that several degrees of holiness are meant."[189]

The point in the current article is not to confirm which view then taken of the various contested verses was or is correct. The point is to confirm that Talmudic Rabbi between 500B.C. and 500A.D. and certainly during the early Christian period, all Jews considered that their God was one and followed a thoroughly monotheistic mindset. But the exchange between the Rabbi Samlaï and his interlocutors serves as a useful introduction to the early Christian theology of God.

---

[186] *Jerusalem Talmud* 150.
[187] Ibid 151.
[188] Ibid. Note that the same monotheistic emphasis comes through from the translation of the Jerusalem Talmud edited by Heinrich W. Guggenheimer (Walter de Gruyter, Berlin and New York, 2000), 605-606. Again, Rabbi Simlai says in "every place where the Christians read heretic meanings, their answer is at that place." He explains that this passage does not say "they created" but that "he created".
[189] Ibid.

Conclusion

In this chapter I have discussed the origin and development of what is now called monotheism in Jewish thought. While I have confirmed that the Jewish rabbis were all thoroughly monotheistic by the time of Christianity's advent, their theological history had a lot more colour in it. That colour included that there were multiple anthropomorphic god-beings though there was always one who presided, whether he was El or Yahweh. While that multiplicity has been interpreted by some modern scholars as proof that the ancient Israelites were polytheists, the modern 'polytheist' label obscures the differences between Israelite worship and the worship of other nations contemporary with them. Though some scholars are happy attaching the polytheist label to ancient Israel, many others are not citing the enduring pre-eminence of Israel's one God at all times. Others are dismissive of such insistence and suggest that it simply identifies the one-God beliefs of the scholar concerned.

It is not the purpose of this book to settle these academic disputes. What is clear is that the Israelite God was not always monotheistic in every modern sense of that label word.

3

CHRISTIANS AS JEWISH HERETICS
THE ORIGINS OF THE IDEA OF TRINITY

Introduction

In chapter two I explained how the idea of monotheism became the established doctrine of Judaism by the time of the coming of Christ. Different sects had developed in Israel after the Exodus, but all of those sects were united in their recognition of the laws given through Moses including the prohibition on worshipping other gods. The prophecies of a Messiah to come existed, but Jesus of Nazareth did not satisfy the criteria set out for the Israelites remaining in Judah in those prophecies primarily because he had suffered an ignominious death and had not redeemed the nation from its occupied status. The suggestion that Jesus was not only the promised Messiah, but that he was also the Son of God was blasphemous if not seditious since it threatened the established religious and political order. The claim that he had been resurrected after his crucifixion was exasperating since it unravelled Jesus' death as an end to the disturbance, and there was no obvious and tidy way to shut down the new claims.

In this chapter I explain that the charge that the Christians were polytheists became the central plank in Jewish intellectual and theological efforts to deny the ongoing claims of Jesus' Messiahship and resurrection. The assertion of Christian polytheism also answered the inflammatory claim that in crucifying Jesus, the Jews had killed their God and rightful King. The reason why the polytheism charge became the most effective anti-Christian weapon of the Jews, was because it cut off the Messiah, God and Jesus resurrection claims at the same time. If there was only one God, which was theology in which all the original Christians were deeply indoctrinated, then Jesus could not be He. And if Jesus was not God as he claimed, then the Messiahship claim was also fraudulent as was the claim of resurrection which no-one but his biased followers claimed to have witnessed. It was an effective and foundational challenge because it was so rhetorically simple and difficult to rebut. Simple denial of the polytheism charge was tantamount to an admission that Jesus was not divine after all, and it was complicated to explain his oneness with the Father when every Jewish schoolboy had been taught that it was sinful to acknowledge more than one God. While the Trinity doctrine was probably not a conversion tool like the claims of Jesus' Messiahship and resurrection, it answered Jewish theological criticism and protected the convictions of the early converts. I will now explain the development of the Trinity doctrine in four Parts.

In the first Part, I will briefly review the antipathy that existed between the early Christians and the Jews. In Part Two, I outline the development of the idea of the Trinity in the early Ante-Nicene Fathers. I do not treat every nuance of that development, but I identify the germs of the idea that were postulated by Justin Martyr, Theophilus and Clement of Alexandria in the second century A.D. In Part Three, I spend more time with Tertullian and Origen because these latter two and particularly Tertullian are considered to be the authors of the orthodox doctrine. But as that discussion reveals, Tertullian's ideas are uncontroversial save for his innovation with the 'one substance' idea - that the unity of Father, Son and Holy Ghost went not just to purpose, but also in some way which he could not explain, to substance. Save in that respect, the mysterious aspects of Trinitarianism are more properly attributed to Saint Augustine and Thomas Cranmer. That is because Tertullian did not write just to rebut the Jewish theological challenge that had subsided by the third century. He wrote to rebut heretical ideas about Jesus and God that were growing out of the existing Trinitarian responses to the Jews. Though Origen disagreed with Tertullian's idea that the Father, Son and Holy Ghost were somehow 'of one substance', the Nicene bishops in due course, did not, although what any of them meant by 'one substance' is not clear.

In Part Four, I briefly survey the contributions of Iraeneus and his disciple, Hippolytus in the third century along with Novatian and Gregory of Thaumaturgus. I conclude that the Trinity doctrine was developed to answer insightful Jewish theological criticism that challenged the foundations of Christian faith. Rather than simply disavow their orthodox Jewish theological ancestry as the early Christians might have done if they had known that Christianity would numerically trump Judaism within three centuries, the post-Apostolic Christian Fathers tried to explain. While those explanations led some to excess, even those named as heretics remained convinced that Jesus was God and that he was one with the Father in a mysterious way not easily understood or explained by mortal man without divine help.

Part One - Early conflict between Christians and Jews

I will shortly review the material in the writings of the Ante-Nicene fathers that support the Jerusalem Talmud view that the Rabbis at the time of the advent of Christianity considered them "bad men"[190] or heretics. But orthodox Jewish antipathy towards Christianity had many levels and theology was just one of the battlefields. The martyrdom of Stephen, Saul's crusade to rid the world of the Christian menace and the various intrigues to later discredit or eliminate him, are recorded Christian anecdotes that suggest that this war became a matter of life and death for them. For orthodox Jews living during the ministries of the Apostles Peter and Paul, Christianity was heresy; the perversion of the law of Moses, the doctrine of God and the Davidic Messiah into a Galilean cult that deified a Nazarene carpenter's son. Like all Reformations, it was at first resisted as the rebellion of a charlatan. Heresy was treason and was capitally punishable under rabbinical law.

Just as the Reformation Protestants were originally persecuted as the

---

[190] *The Talmud of Jerusalem*, Moses Schwab, Translator, (Williams and Norgate, Covent Garden, England 1886) (reprinted by the University of California Libraries using various digital technologies),168.

fanatical dupes of charismatic merchants of treason, so the early Christians were hunted with the venom that is reserved for those who fight the established political order as terrorists. No legislation was too oppressive in the search for security; no punishment too cruel and unusual despite the admonitions of established religious texts about judgment, mercy, patience and faith.[191]

But there are more than legal and political analogies between the Christian Reformation and the advent of Christianity. Just as the Reformers attacked the Catholic doctrines of salvation and the prohibition of universal access to scripture with theses nailed to doors, so the Christian reformers of Judaism, attacked Rabbinism with the 'corrective' doctrines that Jesus Christ had outlined in His Sermon on the Mount. The Law of Moses was about love, reconciliation and forgiveness – about brotherly kindness and secret charity rather than ritual punishment for technical violations of the Oral Law and self-serving public religious observance to be seen of men. The Rabbis defended with all the tools at their disposal. Secret religious police were engaged to expose Christians worshipping behind closed doors and the political and legal authorities were engaged as allies in the witch-hunts, or they turned blind eyes towards the excesses of the religious police when they breached the Roman secular law.

At a theological level, the Rabbis' war was waged with doctrine and claims to orthodoxy. Christianity's deification of Jesus Christ was exposed as a form of polytheism barely removed from the Roman practice of Caesar worship. And theologically, it was this charge of polytheism that stung the early Christians the most. Jewish monotheism had become their badge of civilization, honour and difference. Jewish monotheism distinguished the one true and living religion that was Judaism from the idolatry of the Greeks and Romans that accommodated every savage cult in the empire in the interests of a homogenised multicultural hedonism. Monotheism had become the Jewish badge of righteous honour; a quiet yet very visible and self-serving emblem of peculiar but royal difference.

---

[191] For example, from Jesus himself – Matthew 23:23 perhaps referring to the Hebrew teaching in Hosea 6:6; 12:6 and Micah 6:8.

At first, the Christians did not know how to respond to the derisive epithets that were hurled at them. To be called Christian, was not a term of respect, but it became so as these mostly converted Jews found a familiar spirit in their persecuted peculiarity.[192] But an adequate intellectual response to the charge of polytheism took longer to develop since there was no simple answer to the charge that Christians were just one more example of polytheist infidels.

Theological battle lines

In his twelfth century magnum opus, the Mishneh Torah, Maimonides wrote that "Jesus the Nazarene…[was] a greater stumbling block"[193] to the Jews than anything else in their history. The Messiah was supposed to redeem, save and gather Israel, but this would-be Messiah had caused other nations to scatter, humiliate and destroy her and to replace the Torah rather than to strengthen the commandments.[194]

Maimonides' work was retrospective. Christoph Ochs captures the original Christian theological problem more exactly when he writes that the identity of Jesus was a paradox for the early Christians:

> [I]t would have been far easier to abandon the intellectual embarrassment of a divine-human Christ in favor of a purely human or purely divine Jesus.[195]

Ochs observes that "the question of *how* Jesus came to be understood as divine is much debated"[196] but that the belief was well established by the end of the second century.[197] This belief is what has taken "center stage

---

[192] For example, Deuteronomy 14:2 of the Torah said that Israelite peculiarity was part of what made them holy ("For thou art an holy people unto the Lord thy God, and the Lord hath chosen thee to be a peculiar people unto himself, above all the nations that are upon the earth"). The Apostle Peter similarly taught the early Christians that they were "a chosen generation, a royal priesthood, an holy nation, [and] a peculiar people; [called to] shew forth the praises of him who hath called you out of darkness into his marvellous light" (1 Peter 2:9).
[193] *Hilkhot Melakhim* 11:10–12.
[194] Ibid.
[195] Christoph Ochs, *Matthaeus Adversos Christianos: The Use of the Gospel of Matthew in Jewish Polemics Against the Divinity of Jesus*, (Mohr Siebeck e-book, 2013), 2.
[196] Ibid 2-3.
[197] Ibid 3.

over the discussion of his Messiahship".[198] Quoting Michael Whyshogrod, Ochs says that

> [t]he divinity of Jesus has been rejected by all Jewish (and Muslim) authors as incompatible with true monotheism and [as] possibly idolatrous.[199]

He notes Robert Chazan's agreement that the Christian doctrine of Jesus' incarnation receives "the harshest Jewish criticism of all".[200] That is because the Christian doctrine of incarnation is central to "the definition of God's nature and holiness".[201] Jewish polemicists argued that it belittled God to suggest he had entered into a woman's body to be "born into the world like other men."[202] Though for Christians, this humility did not detract from God's dignity at all but rather enobled Him, for Jews, the very suggestion was a crime of lèse majesté,[203] the greatest heresy of all and thus a treason.

The point of Ochs' work is to show that the New Testament gospel of Matthew was written as 'the gospel for the Jews'. Matthew wrote to convince Jews from their own Old Testament scriptures that Jesus of Nazareth was Jesus Christ, or in other words, their long-awaited Messiah. But Ochs also explains that the Jews used the gospel interpretations of the Old Testament scriptures against the Christians – as for example, when they answered the Christian interpretations of the word 'virgin' in Isaiah chapters 7-9, to explain contextually that the words from which it was translated could also mean 'maid' or 'young woman'.[204]

Ochs says that the Jewish scholars "were not merely defensive, [but]… actively sought out…debate with Christians".[205] On the one hand the Christians used Jewish scripture as a proselyting tool to win Jewish converts for Christ, and on the other hand, the Jews would use the 'faulty' Christian

---

[198] Ibid 5.
[199] Ibid quoting Michael Whyshogrod, "A Jewish Perspective on Incarnation", *Modern Theology* 12 (1996), 195, 197-198.
[200] Ibid quoting Robert Chazan, *Fashioning Jewish Identity in Medieval Western Christendom*, (Cambridge University Press, 2004), 349.
[201] Ibid 6.
[202] Ibid 6 citing Daniel J. Lasker, *Jewish Philosophical Polemics against Christianity in the Middle Ages*, (Littman, 1977), 107-108.
[203] Ibid.
[204] Ibid 10, fn 30.
[205] Ibid 16.

interpretations to win back their misguided brothers and sisters to the true faith of their fathers. Just as the Christians developed interpretations of the Old Testament to explain the Messiahship of Jesus Christ, so scholarly Jews made themselves familiar with the Christian New Testament gospels and letters for their own polemical purposes.[206] While this process developed over centuries and became very detailed during the Middle Ages, it began during the early Christian era. C. Marvin Pate has written that

> [t]he Ante-Nicene church fathers had to assume the role of apologists refuting the claims made against Christianity by Judaism on the one hand and by the Roman Empire on the other hand. Judaism, with its tenacious commitment to monotheism, accused Christianity of polytheism – worshipping two gods (Christ and God) and even three gods (the Trinity).[207]

Pate says the Christians were in trouble with the Romans because they denied the imperial cult which upheld Caesar as the Lord "through which all religions derived their meaning".[208] For first century Jews, the Christian claims that Christ was divine simply contradicted monotheism.[209] Pate says that when Jesus referred to himself as "the great I am",[210] the High Priest Caiaphas rent his priestly garment because Jesus had committed blasphemy by making himself equal with God.[211] More cautious because of the risk of offence to the Jews and the death penalty under sectarian law, Paul and John were both at pains to explain that "Christ's deity did not compromise the *Shema*, Israel's great confession of monotheism".[212] This Jewish antipathy towards Christianity's doctrine of Jesus' divinity continued into the second and third centuries and is manifest by Justin Martyr's *Dialogue with Trypho*.[213] Trypho's very Jewish accusation against Christianity is that 'if Jesus is God, then the Christians must be polytheists.' Justin responded

---

[206] Ibid 17-18.
[207] C. Marvin Pate, *From Plato to Jesus: What Does Philosophy Have to Do with Theology"*, (Kregel Academic and Professional, Grand Rapids, Michigan, 2011), 129.
[208] Ibid.
[209] Ibid.
[210] Ibid citing Mark 14: 61-64.
[211] Ibid.
[212] Ibid referring to the Deuteronomy 6:4 ritualised affirmation – "Hear, O Israel: the Lord our God is one" as distinguished by Paul in 1 Corinthians 8:4-6 and probably (says Pate) John in Revelations 4 & 5.
[213] Ibid. Justin Martyr lived between 100 and 166 AD and his *Dialogue with Trypho* is credited as an authentic second century text.

much as Matthew had done in his gospel and by explaining among other arguments, that Jesus was the "angel of the Lord – God – who appeared to Abraham, Jacob and Joshua".[214] But he did not use the language of the Trinity. Rather he explained that though Jesus Christ is a god, He is not the same as the Lord God and is subject to Him.[215] For Justin Martyr, though Jesus is distinct from God in person, He is one with God "in will" because they have precisely the same purposes and because He does God's bidding as His subordinate.[216]

Initially, the Christian response to the Jewish charge of polytheism was thematically that there was no polytheism. Jesus Christ and the Lord God (and for that matter, the Holy Spirit) were separate and distinct individuals who were united in all their purposes. The language of the Trinity was first used by Clement of Alexandria to explain this very specific kind of purpose unity in the first century,[217] but was not developed into the Trinity doctrine until late in the third century before the Council at Nicaea settled it in a Creed upon which all Christians could agree.

Part Two - Development of the idea of Trinity

Justin Martyr

In the writings of Justin Martyr that have survived, he responded to official persecution of Christians on two fronts. In his *First Apology*, he sought to distinguish Christian theology and practice from the Jewish misinformation that was the cause of their persecution by the Roman authorities as seditious heretics. And, secondly, in his *Dialogue with Trypho*,[218] he explained the different Jewish and Christian conceptions of God from their common scriptures.

---

[214] Ibid 130.
[215] *Ante-Nicene Fathers, The Writings of the Fathers Down to 325AD, Vol 1, The Apostolic Fathers, Justin Martyr, Irenaeus*, "Dialogue with Trypho", American Edition arranged and referenced by A. Cleveland Coxe, Fourth Printing, 2004, 194, 223.
[216] Ibid 223-224.
[217] Theophilus is credited as the first person to use the term "Trinity" but as will be seen below, he did not use the term in the more famous doctrinal sense. Tertullian is also credited as "the first to apply the term 'Trinitas' to the Father, Son, and Holy Spirit" (Robert E. Roberts, *The Theology of Tertullian*, 1924, 22-23.
[218] *Ante-Nicene Fathers, The Writings of the Fathers Down to 325AD, Vol 1, The Apostolic Fathers, Justin Martyr, Irenaeus*, "Dialogue with Trypho", American Edition arranged and referenced by A. Cleveland Coxe, Fourth Printing, 2004, 194.

While we may wonder whether Justin was wise to criticize his Jewish theological cousins when he sought tolerance from their Roman secular lords, he clearly believed that the Jewish and Christian doctrines about God were distinct and different. For the Jews, there was only one God. For the Christians, the Maker of all things and his Son Jesus Christ, were separate and distinct but were one in purpose. Justin Martyr's understanding of the Christian doctrine of God is ironical since the Christian Councils in the fourth century sought to re-align the doctrine of God in the two faiths so that both had only one God. Justin Martyr's teaching that God and Christ were distinct is the reason why he is identified as a 'pagan' in the *New Advent Encyclopedia*.[219] But he is also accepted as an authentic Ante-Nicene Father of Christianity and his understanding of the Christian doctrine of God in the second century A.D., is said to assist understanding how that doctrine developed. Like the Apostle Paul in the first century A.D.,[220] his concerns with apostate teaching are clear and were not authoritatively resolved.

To the Romans

Justin wrote his *First Apology* to defend Christianity before the Roman Emperor Titus, his family, Senate and counselors. He demanded[221] that the Emperor order a judicial investigation into the conduct and faith of the Christians so that "traditional opinions" caused by "mental blindness" about them might be put to rest.[222] This context did not require substantial discussion of the nature and differences between Christian and Jewish doctrines, but Justin explained the doctrine of Christ thoroughly to rebut misinformation that might have come to the Emperor from other sources. He denied the charge that Christians were atheists,[223] and noted that similar mischaracterization of the teaching of Socrates had led to his "death, as

---

[219] < http://www.newadvent.org/cathen/08580c.htm >.
[220] For example, Acts 20:29; 1 Corinthians 11:18; Galatians 1:6; 2 Thessalonians 2: 3; 1 Timothy 1:6; 4:1; 2 Timothy 1:15; 2:18; 3:5; 4:4; and Titus 1:16. Note that Paul was not the only Apostle with concerns about apostate teaching. Peter, John and Jude expressed similar concerns (2 Peter 2:1; 3:17; 1 John 2:18; 4:1; Jude 1:4 and Revelations 2:2; 3:16; 13:7).
[221] *Ante-Nicene Fathers, The Writings of the Fathers Down to 325AD, Vol 1, The Apostolic Fathers, Justin Martyr, Irenaeus*, "The First Apology of Justin", American Edition arranged and referenced by A. Cleveland Coxe, Fourth Printing, 2004, 163.
[222] Ibid.
[223] Ibid 164.

an atheist and a profane person [who was]…introducing new divinities".[224] Christians were god-fearing patriots taught to obey the established secular authorities. Their doctrine that Jesus Christ was born the Son of God, ought not be the subject of persecution since Roman religion also held that Jupiter had sons.[225] But Justin differentiated the Christian idea of God from that of the Jews so that the Romans might understand their differences and treat them separately and respectfully. He said that the Jews worshipped a "nameless God" who spoke to Moses.[226] Christians worshipped Jesus as the Christ or Messiah and as the Son of God. Neither Justin's denigration of Jewish theology, nor the reasons why he so wrote to Caesar are important in our context, but his blunt description of their differences in theology, are. The Jews believed that there was only one God, not two as Justin asserted for the Christians. This was the point of difference in their theology that Justin wanted the Emperor and his advisers to understand. For Justin, this difference proved that the Jews were not really "acquainted with the Father [of the Universe]" because they did not know that He had a Son.[227]

To the Jews

While there is debate as to whether Trypho was a real Jewish rabbi or a fictional character Justin invented to present his message, no one questions the authenticity of Justin's reply or theology.[228]

Justin's core message was that "there is no polytheism" in Christianity. He discussed Moses' account of Abraham's experience "under the oak in Mamre":[229]

> He who appeared to Abraham…is God, sent with two angels in

---

[224] Ibid.
[225] Ibid 170.
[226] Ibid 184.
[227] Ibid.
[228] For example in < http://justus.anglican.org/resources/bio/175.html> the dialogue is "probably a real conversation with a real rabbi" but with "a few good lines that he wished he had thought of at the time". In the *Catholic Encyclopedia*, "according to Eusebius" Tryphon "was 'the best known Jew of that time'" and was perhaps the Rabbi Tarphon at Ephesus (<http://www.newadvent.org/cathen/08580c.htm>), but Jewish sources reject Trypho as the Rabbi Tarphon suggesting that Trypho was simply a fictional device that enabled the presentation of a theological message (Claudia Setzer, *Jewish Responses to Early Christians* (Minneapolis: Fortress Press, 1994) 215 (chapter 9, fn 5)).
[229] Ibid 223.

His company to judge Sodom by Another who remains ever in the supercelestial places, invisible to all men, holding personal intercourse with none, [and] whom [Justin] believe[s] to be the Maker and Father of all things.[230]

But Trypho and his colleagues disagreed with Justin's assertion that these passages proved "that there is any other God or Lord, or that the Holy Spirit says so, besides the Maker of all things".[231] Justin replied, as Pate has observed above,[232] that there is "another God and Lord subject to the Maker of all things; who is also called an Angel, because He announces to men whatsoever the Maker of all things – above whom there is no other God – wishes to announce to them."[233] Again, Trypho does not accept Justin's interpretation and says rather that God "appeared to [Abraham] before the vision of the three"[234] and that the "three whom the Scripture calls men, were angels; two of them sent to destroy Sodom, and one to announce the joyful tidings to Sarah, that she would have a son".[235]

In Justin's account of the dialogue, he tries to explain again and in more detail. He says that this one angel that Trypho had said was sent to proclaim the joyful tidings of Sarah's pregnancy with Isaac, returns and is called God in the scriptural text when He counsels Abraham to accept Sarah's wish that Hagar and her son should leave lest there be a contest over entitlement to Abraham's inheritance.[236] While Trypho concedes that Justin has shown him that the 'angel' who originally announced Sarah's pregnancy was indeed the Creator of all things manifest in angelic or human form,[237] Justin is not satisfied with Trypho's concession and tries to show him from the Psalms, that the angel/god/man who made the pregnancy announcement to Abraham is distinct from God, the Maker of all things, though not in will. Justin's efforts to persuade Trypho and his companions from the Psalms that there is more than one being called God in the Hebrew scriptures, are no more successful than his explanation of

---

[230] Ibid.
[231] Ibid.
[232] Nn 207-216 and supporting text.
[233] Ibid.
[234] Ibid.
[235] Ibid.
[236] Ibid.
[237] Ibid.

Abraham's experience under the oak in Mamre.

What is clear from all Justin Martyr's efforts to persuade Trypho, is that Justin believed that God and Christ are separate and distinct beings but that they are unified in their will and purpose. Christ does the bidding of the Father or Maker of all things. For Justin, Jesus is the God or Lord "who received commission from the Lord who (remains) in the heavens".[238]

In the continuing dialogue, Justin and Trypho discuss what the Hebrew scriptures about the visit to Abraham at Mamre mean when they say that all three who met Abraham ate the food he set before them, and they discuss without any final agreement, God's dealing with Jacob and Moses.[239] Justin insists that the "God who appeared to Abraham, and is minister to God the Maker of all things",[240] is Jesus Christ who was "born of the Virgin, [and] became man, of like passions with all"[241] of us. For Justin, Jesus Christ was begotten of God the Maker before all other creatures and is variously called by the Holy Spirit, "the Glory of the Lord,…the Son,… Wisdom,…an Angel,….God….[and] Lord and Logos".[242] When Jesus Christ "appeared in human form to Joshua the son of Nave (Nun)",[243] "He call[ed] Himself Captain".[244] "He can be called by all those names, since He ministers to the Father's will, and since He was begotten by the Father by an act of will; just as we see happening among ourselves"[245] when we will to do something.

Justin also cites the words "let Us make man after our image and likeness" as another argument in favour of his separate identification of the Father and the Son.[246] For Justin, God the Maker, did not say this to Himself.[247] That is, unlike the present English Monarch, Elizabeth II, the God who is Maker of all things does not use the pronoun "we" when speaking only of Himself. When explaining the creation with the "Let Us" words, the God who is Maker of all things "conversed with someone who

---

[238] Ibid 225.
[239] Ibid 225-227.
[240] Ibid 225.
[241] Ibid.
[242] Ibid 227.
[243] Ibid.
[244] Ibid.
[245] Ibid.
[246] Ibid 228.
[247] Ibid.

was numerically distinct from Himself".²⁴⁸

According to Justin's account, after this explanation, Trypho conceded that Justin had proven a separation between Father and Son (or Angel) in the Hebrew scriptures and they then went on to discuss Christ's incarnation in the flesh.

Justin's interpretation of the words "let us make man after our image and likeness" from Genesis is different from that of the Rabbi Samlaï discussed above from the Jerusalem Talmud.²⁴⁹ But it is not necessary to try and reconcile these different interpretations. Writing before the Christian councils of the fourth century A.D., Justin Martyr believed that God, Christ and perhaps, the Holy Spirit, were separate and distinct.

But Justin Martyr was not the only Ante-Nicene Father who wrote about the Christian doctrine of God in the second century A.D., and the others did not agree with him on all points.

Theophilus

Theophilus is reputed to have been the sixth Bishop of Antioch from perhaps 168 A.D. till his death some time between 181 and 188 A.D.²⁵⁰ He is recognized as the first person to have used the term "Trinity" in writing. But his mention was brief. He wrote:

> In like manner also the three days which were before the luminaries, are types of the Trinity, of God, and His Word, and His wisdom. And the fourth is the type of man, who needs light, that so there may be God, the Word, wisdom, man.²⁵¹

The context surrounding this quotation does not help us understand what Theophilus meant. In discussion with his pagan friend, Autolycus, he seems to be comparing a Trinity of God, the Word and Wisdom to the Christian

---

[248] Ibid.
[249] Chapter Two nn186-188 and supporting text.
[250] *Ante-Nicene Fathers, The Writings of the Fathers Down to 325AD, Vol 2, Fathers of the Second Century, Hermas, Tatian, Athenagoras, Theophilus and Clement of Alexandria (Entire)*, "Theophilus to Autolycus", American Edition arranged and referenced by A. Cleveland Coxe, Fourth Printing, 2004, 88.
[251] Ibid, I, Chapter XV, 100-101.

story of creation confirming that the Christian God is the repository of logic and wisdom.[252] Though Christian apologists have suggested that Theophilus was referring to God, Christ (the Word) and the Holy Spirit (Wisdom) in this reference to Trinity, it is not clear in Theophilus' other writing or in contemporary literature that these references would have been understood as a reference to the triune Christian God. Other surviving second century literature does not use the word Trinity. The most that can be said, is that Theophilus spoke of only one God in his three written answers to this friend. While Theophilus' God is not separated from Christ or the Holy Spirit,[253] Christ and the Holy Spirit are barely mentioned and not in such a way that we can infer that Theophilus saw them as one and the same as the Christian God to whom he constantly referred.[254] The one possible reference to Christ is oblique. Theophilus refers to God, who "made all things out of nothing…[and] willed to make man by whom He might be known". Because he had "His own Word internal within His own bowels, [he] begat Him, emitting Him along with His own wisdom before all things…as a Helper in the things that were created by Him".[255]

After this reference to the separate emanation of the Word from God (and perhaps also of the Holy Spirit as His wisdom), Theophilus retreats to the idea that there is but one God. He says that "He is called 'the governing principle…being Spirit of God, and governing principle and wisdom, and power of the highest, [which] came down upon the prophets".[256] Theophilus repeats that God created all things including man and while he uses the "us" reference in Genesis 1:26, 27,[257] unlike other apologists of the early Christian era, he makes no comment on the significance of this plural pronoun. However, for Theophilus God appears to be unembodied God, since he explains that the Genesis words that have God walking in

---

[252] This interpretation is fair since when Theophilus began his first letter or answer to his friend and described the nature of God, he used these same terms – Word and Wisdom – to describe His attributes – Ibid I Chapter III, 89-90.
[253] Prophets "carry…in them a holy spirit [and are]…inspired and made wise by God" rather than being inspired by a separate manifestation of God as the Holy Ghost or by the Holy Ghost as a personage separate from God (ibid II, chapter IX, 97).
[254] Even when Theophilus is said to explain the "meaning of the name Christian", he does not refer to Jesus Christ or his life (ibid I, Chapter XII, 92).
[255] Ibid II, Chapter X, 97-98.
[256] Ibid 99.
[257] Ibid 99, 101-102.

the Garden of Eden, are simply figurative.[258] The essence of Theophilus' message to his idol worshipping friend, is that Christianity must be true because it relies upon Jewish history to which the only truth in Greek history may be traced.

Clement of Alexandria

Clement's use of the term 'Trinity' and the remnants of some early liturgies that are attributed to him a generation after Justin Martyr and Theophilus,[259] seem to carry modern Trinitarian meaning. But since they come so soon after Justin and since Justin was so emphatic that the unity of Father, Son and Holy Ghost was a unity of purpose only, we must be careful not to impose our modern paradigms on what Clement wrote. Clement's use of the word 'Trinity' comes in his miscellaneous writings or Stromata.[260] In chapter XIV of Book V, he was explaining as Theophilus had done, that the Greeks had plagiarized their history from the Hebrews.[261] When Clement wrote of Trinity, he was commenting on Plato's use of the 'Father and Son' in completely Hebrew terms. He first quoted Plato to make his point and then comments:

> In invoking by oath, with not illiterate gravity, and with all culture, the sister of gravity, God the author of all, and invoking Him by oath as the Lord, the Father of the Leader, and author; whom if we study with a truly philosophical spirit, we shall know.[262]

Clement says that in Plato's address in *Timaeus*, he "calls the creator, Father, speaking thus:"[263]

> Ye god of gods, of whom I am Father; and the Creator of your works

---

[258] Ibid 103.
[259] While there is no absolute certainty as to the times when these three Ante-Nicene Fathers lived, Justin Martyr is thought to have lived between 100 and 166 A.D; Theophilus between 115 and 183 A.D. (holding the Bishopric in Antioch from 168 A.D. till the time of his death), and Clement is reputed to have lived between 150 and 215 A.D.
[260] *Ante-Nicene Fathers, The Writings of the Fathers Down to 325AD, Vol 2, Fathers of the Second Century, Hermas, Tatian, Athenagoras, Theophilus and Clement of Alexandria (Entire)*, "Theophilus to Autolycus", American Edition arranged and referenced by A. Cleveland Coxe, Fourth Printing, 2004, 299-568.
[261] Ibid 465-476.
[262] Ibid 468.
[263] Ibid.

and

> Around the king of all, all things are, and because of Him are all things; and he [or that] is the cause of all good things; and around the second are the things second in order; and around the third, the third.[264]

Clement says that he

> understands [from Plato in these passages] nothing else than the Holy Trinity to be meant; for the third is the Holy Spirit, and the Son is the second, by whom all things were made according to the will of the Father.[265]

Clement does not use the term 'Trinity' again in the remaining works that are attributed to him. By itself, Clement's commentary is not very helpful since the Jews had become emphatic monotheists by this time. Yet when Clement suggests that Plato plagiarized the idea of Father and Son from the Jews, it appears that Clement was asserting a separation between Father and Son in the theology of Judaism during Plato's life.[266]

If Clement was writing to explain and justify Christianity as a religion for educated Greeks and Romans in the second century A.D., and cited Plato (and other Greek philosophers) to prove concurrence between Greek philosophy and pre-Christian Jewish theology as part of his argument, the Trinity reference seems out of place. Not only was Jewish theology becoming thoroughly monotheistic in Plato's time, but the idea that it contained elements of Trinity is anachronistic. Even if Clement was arguing that the origins of Christian Trinity theology could be discerned by thoughtful Greeks in the philosophy they had developed from a Mosaic theology, that does not explain the anachronism. What Clement's use of Trinity language in the Stromata may do is suggest that Trinity language was already commonplace among the Christians of his time since it was such a natural part of his reasoning. But Clement does not explain what he meant when he wrote of "the Holy Trinity". The most that we can say is that Clement's reference to "the Holy Trinity" was ambiguous. For while it may mean that he saw three different aspects of God present in the creation accounts available to him, his words do not reveal whether he believed that the Father and Son were separate beings, united only in

---

[264] Ibid
[265] Ibid.
[266] Plato is believed to have lived between 428 and 347BC, approximately 500-600 years before Clement.

their purposes, or whether they were more substantially united in the later Nicene sense.

In his pedagogical work (*Paedagogus*, roughly translated as 'the Instructor' or 'the Tutor'),[267] Clement explained that Jesus Christ's primary role on earth was to be the teacher or pattern for all mankind. All Christians are Christ's children or sheep,[268] and Christ was the God of the Old Testament.[269] But once again, and probably because Clement was more concerned to explain Christianity to his Gentile contemporaries, he did not write enough to answer the question whether he believed that God and Christ were separate or substantially united. When he touched that issue writing to Gentiles, he was ambiguous. The following quotations demonstrate:

> [O]ur Instructor is like His Father God, whose son He is, sinless, blameless, and with a soul devoid of passion; God in the form of man, stainless, the minister of His Father's will, the Word who is God, who is in the Father, who is at the Father's right hand, and with the form of God is God.[270]

> And man has been proved to be loveable; consequently man is loved by God. For how shall he not be loved for whose sake the only-begotten Son is sent from the Father's bosom, the Word of faith, the faith which is superabundant; the Lord Himself distinctly confessing and saying, "For the Father Himself loveth you because ye have loved Me."[271]

Quoting Esaias, Clement wrote

> *Here am I, and the children that God hath given me* (italics original)[272]

and he observed that

> Isaac...[wa]s a type of the Lord, a child as a son; for he was the son of Abraham, as Christ the Son of God.[273]

Clement also wrote that

> [S]ince Scripture calls the infant children lambs, it has also called Him –

---

[267] Clement, (above n260), 209-296.
[268] Ibid 209-215. We are also His chickens (ibid 212-213).
[269] Ibid 215, 222-225.
[270] Ibid 209-210.
[271] Ibid 211.
[272] Ibid 212.
[273] Ibid 215.

> God the Word – who became man for our sakes, and who wished in all points to be made like to us – "the Lamb of God" – Him, namely, that is the Son of God, the child of the Father.[274]

and that

> The universal Father is one, and one the universal Word; and the Holy Spirit is one and the same everywhere, and one is the only virgin mother.[275]

Finally, from many other Clementine examples that could be used, he wrote

> [T]he Father of all alone is perfect, for the Son is in Him, and the Father is in the Son; it is time for us in due course to say who our Instructor is.

> He is called Jesus....the holy God Jesus, the Word, who is the guide of all humanity. The loving God Himself is our Instructor...[who] provided sufficiently for the people in the wilderness....He who appeared to Abraham.[276]

There are elements of modern Trinitarian doctrine in several of these quotes, but it is not clear that Clement had anything more in mind than the same kind of oneness between Christ and the Father that Christ had sought for his disciples in His intercessory prayer in John 17. What does remain as one reviews this analysis, is a vague concern that these Holy Trinity words may not have been Clement's at all; that their anachronism may be the result of later insertion following an agenda at which we can only guess.

The possibility of later interpolation was referenced by A. Cleveland Coxe when writing about fragments of an early liturgy also attributed to Clement. Writing as the note editor for the second volume of the *Ante-Nicene Fathers, The Writings of the Fathers Down to 325 AD* that deals with the authenticity of these materials, Coxe wrote:

> The age ascribed to [all] these documents depends very much on the temperament and inclination of the inquirer. Those who have great reverence for them think that they must have had an apostolic origin, that they contain the apostolic forms, first handed down by tradition, and

---
[274] Ibid.
[275] Ibid 220.
[276] Ibid 222-223.

then committed to writing, but they allow that there is a certain amount of interpolation and addition of a date later than the Nicene Council. Such words as 'consubstantial' and 'mother of God' bear indisputable witness to this. Others think that there is no real historical proof of their early existence at all – that they all belong to a later date, and bear evident marks of having been written long after the age of the apostles.[277]

Coxe concluded "[t]here can scarcely be a doubt that they were not committed to writing till a comparatively late day."[278]

That being the case, it does not seem wise to accept that Clement believed in the Trinitarian nature of God in the early third century, or that any Nicene-like understanding was common in the early third century A.D. That conclusion means that there is no trace of the 'Trinity' idea from the latter part of the second century for another hundred years.

Part Three – Tertullian and Origen

Tertullian

There are a number of ironies in Tertullian's teaching. For while he is credited as the source of the doctrine that became foundational for Christianity at Nicaea,[279] there are many Christian commentators who are troubled that he should be credited with that much authority.[280] For one thing, he was married,[281] yet was also said to hold the Priesthood as a

---

[277] Ibid 533.
[278] Ibid.
[279] Roberts calls Tertullian's development of "his doctrine of the Trinity... a remarkable foreshadowing of the orthodox position reached at the Council of Nicaea" to the point where it is "difficult to realize that Tertullian belongs to the end of the second and the beginning of the third centuries" (Robert E. Roberts, *The Theology of Tertullian*, 1924, 23, 132, 136-137. Coxe suggests that "subscribers to the Modern Creed of the Vatican have reason to 'speak gently of *their father's* fall" (*Ante-Nicene Fathers, The Writings of the Fathers Down to 325AD, Vol 3, Latin Christianity: Its Founder, Tertullian I. Apologetic: II. Anti-Marcion: III. Ethical*, "Introductory Note", American Edition arranged and referenced by A. Cleveland Coxe, Fourth Printing, 2004, 4) meaning that he should be tributed as the ideological spring from which the Nicene Creed sprang.
[280] For example, *Ante-Nicene Fathers, The Writings of the Fathers Down to 325AD, Vol 3, Latin Christianity: Its Founder, Tertullian I. Apologetic: II. Anti-Marcion: III. Ethical*, "Introductory Note", American Edition arranged and referenced by A. Cleveland Coxe, Fourth Printing, 2004, 4-5. See also Robert E. Roberts, *The Theology of Tertullian*, 1924, 20-21.
[281] Coxe, ibid, 5.

Presbyter of either Rome or Carthage.²⁸² And secondly, there was his dabble in Montanism.²⁸³ Was Montanism, the charismatic and perhaps almost Pentecostal idea that revelation had not ceased because the Holy Spirit continued to minister at least in the African churches, a heresy? And if it was a heresy, should it discredit Tertullian's development of the doctrine of the Christian church in an age when certainty was imperative?²⁸⁴ Tertullian's own inflexible view was that heretics should not even be allowed to read the scriptures, let alone publish treatises about their meaning which could mislead the body of Christ.²⁸⁵ None of these ironies can be conclusively resolved and the result is that orthodox Western Christianity simply accepts what Tertullian wrote because he was the strongest original contributor of the Trinitarian ideas that were improved by the Cappadocians,²⁸⁶ and approved at Nicaea.

While there is debate about whether Tertullian knew Hebrew or whether he simply preferred to rely on the Greek or Latin version of the apostolic writings²⁸⁷ because there was no canonized New Testament when he wrote, the Rule of Faith was his surest guide. He would not rely on anything unless he knew it had been "handed down from Christ through the apostles and the churches".²⁸⁸ The Rule of Faith was the tradition "by which even the Scriptures were to be tried."²⁸⁹ But Roberts has pointed out that the

> Rule of Faith was not as 'constant', and 'immoveable and irreformable' as Tertullian would have us suppose…[for] Tertullian did not hesitate to import into it whatever was necessary to refute the views of heretics or

---

[282] Ibid.

[283] Ibid 3-5; Roberts, (above n279), 20-21.

[284] Coxe says Tertullian was "cut off by his own act" meaning that he departed from Rome because he was drawn to the life and authority he felt in Montanism in North Africa (ibid, 4).

[285] *Ante-Nicene Fathers, The Writings of the Fathers Down to 325AD, Vol 3, Latin Christianity: Its Founder, Tertullian I. Apologetic: II. Anti-Marcion: III. Ethical*, "The Prescription against Heretics", American Edition arranged and referenced by A. Cleveland Coxe, Fourth Printing, 2004, 243-265, but note particularly chapter XV-XIX (250-252).

[286] Roberts, (above n279), 132, 136-137.

[287] *Ante-Nicene Fathers, The Writings of the Fathers Down to 325AD, Vol 3, Latin Christianity: Its Founder, Tertullian I. Apologetic: II. Anti-Marcion: III. Ethical*, "Introductory Note", American Edition arranged and referenced by A. Cleveland Coxe, Fourth Printing, 2004, 7.

[288] Roberts, (above n279), 18 <http://www.tertullian.org/articles/roberts_theology/roberts_01.htm>.

[289] Ibid.

to convey his own opinions.²⁹⁰

Roberts concludes that while Tertullian adopted the "essentials [of the Rule of Faith] from his predecessors",²⁹¹ his "additions"²⁹² included

> the priority of the Son to all creatures,...His agency in the work of the creation,...and the qualification of the assertion of the Unity of God by the introduction of the notion of the divine *oi)konomi/a.*²⁹³

Tertullian wrestled to provide definite answers to questions about the nature of the Christian God, but he was hamstrung by an absence of authoritative source material. He defended Christianity against Greek philosophy, Gnosticism and Marcionitism,²⁹⁴ but he improvised when he felt he had to and felt justified in doing so because the Holy Spirit was working in him, Montanist-style.

Tertullian's Trinitarianism

Robert E. Roberts says that two "passages in Tertullian's writings ["The Apology" and "Against Praxeas"]...are of greatest importance for ascertaining his doctrine of the Trinity".²⁹⁵ In the first shorter passage, Tertullian says his purpose is to make "a remark or two as to Christ's divinity".²⁹⁶ He does not mention the Holy Spirit at all, but he does seek to explain how the Father and Son are one and that they are spirit. He observes that Christ's coming and birth were announced by God²⁹⁷ and that he had no reason to be ashamed of either his paternal or his maternal origins, since his Father was God and his Mother was a virgin.²⁹⁸ And then Tertullian wrote:

> He proceeds forth from God, and in that procession He is generated; so that He is the Son of God, and is called God from unity of substance

---

²⁹⁰ Ibid 15-16.
²⁹¹ Ibid 16.
²⁹² Ibid.
²⁹³ Ibid.
²⁹⁴ Ibid 13.
²⁹⁵ Roberts, (above n279), 130-131.
²⁹⁶ *Ante-Nicene Fathers, The Writings of the Fathers Down to 325AD, Vol 3, Latin Christianity: Its Founder, Tertullian I. Apologetic: II. Anti-Marcion: III. Ethical*, "Apology", American Edition arranged and referenced by A. Cleveland Coxe, Fourth Printing, 2004, 34.
²⁹⁷ Ibid.
²⁹⁸ Ibid.

with God. For God, too, is a Spirit. Even when the ray is shot from the sun, it is still part of the parent mass; the sun will still be in the ray, because it is a ray of the sun – there is no division of substance, but merely an extension. Thus Christ is a Spirit of Spirit, and God of God, as light of light is kindled. The material matrix remains entire and unimpaired, though you derive from it any number of shoots possessed of its qualities; so too, that which has come forth out of God is at once God and the Son of God, and the two are one. In this way also, as He is Spirit of Spirit and God of God, He is made a second in manner of existence – in position, not in nature; and he did not withdraw from the original source, but went forth. This ray of God, then, as it was always foretold in ancient times, descending into a certain virgin, and made flesh in her womb is in His birth God and man united. The flesh formed by the Spirit is nourished, grows up to manhood, speaks, teaches, works, and is the Christ.[299]

Roberts says that this statement follows Tatian,[300] but that Tertullian is more clear that the Logos or Word is Jesus Christ[301] and that He was the Creator or Logos consistent with heathen philosophy.[302] But for Roberts,

---

[299] Ibid 34-35.

[300] Tatian lived from 117-172AD. In the "Introductory Note" to "Tatian's Address to the Greeks" in the *Ante-Nicene Fathers, Vol II*, the editor says that Tatian was "half Father and half heretic" (61). He "laid the egg which Tertullian hatched and invented terms which [Tertullian] raised to their higher power" (62). And that editor says that between them, Tatian and Tertullian promoted the Montanist ideas that some should be forbidden to marry and that it was appropriate to command Christians to abstain from meats [see also *Ante-Nicene Fathers, Vol II*, "Fragments", 82], despite Paul's letter to Timothy [1 Timothy 4:3] which identified such teaching as heresy (ibid). That editor also observes that after Justin's death, Tatian "fell under the influence of the Gnostic heresy and founded an ascetic sect" (ibid 63). In Chapters IV and V of the "Address of Tatian to the Greeks" (*Ante-Nicene Fathers, Vol II*, 66-67) Tatian says that the Christians worship one Spirit God alone who is beyond time. He then explains that God in the beginning was alone and that all existence came from Him by Logos-power. Similarly, the Logos Himself also came forth "by His simple will". The Logos was "the first-begotten work of the Father" and through the Logos, the world began. Tatian uses a torch rather than a sun-ray analogy. God lit the torch of the Logos but was not diminished by doing so.

[301] Roberts, (above n279), 130-131.

[302] *Ante-Nicene Fathers, Vol III*, 34 where Tertullian says:
We have already asserted that God made the world, and all which it contains, by his Word, and Reason, and Power. It is abundantly plain that your philosophers, too, regard the Logos – that is, the Word and Reason – as the Creator of the universe.

it is the later more detailed statement in "Against Praxeas"[303] where Tertullian

> set[s] out the Trinitarian doctrine in a form, which despite its limitations and imperfections, supplied the framework for the later presentation of the doctrine at the Council of Nicaea, and by the Cappadocians.[304]

The following extract abbreviated from "Against Praxeas", is Tertullian's longer exposition of the Trinity doctrine to which Roberts referred above. Tertullian wrote:

> We…believe that there is one only God, but only under the following dispensation, or *oikovouia*, as it is called, that this one only God has also a Son, His Word, who proceeded from Himself, by whom all things were made, and without whom nothing was made. Him we believe to have been sent by the Father into the Virgin, and to have been born of her – being both Man and God, the Son of Man and the Son of God, and to have been called by the name of Jesus Christ; we believe Him to have suffered, died and been buried, according to the Scriptures, and, after He had been raised again by the Father and taken back to heaven, to be sitting at the right hand of the Father, and that He will come to judge the quick and the dead; who sent also from heaven from the Father, according to His own promise, the Holy Ghost, the Paraclete, the sanctifier of the faith of those who believe in the Father, and in the Son, and in the Holy Ghost. That this rule of faith has come down to us from the beginning of the gospel, even before any of the older heretics, much more before Praxeas, a pretender of yesterday.[305]

Tertullian then briefly explained Praxeas' error which was that Praxeas believed "one cannot believe in One Only God in any other way than by saying that the Father, the Son, and the Holy Ghost are the very selfsame Person."[306] Tertullian corrected that error by saying its mistake was to imply

---

[303] *Ante-Nicene Fathers, The Writings of the Fathers Down to 325AD, Vol 3, Latin Christianity: Its Founder, Tertullian I. Apologetic: II. Anti-Marcion: III. Ethical*, "Against Praxeas", American Edition arranged and referenced by A. Cleveland Coxe, Fourth Printing, 2004, 597-627. See below in connection with nn305-325 and associated text.

[304] Roberts, (above n279), 130-131.

[305] *Ante-Nicene Fathers, The Writings of the Fathers Down to 325AD, Vol 3, Latin Christianity: Its Founder, Tertullian I. Apologetic: II. Anti-Marcion: III. Ethical*, "Against Praxeas", American Edition arranged and referenced by A. Cleveland Coxe, Fourth Printing, 2004, Chapter II, 598.

[306] Ibid.

> one were not All, in that All are One, by unity (that is) of substance; while the mystery of the dispensation is still guarded, which distributes the Unity into a Trinity, placing in their order the three Persons – the Father, the Son and the Holy Ghost: three, however, not in condition, but in degree; not in substance, but in form; not in power, but in aspect; yet of one substance, and of one condition, and of one power, inasmuch as He is one God, from whom these degrees and forms and aspects are reckoned, under the name of the Father, and of the Son, and of the Holy Ghost[307]

and Tertullian said his further exposition clarified "[h]ow they are susceptible of number without division".[308] In that exposition, one can also see Tertullian maintaining the Trinity doctrine as a defence against enduring Jewish criticism, and identifying contemporary Christian teachers who had misunderstood the correct Trinity doctrine. He wrote:

> They are constantly throwing out against us that we are preachers of two gods and three gods, while they take to themselves pre-eminently the credit of being worshippers of One God; just as if the Unity itself with irrational deductions did not produce heresy, and the Trinity rationally considered constitute the truth. We, say they, maintain the Monarchy (or, sole government of God)....As for myself, however, if I have gleaned any knowledge of either language [Latin or Greek], I am sure that *μοναρχία* (or Monarchy) has no other meaning than single and individual rule; but for all that, this monarchy does not, because it is the government of one, preclude him whose government it is, either from having a son, or from having made himself actually a son to himself, or from ministering his own monarchy by whatsoever agents he will.....If moreover, there be a son belonging to him whose monarch it is, it does not forthwith become divided and cease to be a monarchy, if the son also be taken as a sharer in it; but it is as to its origin equally his, by whom it is communicated to the son; and being his, it is quite as much a monarchy (or sole empire) since it is held together by two who are so inseparable. Therefore, inasmuch as the Divine Monarchy also is administered by so many legions and hosts of angels, according as it is written, "Thousand thousands ministered unto Him, and ten thousand times ten thousand stood before Him;" [referring to Daniel 7:10] and since it has not from the circumstance ceased to be the rule of one (so as to no longer be a monarchy), because

---

[307] Ibid.
[308] Ibid.

it is administered by so many thousands of powers; how comes it to pass that God should be thought to suffer division and severance in the Son and in the Holy Ghost, who have second and the third places assigned to them, and who are so closely joined with the Father in His substance, when He suffers no such (division and severance) in the multitude of so many angels? Do you really suppose that Those, who are naturally members of the Father's own substance, pledges of His love, instruments of His power itself and the entire system of His monarchy, are the overthrow and destruction thereof?....the overthrow of a monarchy... [rather occurs] when another dominion, which has a framework peculiar to itself (and is therefore a rival) is brought in over and above it: when, *e.g.,* some other god is introduced in opposition to the Creator, as in the opinions of Marcion; or when many gods are introduced, according to your Valentinuses and your Prodicuses. Then it amounts to an overthrow of the Monarchy, since it involves the destruction of the Creator.[309]

Roberts summarises the scholarly analysis of Tertullian's Trinity statements. All the scholars make comparisons with the later Nicene Creed and most find connections. The orthodox ignore the material that is inconsistent with the Creed as in Tertullian's affirmation that there was a time when Jesus did not exist. They also avoid some of his 'less than perfect analogies' to the Trinity (sun, ray and apex; root, tree and fruit; well, spring and river) because "all figures of the Trinity" are inherently imperfect.[310]

Petavius is unsatisfied because Tertullian did not acknowledge "the eternity of the Word".[311] But Bishop Bull thought that came through loud and clear. Bishop Bull says that although Tertullian taught that "the Son of God was made, and was called the Word from some definite beginning",[312] it is very clear that Tertullian believed the hypostasis (a synonym for 'the Word' in Tertullian's text) is eternal.[313]

Bishop Kaye considered Tertullian orthodox but said that he was less precise than later writers who learned to avoid controversial language.[314]

---

[309] Ibid, Chapter III, 599.
[310] Roberts, (above n279), 133.
[311] Ibid 131.
[312] Ibid.
[313] Ibid.
[314] Ibid 132.

But Harnack said that Tertullian's 'economic Trinity' was defective because it held that the Son and the Holy Spirit only existed to do the work of creation and revelation; only possessed a portion of the Father's fullness; were subordinate to Him and were thus little more than "transitory manifestations".[315]

Tertullian seemed to expect further revelation or insight himself when he said that the mystery "which distributes the Unity into a Trinity"[316] was still guarded, but that did not prevent him from trying to explain. His explanation was that there is an order between the three persons of the Trinity, and their difference is a difference in degree, form and aspect, rather than of condition, substance or power.[317] But then Tertullian appears to contradict himself by saying that the difference of the three persons who make up the Trinity is one of substance, condition and power after all.[318]

If Praxeas was not a believer in Christ in some degree already, it is likely that he was confused by some of the distinctions Tertullian made but then substantially qualified. Perhaps human language does not lend itself to explanation of matters which human experience cannot comprehend by itself. And though some of Roberts' scholarly analysts are critical of Tertullian's less than perfect analogies, it is noteworthy that Tertullian did not qualify his analogies as he did his theological explanations. Tertullian thus seems satisfied to say that Jesus is made of the same substance as the Father in the same way as a sunray is of the same substance as the Sun, but he is not satisfied that Jesus and the Father are not different in condition, substance or power. Perhaps as in Jesus' own scriptural teaching, parables and analogies are more effective at inspiring human conduct improvements than theological exegesis. We can conjecture at the reasons why, but for both Tertullian and Jesus, leaving hearers with parables and analogies seems to have something to do with letting the hearers come to their own conclusions as to what the teacher meant with only the personal interpretive assistance of the Holy Spirit.

Though Tertullian is said to have deplored Greek philosophy and Hellenism

---

[315] Ibid.
[316] Ibid.
[317] Ibid.
[318] Ibid.

in general,[319] he engaged a number of its tools in these explanations of the Trinity but seems to have been more satisfied with his analogies however imperfect those of a philosophical bent may find them.

Though I have suggested that Tertullian's explanations of the Trinity were sourced in the need to respond to Jewish criticism, the closing sentences of the explanation to Praxeas above show that Tertullian was also responding to heretical views sponsored within the Christian Church by Marcion,[320] Valentinus[321] and Prodicus.[322] But that does not mean that the genesis of the ideas to which these three (named heretics by Tertullian) responded were not Jewish. It is more likely, that these named heretics had previously responded to Jewish criticism of Christian polytheism, but had made mistakes in doing so. Thus, while Tertullian did not directly respond to Jewish criticism of Christian polytheism, that criticism still underlay the doctrinal mistakes he was trying to correct. Many of the Christian heresies in Ante-Nicene Christianity may be traced

---

[319] For example, see Roberts, (above n279), 68.
[320] Marcion (85-160AD) expounded an unashamed doctrine of two Gods, but held that Jesus, as the forgiving God of the New Testament, was superior to the wrathful God of the Old Testament and had effectively taken over from Him.
[321] Valentinus (100-160AD) taught that the Godhead consisted of three hidden spiritual realities (hypostases). He is reputed to have been a gnostic follower of Theudas who claimed to have received special secret wisdom from Paul (after his vision of the third heaven in 2 Corinthians 12: 2-4).
[322] Little is known of Prodicus but he is thought to have taught similar doctrine to Valentinus.

to the watershed of Jewish criticism.[323]

For our purposes in reviewing the development of the Trinitarian doctrine, it is clear that Tertullian intended more than that Father, Son and Holy Ghost were unified in purpose. If that was his intent, he had no need to go further than to analogise to a Monarchy. But he did not stop there. He quite expressly said that the unity of the Father, Son and Holy Ghost was much more than a simple unity of purpose. Their unity extended to their very substance. But it is clear from Tertullian's earlier ambiguity (as to condition/degree; substance/form; and power/aspect),[324] that he had not been able to find a better philosophical or theological way to explain that unity in substance, if he fully understood it himself.[325] Tertullian's statement that the sunray is made of the same substance as the sun itself, is as far as he goes and that says no more than that they were composed of the same genetic material.

While Tertullian wrote more about how the Son came forth from the Father, further analysis of his formulation of the Trinity does not help

---

[323] Kenneth D. Whitehead provides a list of Christian heresies in the Appendix to his book, *A Short Guide to Ancient Heresies* (e-book). The following precede the Council at Nicaea and all concern the nature of God and Christ: Adoptionism (first expounded in the 2nd century AD by Theodotus of Byzantium); Anomeanism (a 4th century AD anti Arian sect); Appollinarianism (the 4th century AD view taught by Appollinaries of Laodicea that Jesus had a human body and lower soul, but a divine mind); Arianism (which, beginning in the 3rd century AD, was said to deny the divinity of Jesus Christ in holding that Jesus was created and so had a beginning unlike God); Macedonianism (a 4th century AD Arian sect which denied the divinity of the Holy Spirit, holding that the Holy Spirit emanated not from God but that it was a creation of the Son); Marcionism (from the 2nd century AD holding that Jesus came from God but that he was not the wrathful God of the Old Testament); Modalism (a form of Trinitarianism from the 2nd and 3rd centuries AD which held that God manifested Himself in different modes); Priscillianism (a Spanish form of Gnosticism, which from the 4th century AD, denied that Christ was either human or divine); Sabellianism (a 3rd century AD version of Modalism above); Subordinationism (a name for a collection of 4th century AD heresies that admitted that only God the Father was God); and Valentinianism (the idea beginning in the 2nd century AD, that the visible world had been created by the God of the Old Testament; that only the unseen invisible world was real and that Christ had come to deliver mankind from its bondage to matter). Indeed, from Whitehead's list of early Christian heresies only Donatism, Gnosticism, Novatianism and Pelagianism originated before the Nicene Council and did not directly concern the nature of God in some way.

[324] Nn306-308 above and supporting text.

[325] That is, once again, it seems in his reference to "the mystery of the dispensation" in Chapter II, that he is waiting for more information to be revealed to him in accordance with Montanist ideology to which he subscribed by the time he wrote "Against Praxeas".

identify what it contributed to the Nicene creed. We have identified Tertullian's Trinity theology; we can see that in part, he followed the earlier theological thinking of Tatian, but we can also see his innovation. Tertullian's original contribution was that the Father and Son were as unified in substance as they were in purpose. In Justin Martyr's understanding, a unity in purpose was sufficient to rebut Jewish criticism of Christian polytheism, but Tertullian felt the need to explain that the unity of Father and Son went deeper than unity of purpose. He explained that greater depth with the word substance, but the analogies which he preferred as explanatory devices, do not merge the personalities of the Father and the Son. A monarch is still a monarch even if he assigns his genetic son as an executive in the kingdom. And a sunray is still made of the same substance as the sun from which it was sent forth even though it is physically separated from that source. The Father and Son were still separate personages as they had been in Justin Martyr's understanding, but their oneness was deeper than a mere unity of purpose which man can understand. While Christian doctrine might still be charged with polytheism by Jewish theologians who had renounced or forgotten their monarchical conception of a Divine Council presided over by the 'Supreme God or Maker of all things' (Justin's words), there was no need to mislead Christian believers as Marcion, Valentinus and Prodicus had done.

Origen

Like Tertullian, Origen was a prolific theologian whose reliability has been questioned because of some views he held that were later deemed heretical.[326] He was a disciple of Clement of Alexandria who lived between 185 and 254 A.D. and stood upon the shoulders of his predecessors when it came to the theology of the Trinity. A. Cleveland Coxe apologises for the fact that some have considered him a heretic:

> Justly has it been urged that to those whose colossal labours during the

---

[326] For example, the Second Council of Constantinople in 553AD is said to have anathematized his teachings concerning the pre-existence of the soul, the idea that animals also have spirits, and his denial that there was any lasting resurrection of the physical body ("The Anathemas Against Origen". *Nicene and Post-Nicene Fathers: Series II, Volume XIV (The Seven Ecumenical Councils)*, Philip Schaff, ed., Hendrickson Publishers, Peabody, Massachusetts, 1994). Note that these teachings are difficult to find because the result of the declaration of anathema was that these works were either burned, stricken out, or rewritten in a form that conformed to orthodoxy.

Ante-Nicene period exposed them to hasty judgment, and led them into mistakes, much indulgence must be shown. The language of theology was but assuming shape under their processes, and we owe them an incalculable debt of gratitude: but it was not yet moulded into precision; nor had great councils, presided over by the Holy Ghost, as yet afforded those safeguards to freedom of thought which gradually defined the limits of orthodoxy. To no single teacher did the Church defer…Over and over again were the bishops of patriarchal and apostolic sees, including Rome, adjudged heretics, and anathematized by the inexorable law of truth….Before the great Synodical period (A.D. 325 to 451), while orthodoxy is marvelously maintained and witnessed to by Origen and Tertullian themselves, their errors, however serious, have never separated them from the grateful and loving regard of those upon whom their lives of heroic sorrow and suffering have conferred blessings unspeakable. The Church cannot leave their errors uncorrected. Their persons she leaves to the Master's award: their characters she cherishes, while their faults she deplores.[327]

Thus, the orthodox western branch of Christianity claims Origen, but Jerome[328] worried that some of Origen's writing concerning the doctrine of the Trinity in *De Principiis* was a departure "from the Catholic Faith"[329] and had been corrupted by the translator Rufinus.[330]

More recent scholars who have been less concerned to identify the differences between Origen's version of the doctrine of the Trinity and what was ruled orthodox in the 'Great Councils', have seen Origen as one of the builders of the "theological system that weds the church's three-fold understanding of God".[331] Nathan says that Origen incorporated all the Trinity understanding of his predecessors and systematized it in *On First Principles (De Principiis)*.[332] Justin Martyr defended Christianity against the charge of atheism by linking the 'logos' notion (a triad of God, Logos and Psyche) from Stoicism and Platonism with the Christian triad of Father,

---

[327] *Ante-Nicene Fathers, The Writings of the Fathers Down to 325AD, Vol 4, Fathers of the Third Century: Tertullian, Part Fourth; Minucius Felix; Commodian; Origen, Parts First and Second*, "Introductory Note", American Edition arranged and referenced by A. Cleveland Coxe, Fourth Printing, 2004, 223.
[328] Lived 347-420 A.D.
[329] *Ante-Nicene Fathers, Vol 4*, "Introductory Note", 233.
[330] Ibid.
[331] N.A. Nathan, "The Trinity according to Origen", 1.
[332] Ibid.

Son and Holy Ghost.[333] In the following century, Iraneus, Tertullian, Hippolytus and Clement, warn the vulnerable church against various heresies concerning the nature of the God triad and begin to explain how God is "both one and three" in Christian understanding.[334] But their 'Economic Trinitarianism' is confusing even though it sharpens understanding of "the distinct individuality of the Logos immanent eternally in the Godhead",[335] because it leaves unanswered questions and suggests that though the Son began before the creation, he somehow postdated the Father.[336] Certainly Tertullian had moved to resolve these conundrums by explaining that the Son and Holy Ghost shared in the 'substantia' of the Godhead,[337] but it was Origen's work to "harmonise...the Church's threefold understanding of God to the categories of Middle Platonism".[338] Nathan says that Origen was "never content...to repeat his predecessors".[339] He "seizes these grey areas" and by speculation, theological research and sheer effort of mind, escapes the "stereotypes of his mind [to]...chart a new course".[340] While Origen relies on scripture and the Rule of Faith revered by his predecessors where it has a contribution to make, he feels quite at liberty to speculate when there is a vacuum in understanding.

Following the first chapter of the Gospel of John, Nathan says that

> Origen explains that this one God is the God-in-Godself and his divinity is his own and not derived whereas the Logos is simply called God because his divinity, though real and true, is derived from the Supreme God. This supreme God who is generating a Son and breathing forth the Spirit also constitutes a Trinity, Father, Son and Holy Spirit. This is the triadic understanding of God which Christian faith confesses and which forms the basis of salvation.[341]

But Origen is also confusing because while his use of the term *hypostases* (to "signif[y] the distinct and individual existence of the members of the

---

[333] Ibid 2.
[334] Ibid 2-3.
[335] Ibid 3.
[336] Ibid.
[337] Ibid.
[338] Ibid 4.
[339] Ibid 5.
[340] Ibid.
[341] Ibid.

Triad"[342]) corresponds with *prosopon* in Hippolytus and *persona* in Tertullian, it "can also refer to the being or substance of something and was identical with the Latin term *substantia*."[343] But he does "break with predecessors" when he asserts that the Son and the Holy Spirit are co-eternal with the Father.[344] For Nathan, this is where Origen displays his originality.[345] He has moved away from the Stoic idea of "the immanent expressed in the Logos"[346] from which his predecessors had drawn their understanding of the Triad, and has found the co-eternality idea which resonated with the Council at Nicaea.[347] That original insight is best demonstrated with a quotation from *De Principiis* where Origen is concluding his chapter on how the Holy Spirit is a co-eternal part of the Godhead:

> [N]othing in the Trinity can be greater or less, since the fountain of divinity alone contains all things by His Word and Reason, and by the Spirit of His mouth sanctifies all things which are worthy of sanctification… There is also a special working of God the Father, besides that by which He bestowed upon all things the gift of natural life. There is also a special ministry of the Lord Jesus Christ to those upon whom he confers by nature the gift of reason, by means of which we are enabled to be rightly what we are. There is also another grace of the Holy Spirit, which is bestowed upon the deserving, through the ministry of Christ and the working of the Father, in proportion to the merits of those who are rendered capable of receiving it…From which it most clearly follows that there is no difference in the Trinity, but that which is called the gift of the Spirit is made known through the Son, and operated by God the Father….Having made these declarations regarding the Unity of the Father, and of the Son, and of the Holy Spirit, let us return to the order in which we began this discussion. God the Father bestows upon all, existence; and participation in Christ, in respect of His being the word of reason, renders them rational beings. From which it follows that they are deserving either of praise or blame, because capable of virtue or vice. On this account, therefore, is the grace of the Holy Ghost present, that those beings which are not holy in their essence may be rendered holy by participating in it. Seeing then, that firstly, they derive

---

[342] Ibid.
[343] Ibid.
[344] Ibid 6. See also *Ante-Nicene Fathers, Vol 4*, "Origen De Principiis", Chapter III, 251-256.
[345] Ibid.
[346] Ibid.
[347] Ibid.

their existence from God the Father; secondly, their rational nature from the Word; thirdly, their holiness from the Holy Spirit, - those…..will…by the ceaseless working of the Father, Son and Holy Ghost in us, …be able at some future time…to behold the holy and blessed life.[348]

Nathan opines that Origen overstated the distinctions in the Trinity, the subordination of the Son and the limitations of the Holy Spirit too much for the later church.[349] But he says that Origen still laid the theological foundations upon which Athanasius and the Cappadocians built the "great doctrinal formulas"[350] which were sanctioned by the Great Councils.

Part Four - Other Ante-Nicene theologians

Other Ante-Nicene Fathers wrote about the nature of God and even about the Trinity, but none contributed as much to the Nicene doctrine as those discussed above. For Irenaeus[351] as for Justin Martyr, there is no suggestion of a consubstantial being. The Father, the Son and the Holy Ghost are separate and distinct but unified in purpose.[352] Hippolytus,[353] a disciple of Irenaeus, expresses the Trinitarian idea that "[t]he Father

---

[348] *Ante-Nicene Fathers, Vol 4*, "Origen De Principiis", Chapter III, 255.
[349] N.A. Nathan, "The Trinity according to Origen", 7.
[350] Ibid.
[351] Lived 130-202 A.D.
[352] See for example, *Ante-Nicene Fathers, The Writings of the Fathers Down to 325 AD, Vol 1, The Apostolic Fathers, Justin Martyr, Irenaeus*, "Irenaeus Against Heresies", American Edition arranged and referenced by A. Cleveland Coxe, Fourth Printing, 2004, Book I, Chapter IX, 329 where in refuting heretics who held there was another Saviour and Logos, Irenaeus states:

> For when John, proclaiming one God the Almighty, and one Jesus Christ, the Only-Begotten, by whom all things were made, declares that this is the Son of God, this the Only-begotten, this the Former of all things, this the true Light who enlighteneth every man, this the Creator of the world, this that came to His own, this He became flesh and dwelt among us….that Jesus who suffered for us, and who dwelt among us, is Himself the Word of God.

> Similar indirect statements which seem inconsistent with the later doctrine of the Trinity appear in Book I, Chapter X (330-332), Book I Chapter XXII (347) where he says "there is one God Almighty…[and] He is the Father of our Lord Jesus Christ" and in Book II, III, and IV where he objects to the idea that the Supreme God is somehow, a compound being.

[353] Lived 170-235 A.D.

decrees; the Word executes and the Son is manifested".[354] The context is not very Trinitarian but suggests that again, he was writing in response to Jewish criticism:

> If, then, the Word was with God, and was also God, what follows? Would one say that he speaks of two Gods? I shall not indeed speak of two Gods, but of one; of two Persons however, and of a third economy (disposition), viz., the grace of the Holy Ghost. For the Father indeed is One, but there are two Persons, because there is also the Son; and there is the third, the Holy Spirit.

This statement is followed by the quote about the role of Father in decreeing and the Word in executing and Hippolytus continues

> The economy of harmony is led back to one God; for God is One. It is the Father who commands, and the Son who obeys, and the Holy Spirit who gives understanding: the Father who is above all, and the Son who is through all, and the Holy Spirit who is in all. And we cannot otherwise think of one God, but by believing in truth in Father and Son and Holy Spirit. For the Jews glorified (or gloried in) the Father, but gave Him not thanks, for they did not recognise the Son.[355]

And then he summarises, but without further detail –

> And by this He showed, that whosoever omitted any one of these, failed in glorifying God perfectly. For it is through this Trinity that the Father is glorified.[356]

In effect, Hippolytus uses the Trinity expression to repeat his criticism of the Jews. They failed to glorify the Father whom they purported to worship because they did not recognize, worship and glorify His Son. To fail to recognize Jesus Christ as the Father's Son and Agent was to deny the Father.

The most specific work on the Trinity, *De Trinitate*[357], was written by

---

[354] *Ante-Nicene Fathers, The Writings of the Fathers Down to 325 AD, Vol 5, Fathers of the Third Century, Hippolytus, Cyprian, Caius, Novatian, Appendix*, "Against the Heresy of One Noetus", American Edition arranged and referenced by A. Cleveland Coxe, Fourth Printing, 2004, 228.
[355] Ibid.
[356] Ibid.
[357] *Ante-Nicene Fathers, The Writings of the Fathers Down to 325 AD, Vol 5*, "A Treatise of Novatian Concerning the Trinity", American Edition arranged and referenced by A. Cleveland Coxe, Fourth Printing, 2004, 611-644.

the later anti-Pope Novatian[358] after the Sabellian heresy[359] and therefore probably in 257 A.D. Though some have interpreted his "emulation of the episcopal office"[360] and subsequent cause of schism as a gross form of apostasy,[361] more charitable benefactors who accept that we only have the story from his enemies,[362] have defended his orthodoxy.[363] They say that he was only ever deemed to be heretical in respect of church discipline since he would not forgive and allow the rebaptism of those whose faith had once lapsed.[364] A. Cleveland Coxe says that his "work upon the Trinity….is a most valuable contribution to ante-Nicene theology".[365]

In thirty-one chapters, Hippolytus sets forth from reason and the scriptures, the nature of God. He contains all things and is inexplicable;[366] He is infinite;[367] His anger, indignation and hatred are not human in nature;[368] He does not have a bodily nature;[369] but Jesus Christ was truly man;[370] and God also;[371] it was Jesus Christ that appeared to Abraham;[372] to Jacob;[373] He is distinct from the Father;[374] suffered death but the Father did not;[375] but there are not two Gods.[376]

When one compares the doctrinal teachings of the ante-Nicene fathers, one can see that the closer they approach the Council at Nicaea in time, the

---

[358] Lived 200-258 A.D.
[359] In his "Introductory Notice to Novation, A Roman Presbyter" in *Ante-Nicene Fathers, The Writings of the Fathers Down to 325AD, Vol 5*, at 608, A. Cleveland Coxe says that "the heresy of Sabellius…appeared 256 A.D.".
[360] Ibid 607-608.
[361] Ibid 607.
[362] Ibid.
[363] Ibid.
[364] Ibid 608.
[365] Ibid 607.
[366] *Ante Nicene Fathers, The Writings of the Fathers Down to 325AD, Vol 5*, "A Treatise of Novatian Concerning the Trinity", 612-613.
[367] Ibid 614-615.
[368] Ibid 615.
[369] Ibid 615-616.
[370] Ibid 619-620.
[371] Ibid 620-626.
[372] Ibid 627-629 which is the same argument that Justin Martyr made in his "Dialogue with Trypho" discussed above.
[373] Ibid 629-631.
[374] Ibid 634-640
[375] Ibid 635-636 which is a restatement of another argument against the Patripassian heresy that God suffered everything that his Son Jesus Christ suffered including, the cross.
[376] Ibid 641-644.

closer their orthodoxy came to its expression in the creed that was born there.

But Novatian was not the only theologian of the third century A.D. prompted to write about the Trinity because of the Sabellian heresy. Gregory Thaumaturgus[377] who was a disciple and apologist for Origen and became the Bishop of New Caesarea,[378] also responded, but his reasoning is confusing and seems inconsistent, though that may simply be an indication of his close proximity to the time of the Councils and the need for them.[379] For on the one hand he has written

> [S]ome treat the Holy Trinity in an awful manner, when they confidently assert that there are not three persons, and introduce (the idea of) a person devoid of substance. Wherefore we clear ourselves of Sabellius, who says that the Father and the Son are the same….We foreswear this, because we believe that three persons – namely, Father, Son and Holy Spirit – are declared to possess the one Godhead; for the one divinity showing itself forth according to nature in the Trinity establishes the oneness of the nature…'There is one God the Father'; and there is divinity hereditary in the Son, as it is written, 'The Word was God;' and there is divinity present according to nature in the Spirit – to wit, what subsists as the Spirit of God – according to Paul's statement, 'Ye are the temple of God, and the Spirit of God dwelleth in you'. Now the person in each declares the independent being and subsistence…wherefore, if the divinity may be spoken of as one in three persons, the trinity is established and the unity is not dissevered….Wherefore if there is one God, and one Lord, and at the same time one person as one divinity in one lordship, how can credit be given to (this distinction in) the words 'of whom' and 'by whom' as has been said before?[380]

---

[377] Lived 213-270 A.D. Note that his surname means "Wonder-worker" and is considered to be a reference both to his success in converting his city and to his working of miracles (*Ante-Nicene Fathers, The Writings of the Fathers Down to 325AD, Vol 6, Gregory Thaumaturgus, Dionysius the Great, Julius Africanus, Anatolius and Minor Writers, Methodius, Arnobius,* "Introductory Note to Gregory Thaumaturgus", American Edition arranged and referenced by A. Cleveland Coxe, Fourth Printing, 2004, 6).

[378] *Ante-Nicene Fathers, The Writings of the Fathers Down to 325AD, Vol 4, Fathers of the Third Century: Tertullian, Part Fourth; Minucius Felix; Commodian; Origen, Parts First and Second,* "Introductory Note", American Edition arranged and referenced by A. Cleveland Coxe, Fourth Printing, 2004, 228-229.

[379] Note that the editors of the *Ante-Nicene Fathers Vol 6*, label these writings ("A Sectional Confession of Faith", Ibid 40-47), "Dubious or Spurious" (ibid 40).

[380] Ibid 42.

But then he continues

> We acknowledge that the Son and the Spirit are consubstantial with the Father, and that the substance of the Trinity is one....And those who have fellowship with men that reject the consubstantiality as a doctrine foreign to the Scriptures, and speak of any of the persons in the Trinity as created, and separate that person from the one natural divinity, we hold as aliens.[381]

The answer to the inconsistency seems to lie in the editor's concerned label – "dubious or spurious writings".[382] This last paragraph and some of the material that follows it, appears to be the sloppy work of someone correcting the material later,[383] for it is generally accepted that the concept of consubstantiality came later than 257 A.D.[384] More likely it is that Gregory of Thaumaturgus "believe[d]", as he testified, just before the probable interpolation,

> in one God, that is in one First Cause, the God of the law and of the Gospel, the just and good; and in one Lord Jesus Christ, true God, that is, Image of the true God, Maker of all things seen and unseen, Son of God and only-begotten Offspring, and Eternal Word, living and self-subsistent and active, always being with the Father, and in one Holy Spirit.[385]

---

[381] Ibid 45.
[382] The editors of the *Ante-Nicene Fathers Vol 6*, (above n379).
[383] Sloppy because the consubstantiality assertion does not have any credibility when all that has been written before it denies consubstantiality.
[384] See for example Roberts, (above n279), 22-23, 165 where he quotes Bishop Bull and observes gently that Tertullian so aptly described the notion of consubstantiality without using the term, that you would think he was writing after the Nicene Council. The Editors of Volume 7 of the *Ante-Nicene Fathers* are rather more blunt. When they dismiss the antiquity alleged for some of the early liturgies attributed to Clement of Alexandria, they write:

> The age ascribed to these documents depends very much on the temperament and inclination of the inquirer. Those who have great reverence for them think that they must have had an apostolic origin, that they contain the apostolic form, first handed down by tradition, and then committed to writing, but they allow that there is a certain amount of interpolation and addition of a date later than the Nicene Council. Such words as "consubstantial" and "mother of God" bear indisputable witness to this. Others think that there is no real historical proof of their early existence at all, - that they all belong to a later date, and bear evident marks of having been written long after the age of the apostles (ibid 533).

[385] *Ante-Nicene Fathers Vol 6*, 45.

Dionysius of Rome[386] also wrote briefly against the Sabellians.[387] He said that the Sabellian heresy would rend the "Church of God, into… three powers and distinct substances (hypostases), and three deities, [and] destroy it".[388] He continued that "the doctrine that there are three gods is neither taught in the Old nor in the New Testament."[389] He continued in what Trinitarian scholars must consider, a very advanced vein:

> It is therefore not a trifling, but a very great impiety, to say that the Lord was in any wise made with hands. For if the Son was made, there was a time when He was not; but He always was, if, as He Himself declares, He is undoubtedly in the Father.[390]

Conclusion

And so we complete our analysis of the teachings of the Ante-Nicene Fathers concerning the nature of God.

In the first half of the second century A.D., Justin Martyr believed that God and Jesus Christ were separate and distinct individuals but that they are united in their purposes. He wrote to respond to Trypho's Jewish criticism that the Christians were polytheists and he sought to demonstrate from the Hebrew scriptures, that they also worshipped more than one God. Writing later in the second century, Theophilus was the first of the Christian writers to use the term 'Trinity', but he did not use it in connection with God, Jesus Christ or the Holy Spirit or to explain their nature. Rather, he used the term to persuade an intelligent pagan friend named Autolycus, that the Christian God was the repository of all logic and wisdom in an attempt to build a bridge of understanding for his friend using concepts familiar from Greek philosophy. While some Christian apologists have observed that the use of the word logic as logos refers to Jesus Christ as the Son or Word of God, and the personification of wisdom in ancient Hebrew texts adds the Holy Spirit in to Theophilus' Trinity, that is an academic stretch.

---

[386] He died in 268 A.D.
[387] *Ante-Nicene Fathers, The Writings of the Fathers Down to 325AD, Vol 7, Lactantius, Venantius, Asterius, Victorinus, Dionysius, Apostolic Teaching and Constitutions, 2 Clement, Early Liturgies*, "Against the Sabellians", American Edition arranged and referenced by A. Cleveland Coxe, Fourth Printing, 2004, 365-366.
[388] Ibid 365.
[389] Ibid.
[390] Ibid.

A generation later crossing over into the third century A.D., there are suggestions that Clement of Alexandria drew the term 'Trinity' further into Christian theology. He is said to have explained that some of the coincidence between Greek philosophy and Christian thought arose because the Greek philosophers had used Hebrew scripture as a major source for their history. But the anachronistic suggestion that Greeks and Jews in the fifth century B.C. believed in the same multiple Gods, raises questions about Clement's authorship of the Trinity passages attributed to him and in any event, those passages do nothing to assist understanding of the relationship between Father, Son and Holy Spirit.

But 700 miles away from Clement's theology school in Alexandria, Clement's near contemporary Tertullian in Carthage was focused on rebutting heresies. Though he has been described as a Montanist heretic by some later commentators, Tertullian is widely credited as the source of the Trinitarian understanding that was accepted at Nicaea. He affirmed that the Son not only shared the same mind with the Father, but because he came forth from the Father, he was also of the same substance though the nature of that oneness has not been fully revealed. Though Tertullian did not directly respond to Jewish criticisms of Christian belief about God, most of his writing was directed at correcting Christian writers who had made mistakes as they sought to defend Christianity against Jewish criticism of Christian polytheism.

Another generation later but still in the third century A.D., Clement's disciple Origen summarized and systematized all that his predecessors had written about the Trinity. Origen charted a new course by harmonizing previous understanding with "the Church's threefold understanding of God to the categories of Middle Platonism".[391] He developed the Stoic idea of the immanence of the Godhead into the new idea that the three hypostases that comprised it, were co-eternal. While Origen made distinctions between the different persons in the Godhead that were set aside at Nicaea, his co-eternality explanation of their timelessness, resonated with those called upon to resolve the Arian controversy there. Save for those who later rebutted Arius' forceful assertion that the Son was less than the Father, the ideas that were expressed at Nicaea had all been seeded by the time that

---

[391] N.A. Nathan, "The Trinity according to Origen" Ibid., 4.

Tertullian and Origen had finished their work. There is nothing particularly novel in what Novation and Dionysius wrote of the Trinity to answer Sabellian heretics, and what is attributed to Gregory Thaumaturgus on that score is properly dismissed as anachronistic since it bears the clear marks of later interpolation.

When the idea of the Trinity developed by the Ante-Nicene fathers is traced to source, it originated as a response to the Jewish criticism that the Christians were heretics because they believed in more than one God. The idea that the Father or Maker and Jesus Christ were the same being in any physical way, may be detected in the writing of Tertullian and Origen about their common substance but neither of them suggest that the Father and Son are the same person. For everyone earlier, Christ was completely unified with His Heavenly Father in purpose, but did His bidding. And Jesus sought that same oneness for all who believed what He taught. There was nothing of nirvana in Jesus' aspiration in His intercessory prayer, nor was there any suggestion of physical identity between Father and Son in the gospels. The Son sought simply to completely and exactly obey the Father, and to please Him.

Upon this foundational understanding of the origin of the doctrine of the Trinity in response to Jewish criticism and mistaken Christian teaching, we can now discuss the political context for the Council of Nicaea and the theological discussion that occurred during six weeks between May and July in 325 A.D.

4

WHY THE NICENE COUNCIL AND WHAT DID IT DECIDE?

Introduction

In this chapter, I will suggest that by the time the Nicene Council was convened, the Christianity's need to defend against Jewish criticism of their theology was only important to the extent that it provided context for Christianity's unswerving commitment to monotheism. My purpose in this chapter is to identify the arguments about the nature of Christ and his relationship with the Father that the Nicene Council was convened to resolve, and to place those arguments in their historical and political context. Though the Nicene Council also settled the date when Christians would celebrate Easter in future and promulgated twenty new church laws or canons, those issues are not a part of the discussion that follows because they do not bear on the nature of Christ's godhood, nor his relationship with the Father.

I have divided my discussion of the history, politics and theology at Nicaea in this chapter into five parts. In the first part, after briefly refreshing the history of the debate between Christians and Jews over the nature of God, I discuss the imperial and church politics that were brought to a head at Nicaea. I note that even though the Emperors Constantine and Licinius were probably both Christians, were related by marriage and had jointly issued the Edict of Milan as the first international law establishing religious tolerance in 313 A.D., they were not able to settle their political differences in peace. Constantine finally defeated Licinius and put him to death even though he had promised his wife that there would be no execution. I explain that before Constantine's conquest reunited the empire, dissent within the Christian Church was a large political issue for both emperors and both had experimented with different ways of resolving the conflict. Both had witnessed the oppression and persecution of Christians and while both had come to prefer policies of toleration, their direction that Church Councils were not to be convened without imperial consent, had not resolved the underlying arguments.

In Part Two, I discuss Constantine's efforts to resolve theological arguments inside the church using Bishop Ossius of Cordoba as imperial legate before Constantine himself invited all the Bishops to the Council near his summer residence. That discussion notes the heavily Eastern attendance and doubts some accounts which suggest that the resulting theology was of Western provenance. In Part Three, I discuss how the Christology debate unfolded before discussing the *homoousios* concept in Part Four which has been at the core of the Trinity theology ever since. The *homoousios* discussion confirms that Constantine personally introduced this word as a possible solution though we cannot be sure whether he was alert to the theological baggage this word carried for some of those present. In Part Five, I explain that there was no consensus on Christology at the Council. Though the Creed was developed in the same way as declarations at modern conventions, a small number of those attending would not sign it, mostly because they would not agree to the added anathemas. The non-signers were sanctioned though all were returned to Constantine's favour within two years.

I conclude that Constantine convened the Nicene Council as part of his strategy of unity in the empire. His quest was to find a theological solution that was general enough to accommodate everyone. As he had earlier written in his letter to Arius and Athanasius, Constantine expected these ministers of Christ to be able to resolve their differences peacefully as an example for others. He expected general resolutions which accommodated differences since the trifles they were fussing about were matters of mere conjecture.

Part One - The history and politics surrounding Nicaea

In the first section of this book, I traced the idea of monotheism from its first appearing in Egypt in the second millennium B.C. through its Jewish adoption a millennium later to protect sacred theology from persecution and admixture during the successive Assyrian, Babylonian, Greek and Roman occupations of Palestine. I suggested in particular that when the Jews were ruled by the Romans and Greeks, they did not want their 'divine council' confused with or syncretized into the God pantheons those two ancient super powers adopted as a part of their approach to the management of religious difference in their empires. I further suggested that Jewish monotheism was so defensively entrenched in orthodox Jewish theology after the Babylonian captivity, that their old 'divine council' theology had been lost. That theology had recognized four different levels of beings created in the image of God. I explained that when Christianity began, it was treated as heresy by orthodox Jews in the 1st century A.D. The Christian teaching that Jesus Christ was divine was attacked as a polytheistic heresy like those that good Jews had resisted through Greek and Roman sovereignty. But by the time the Council at Nicaea was convened, Christianity was no longer simply a minority sect that had grown out of Judaism. By the 4th century A.D., Christianity's sheer size had seen it transcend its Jewish origins and it had become a world religion with adherents that included members of the imperial staff and family. In that context, the first and second century Jewish criticism that Christian theology was polytheistic had subsided in importance and the contemporary questions that divided the Christian faith and with it, the empire, concerned the nature of the Father and the Son and their relationship with each other.

The Councils that were convened in the fourth century, were Christianity's attempt to find common cause; to agree on an orthodox theology; to identify and debunk non-orthodox teaching and to call those exposed as heretics to repentance. Many Christians claim that the councils settled and implemented their creeds democratically, and because they thus present as the majority will of the whole church, they are said to have settled church doctrine for all practical purposes. Other Christians then and since, maintain that truth cannot be settled by a majority. Absent clarification from the Father, Son and Holy Ghost, no mortal or group of mortals can settle the Christological issues that were contested at Nicaea. Neither this chapter nor this book as a whole will seek to do that. All that is intended here is to provide context to enable and facilitate contemporary debate with humility and respect.

Part Two – Constantine's unity agenda

While the Emperor Constantine invited all Christian Bishops to the Council he convened at Nicaea, there is disagreement about the level of his interest and involvement in the theology that was discussed there.[392] Robert M. Grant's seminal 1975 summary of the politics behind the Council concludes that

> The Council of Nicaea was ecumenical only in the sense that the participants came from the Roman world and, indeed, only from the eastern half of it…[and] the so-called Nicene Creed was actually set forth not at Nicaea but at Constantinople in 381.[393]

Grant also confirms that "the Roman Emperor took his seat among the bishops and discussed theology with them."[394] But the great majority of the bishops who attended came from the Eastern half of the empire and came at Constantine's request. Grant continues that Constantine convened the Council because by 312, in "his campaign for supreme power" he had perceived "how helpful the Christian church could be"[395] despite his previous use of the persecution favoured by his predecessors.

When Constantine came to the Imperial throne in the West, he came to the throne of a divided Empire. His brother-in-law, Licinius, ruled in the East and Constantine had claimed the West by virtue of his civil war victories over Maxentius. While Constantine and Licinius initially co-existed in peace and jointly authored and promulgated the Edict of Milan in 313 that curtailed the ongoing official persecution of Christianity, Constantine

---

[392] For example, see James R. White who suggests that Constantine's only interest was in a unified church and John D. Hagen Jr. who is anxious to rebut Dan Brown's *Da Vinci Code* idea that "Constantine invented Jesus' divinity and imposed it through a relatively close vote at the Council of Nicea".

[393] Robert M. Grant, "Religion and Politics at the Council at Nicaea", *The Journal of Religion*, Vol. 55, No. 1 (January 1975), University of Chicago Press, 1-12 (1).

[394] Ibid.

[395] Ibid.

distrusted Licinius and the alliance did not hold. There were intermittent wars between them from 314 till Licinius was finally defeated and spared following the battle of Chrysopolis on 18 September 324. However Licinius was executed on suspicion of treason during the following year.

While Constantine portrayed Licinius as a pagan so as to portray himself as the great Christian liberator,[396] Licinius' policy of toleration towards Christians after his marriage and the Edict of Milan, appear to have been sincere.[397] His wife, Constantine's half-sister, was a devout Christian and Licinius' implementation of the Edict of Milan[398] ended the Christian persecution which had been Diocletian's policy in his half of the empire. Licinius' took a variety of steps to enable church unity, and his practice of inviting bishops to extended council meetings, foreshadowed councils convened later by Constantine including the famous Council of Nicaea. Like Constantine after his famous conversion experience at the Battle of Milvian Bridge in 313, Licinius had his armies display Christian insignia

---

[396] Canduci, Alexander (2010). *Triumph & Tragedy: The Rise and Fall of Rome's Immortal Emperors*. Pier 9, 125. See also Peter J. Leithart, *Defending Constantine: The Twilight of an Empire and the Dawn of Christendom*, (Intervarsity Press, Downers Grove, Illinois, 2010), 101.

[397] Note however, that some commentators interpret Licinius' marriage to Constantine's half-sister as self-protection with the further suggestion that the only reason that Licinius practiced any degree of toleration towards Christians was because that was the policy of his more powerful co-emperor and brother-in-law. Similar political correctness is attributed to the fact that his armies fought under Christian insignia after the joint proclamation of the Edict of Milan in 313 A.D. The truth of Licinius' sincerity is impossible to establish particularly given his execution as a traitor and Constantine's subsequent spin as victor to reinforce his own spiritual credentials as the better Christian tolerator. See for example, Francis C. Betten, "The Milan Decree of A.D. 313: Translation and Comment", *The Catholic Historical Review*, Vol. 6, No. 2, (July 1922), 191-197 (191). The Encyclopedia Britannica notes that "Licinius…made his army use a monotheistic form of prayer closely resembling that later imposed by Constantine" during his campaign against Maximinus shortly after the joint Edict of Milan in 313 A.D. However, the Britannica accepts that Licinius became "alienated from Christians…and initiated a mild form of persecution against them". Robert M. Grant however (above n393) says that unlike Constantine, Licinius "maintained absolute toleration from the beginning of his reign" as Emperor (ibid 2).

[398] Michael DiMaio Jr., "Licinius (308-324 A.D.)", *De Imperatoribus Romanis*, 1997, says that the Edict of Milan was issued as a celebration of the marriage of Licinius and Constantine's half-sister but was not original. It was a reissue of an edict earlier issued by Galerius, Licinius' friend and patron. Note however that the Reverend Francis S. Betten SJ has called Galerius "the arch-persecutor" and says he had only "grudgingly permitted the Christians to practice their religion" and his edict went nowhere near as far as the Edict of Milan in restoring confiscated church properties and giving Christians full citizen rights (Betten, (above n397), 191).

following the Edict of Milan.[399]

Grant considers that Licinius was tolerant toward Christianity throughout his reign.[400] But other historians have treated Licinius less kindly, probably because of the influence of Constantine's propaganda.[401] Grant states

> An inscription dated in 318 shows the Marcionites, a sect viewed as heretical by most Christians, were free to build churches. The more orthodox Christian bishops were free to meet in provincial synods and create church legislation on moral problems.[402]

However Grant has also observed that by A.D. 321, Licinius was concerned that a doctrinal argument that had broken out between Alexander, the Bishop of Alexandria and one of his presbyters named Arius, stood to fracture his half of the empire.[403] The ban on bishops' meetings that he imposed to preserve the peace was unpopular. It saw "some Christians…refus[e] to take part in sacrifices to celebrate the fifteenth year of his reign"[404] in 323 A.D. and Licinius never had the opportunity to resolve the matter because he was defeated by Constantine just one year later.

Following this victory,[405] Constantine maintained both Licinius' religious toleration and his policy ban on bishops' conferences without imperial approval pending a review of the Arian disturbance by his ecclesiastical advisor, Bishop Ossius of Cordoba. To fulfill this imperial commission, Ossius went personally to Alexandria with a personal letter from Constantine that held both parties responsible for the breach in the "peace, harmony and unity"[406] of the empire which had resulted from their dispute. Ossius' instructions confirmed the policy that Alexander and Arius were to "refrain from further discussions"[407] without imperial

---

[399] See above n397 where the display of Christian insignia by Licinius' army has been interpreted as deference to Constantine as the Senior Augustus per the Edict of Milan in 313 A. D.
[400] Grant, (above n393), 2.
[401] See discussion above n397.
[402] Grant, (above n393), 2.
[403] Ibid 3.
[404] Ibid. Licinius' rule as a Roman Emperor lasted from 308-324 A.D.
[405] This victory united the empire for the first time since Diocletian had appointed Maximian as his co-emperor in 286 A.D.
[406] Grant, (above n393), 3. The full text of the letter may be found in the Appendix.
[407] Grant, ibid.

approval.

Though Alexander had asserted wide ranging support for both his position and his theology, Ossius' inquiries revealed that not everyone agreed with him. Alexander's views were not universally supported, particularly in three of the Western provinces of Asia Minor and provinces further East "where the influence of [Eusebius,] the bishop of Nicomedia was strong."[408] Ossius therefore travelled to Antioch to hear Alexander's opponents for himself. Ossius' arrival in Antioch coincided with the death of the incumbent bishop whom he replaced, exercising imperial authority, with Eustathius of Beroea.[409] Ossius then convened a Council which was well attended by bishops who did not support Alexander.[410]

Grant reports that the only trace of the debate that took place in that bishops' council "lies in a fragment preserved by Eusebius of Caesarea".[411] In that brief fragment, Ossius was said to have asked a Cilician bishop if he believed in two 'essences' [Father and Son], but when the bishop replied that he believed in three [Father, Son and Holy Ghost], the anti-Arians were "scandalized…and the council agreed to expel the Arian supporters."[412]

Though Grant says that Ossius had imperial authority "to… undertake…excommunications on his own initiative", his view of how the issue should be resolved had been endorsed by the "bishops from six eastern provinces…who had all agreed on an anti-Arian formula". Eusebius of Caesarea was one of those "suspended from office" pending repentance. Ossius' enduring problem was that the suspended were not inclined to repent and Eusebius in particular continued preaching that "the Son of God was a created being."[413] Ossius therefore proposed a further council at Ancrya but Constantine transferred it to Nicaea because it "would be more convenient for the western representatives… [being] nearer Italy and the rest of Europe[,…] had a milder climate[,…]

---

[408] Ibid.
[409] Ibid 4.
[410] Ibid.
[411] Ibid.
[412] Ibid.
[413] Ibid.

and was close to the emperor's own residence at Nicomedia."[414]

At Nicaea, Constantine would be able to personally "participate in council's sessions" and in Grant's words, "keep the bishops under his control."[415] Though we do not have the terms of Ossius' appointment, it is clear that he held and exercised imperial authority to fill vacant bishops' sees and to excommunicate the unorthodox. No one suggests that Ossius thereby exceeded his authority. But it is unclear whether the bishops acquiesced in Ossius' action and the direct imperial involvement that followed for political reasons, or because they accepted imperial intervention on theological grounds.

The Council of Nicaea – attendance

Grant says that Constantine's engagement with the Christian Church was pragmatic. Early in his reign in the West, he had "sent funds to support the more reliable clerics" and he had "subsidized…church councils at Rome and at Arles", but he had found "that money could not buy unity".[416] He had then "tried persecution and confiscation" but "finally turned to toleration only because he had to do so."[417] After that experimentation early in his Western reign, he became more committed to toleration both because of the commitments he had made at Milan, and because toleration proved more effective in practice. When he defeated Licinius and united the empire, he found the Christian churches of the East were "divided just as those of the [W]est had been divided a decade earlier."[418] Because Ossius had not been successful in resolving "the episcopal squabbles",[419] he intervened personally to transfer the "great and hieratic council"[420] that Ossius had called, from Ancrya to Nicaea. His three reasons for the transfer given above[421] were mere pretext for his personal intervention.

---

[414] Ibid.
[415] Ibid.
[416] Ibid 2.
[417] Ibid.
[418] Ibid 3.
[419] Ibid 4.
[420] Ibid.
[421] Above n414 and supporting text.

Grant concedes historical differences in dates given for the great council. But he confirms that its opening on May 20, 325 is now well documented by contemporary legal documents and he confirms that it was over by July 30th since Constantine was back at Nicomedia by that date. What remains unclear is how many bishops and support staff attended, and who they were.

Numerical uncertainty swirls around the attendance number because the reported attendance of 318 is very conveniently the same number as had become sacred because the book of Genesis says that Abraham mustered 318 for 'the battle of the kings in Genesis 14:14.[422] Grant suggests that even attendance of between 250 and 300 according to early witnesses may be exaggerated,[423] but most commentators agree that the great majority of the bishops who did attend, came from what was formerly Licinius' Eastern half of the Empire.[424] Those same commentators agree with Grant's assessment that we cannot be sure of the names of the bishops who attended from the West in person because "their names may well have been added after they expressed their agreement with the council's decisions."[425] Other sources suggest that Constantine had invited all of the then 1800 bishops from the Christian Church – perhaps 1000 in the East and 800 from the West – and that the actual attendance "of accompanying priests, deacons and acolytes" was more than 1500 since each bishop "had permission to bring with him three priests and two deacons".[426]

Most of the enduring debate surrounding the Nicene Council concerns what it decided, how those decisions were made and which factions may or may not have influenced the outcomes. While the answers to the theological questions have received more attention in

---

[422] Sacred also because in Greek the number 318 is written 'TIH', "the Tau also referring to the cross and the IH to the first two letters in the name of Jesus" (Grant, (above n393), 5). See also Jörg Ulrich, "Nicaea and the West", *Vigiliae Christianae*, Vol. 51, No. 1 (March 1997) 10, 12-13.

[423] Grant, (above n393), 5. See also RPC Hanson, *The Search for the Christian Doctrine of God*, (T & T Clark, Edinburgh, 1987), 156.

[424] See for example Ulrich, (above n422), 12-14.

[425] Grant, (above n393), 5. Ulrich gives the names of six western empire bishops as "participants in the council" – "Ossius of Cordoba, Vicentius and Victor as representatives of the bishop of Rome, Silvester, Markus from Calabria, Caecilian of Carthage, Domnus from Pannonia, and Nikasius from Gaul" (Ulrich, (above n422), 14).

[426] <http://www.newworldencyclopedia.org/entry/First_Council_of_Nicaea>.

subsequent centuries, the Council's decision-making methodology is also important since deference to a senior ecclesiastical leader could have pre-empted any factional lobbying that would otherwise have been influential. Similarly, deference to the will of the emperor could also have mitigated the power of any single factional view, though factional lobbying may also have influenced the views of the emperor.

Part Three - The Council of Nicaea – methodology

Neither the Bishop of Rome, later revered as the Pope in Roman Catholicism, nor any of the patriarchs from the various strains of Eastern Orthodoxy, attended the Council. The Papacy had not yet been formally recognized, nor had the five Eastern Orthodox Patriarchates been formed. Though two presbyters attended Nicaea from Rome, and Ossius (the bishop appointed to preside by Constantine) is said by the New World Encyclopedia to have represented the Pope from Rome,[427] none of the authorities are certain of that representation nor of the authority of these three to bind the see of Rome in matters of theology or practice. Again, the New World Encyclopedia credits Alexander of Alexandria, Eustathius of Antioch (recently appointed as Bishop by Ossius) and Macarius of Jerusalem as being first in rank from the East.[428] But this ranking simply recognises the later pre-eminence of their bishoprics in Eastern Christianity. It has also been suggested that the aged bishop Metrophanes of Constantinople was represented by his deputy and successor, the presbyter Alexander. But other records suggest that Bishop Metrophanes attended in his own right or that Alexander who later became the first archbishop of Constantinople, was already a bishop in his own right by this time and that Metrophanes would have been 117 years old if he was alive to attend the Council.[429]

Grant accords Ossius the role of presiding officer at the Council because he had presided so recently at the council he had called at Antioch

---

[427] Ibid, see also Grant, (above n393), 5.
[428] New World Encyclopedia, ibid.
[429] Smith, I.G., "Alexander of Byzantium" in Wace, Henry and Piercy, William C., *Dictionary of Christian Biography and Literature to the End of the Sixth Century*, 3rd ed., (London, John Murray, 1911).

exercising his imperial authority and because he was "close to Majesty".[430] But Grant also concedes that many of "[t]he ancient historians disagree completely".[431] The authors of the New World Encyclopedia concur in Grant's conclusion because "the council was convened by Constantine I upon the recommendation of a synod led by Hosius of Cordoba in Eastertide of 325 C.E."[432] But it is also reasonable to surmise that Ossius was more of a conducting officer than a presiding official since his authority and the authority to convene the Council, clearly emanated from Constantine himself.

Grant's description of the venue and seating arrangements suggest the deference that was accorded the Emperor:

> The meeting place symbolized imperial concern for church affairs [in a palace at Nicaea recently taken from Licinius];…the bishops sat along the sides of the main hall, to the right and left of the chair reserved for the emperor. All stood up when he entered with his bodyguards; he graciously remained standing until they invited him to sit.[433]

But the authors of the New World Encyclopedia leave a slightly different impression with a quote from Warren H. Carroll:[434]

> Resplendent in purple and gold, Constantine made a ceremonial entrance at the opening of the council…but respectfully seated the bishops ahead of himself.[435]

The Encyclopedia authors continue summarizing Carroll:

> [The Emperor] was present as an observer but did not vote. Constantine organized the Council along the lines of the Roman Senate. 'Hosius (Ossius) presided over its deliberations; he probably, and the two priests of Rome certainly, came as representatives of the Pope.'

Because of subsequent schisms in Christianity and the apologetic nature of the historical summaries, it is difficult to be sure who attended and how much delegated authority they brought with them. But it is also difficult to resist the conclusion, since Constantine was present for the

---

[430] Grant, (above n393), 5.
[431] Ibid.
[432] New World Encyclopedia, (above n426).
[433] Grant, (above n393), 5.
[434] Carroll WH, *The Building of Christendom*, (Christendom Press, 1987).
[435] Ibid 11.

full six weeks of deliberation, that his influence was profound even if he did not vote.

The New World Encyclopedia identifies six topics on the Council's agenda:

1. The Arian question;
2. The celebration of Passover;
3. The Meletian schism;
4. The Father and Son are one in purpose or in person;
5. The baptism of heretics;
6. The status of the lapsed in the persecution under Licinius.[436]

While Grant acknowledges the agenda items and identifies distrust among the bishops since some were suspected of having informed on others,[437] Constantine would not buy into any of these recriminations since that would have detracted from "[h]is policy…of conciliation and harmony".[438] Indeed, "Constantine demonstrated his moral superiority and political skill" after all the bishops had informed on one another in writing, "by burning the accusations without reading them" and telling them thereafter to start again. "In effect, [he] treat[ed] all the accusations as anonymous"[439] so that the Council could "reach unanimous consensus on the Christological views of Arius."[440]

Grant confirms that after Constantine had thus symbolically set all personal animus aside, the Council proceeded to its core theological business. None of that interlocutory action is consistent with the view that Constantine was a mere observer at the Council.

The deliberation concerning Christology

Grant suggests that bishop "Eusebius of Nicomedia, made a move fairly early in the proceedings"[441] perhaps because he thought the Arians had a chance of "winning"[442] the debate. It is also possible that he acted in

---

[436] New World Encyclopedia, (above n426).
[437] Grant, (above n393), 6.
[438] Ibid.
[439] Ibid.
[440] Ibid.
[441] Ibid.
[442] Ibid.

good faith and simply focused the issue by placing the Arian teaching up front and centre from the outset. Grant notes that Arius claimed support from both Eusebius of Nicomedia and Eusebius of Caesarea. Eusebius of Caesarea was a "historian and biblical scholar"[443] who had convened a council of Palestinian bishops and "supplied additional New Testament texts"[444] in favour of Arius before Nicaea. Eusebius of Nicomedia, "the chief bishop of the eastern empire",[445] had followed Eusebius of Caesarea in supporting Arius by previously convening a similarly supportive council at Bithynia.[446]

In any event, Grant reports that Eusebius of Nicomedia's possibly pre-emptive move at Nicaea, was a "lead balloon".[447] Grant quotes Eusebius' "vindictive opponent Eustathius of Antioch":[448]

> When they began to investigate the formulation of the faith, the statement of Eusebius was brought forth, with clear evidence of its blasphemy. When it was publicly read, it produced immeasurable grief...for the audience and inflicted irremediable shame for its author. The workshop of the Eusebians was plainly convicted and the lawless document was torn up in the sight of all. Some, however, on the pretext of peace, put to silence all those who were accustomed to speak the best.[449]

Grant suggests that there is more than a little disappointment in Eustathius' reference to silence, since it infers that Constantine's insistence on comity, denied Eustathius the public rout he sought.[450] The truth was that the proposal from the Bishop of Nicomedia had the support of at least "twelve prominent bishops" and again, the shredding of the documents which captured all the disagreement, prevented the dissolution of the Council in hopeless disarray. The inference is thus that Constantine's presence and his commitment to unity more than once prevented walk-outs.[451]

---

[443] Ibid 2.
[444] Ibid.
[445] Ibid.
[446] Ibid 3.
[447] Ibid 6.
[448] Ibid.
[449] Ibid.
[450] Ibid.
[451] Ibid 6-7. Lewis Ayres has also opined that Constantine convened the Council to put an end to the divisive Christological dispute (*Nicaea and its legacy*, (Oxford University Press, 2004), 18, 87). See also Hanson, (above n423), 152.

Grant says that those who were eventually found orthodox, were concerned to avoid getting caught up in the irreverent language of the Arians. Perhaps anxious to redeem his reputation after censure several months previously at the Antioch Council convened by Ossius, Eusebius of Caesarea suggested the key to resolving the Christological problem lay in the scriptural language in the gospel of John and in Paul's letter to the Colossians. Grant says this initiative was rewarded when Constantine personally intervened and endorsed him. Constantine confirmed not only Eusebius of Caesarea's orthodoxy and his personal agreement with his interpretation of the scriptures he had cited, but he also recommended that the other bishops endorse Eusebius' formulation. Once again, it is difficult to accept the proposition that Constantine was a passive observer of the proceedings.

Ulrich rejects the idea that Western Christology was prominent in the Nicene Council discussion. The focus was all on resolving Eastern theological arguments. Ulrich is emphatic that despite the fact that after the Arian controversy 'had started at Alexandria in A.D. 318, [and]… spread surprisingly quickly over the whole Greek speaking part of the Roman empire",[452] it did not engage the West. While Tertullian in the West had earlier used the term 'Trinity' to describe the unity of Father, Son and Holy Spirit,[453] his purpose was to "refute…modalistic opponents",[454] and the speculative Trinitarian theology came out of the Greek philosophical and theological schools rather than from the West.[455] Ulrich says that he cannot find any Western engagement in "the dogmatic discussions on the Trinity at Nicaea until the forties of the fourth century"[456] which is fifteen to twenty years too late.

Part Four - The *homoousios* idea

Grant says that Constantine endorsed the orthodoxy of doctrinal statements by Eusebius of Caesarea because they came so close to ideas which he had already agreed with Ossius. Only one word of final

---

[452] Ulrich, (above n422), 12.
[453] Ibid 11.
[454] Ibid.
[455] Ibid.
[456] Ibid 10.

clarification was necessary to finalise consensus and that word was "the famous *homoousios*".[457] But Grant is not certain where the 'same essence' idea came from and why that expression of the essential argument resonated around the great council chamber. While Grant concedes that Ossius and Alexander of Alexandria had already agreed on it, few of the other bishops attending the Council could have been aware of the word's questionable Christian history descending as it did from the Valentinian gnostics of the second century, who had used it to describe their spiritual union with God.[458] When introducing the word into the Nicene discussion, Constantine "gave it a semi-philosophical interpretation and added that it was suitable 'to understand such (theological) matters with divine and ineffable terms.'"[459] Whether the introduction of the word *homoousios* should thus be presented as Constantine's stroke of genius which enabled settlement of the debate, or whether Christian doctrine was thus corrupted by Greek philosophy forever, depends on one's perspective.

Grant may here beg one of the underlying questions at Nicaea, since he attributes the introduction of the term *homoousios* to Constantine himself and that again places the Emperor at the centre of the theological discussion and in the theological settlement which followed.[460] Christians who argue that the Nicene creed does not accurately represent the doctrine of Christ's Godhood, question why the core of this creed could validly have come from a secular emperor who may not even have been a

---

[457] Grant, (above n393), 7.
[458] Ibid. In Grant's words, these gnostics used the term to explain that spiritual men like themselves "had the same essence" with God.
[459] Ibid 8.
[460] RPC Hanson refers to Eusebius of Nicomedia's direct involvement in the homoousios discussion and his insistence that though the word was included, it should be glossed so as to make it less offensive to Arians (above n423), 170).

true believer or a member of the Christian church at the time.[461]

Ulrich confirms that "Constantine was very much in favour of the *'homoousios'* being incorporated in the creed",[462] and he credits Eusebius of Nicomedia as his source for the fact "that the emperor personally inserted the *'homoousios'*"[463] idea in the creed. But after canvassing the various theories as to who drafted the creed,[464] Ulrich also agrees with Christopher Stead's conclusion that Ossius of Cordoba could not have been the draftsman since Eusebius spoke "derogatively" about the drafting but positively characterized Ossius as a "peacemaker" at Nicaea.[465]

While some critics of the Nicene creed may take delight in this evidence of Constantine's personal involvement in the formulation of the creed at Nicaea, with respect it does not prove or disprove the creed's value or its divine provenance. That is a matter that individual believers must settle for themselves with the assistance of the Holy Spirit. What is more useful here is to identify just what those attending the council understood they were agreeing to, and in particular what the word *homoousios* meant to them.

The central question at the council was of course, whether Christ the Son was subservient to God the Father in some way. Those later

---

[461] Note that there is disagreement in scholarship as to the date and the sincerity of Constantine's conversion. Many point to his vision at the battle of the Milvian Bridge in A.D. 312 as the date of his conversion and suggest that Constantine thereafter considered himself a Christian (eg K.E. Carr, "Constantine's Conversion". Others point to the fact that he delayed his baptism till his deathbed on May 22, 337 where the ordinance was administered by Eusebius, the bishop of Nicomedia who had been exiled following his resistance at the council of Nicaea but who had been reinstated and was held in "high favour" by 329 A.D. Others see the delay in his baptism as typical during a period when many Christians believed one could not be forgiven following baptism. Others again suggest that engagement with the Christian church by Constantine was never anything more than a matter of wise political expediency.

[462] Ulrich, (above n422), 15.
[463] Ibid.
[464] Ulrich notes that Athanasius said that Ossius was the draftsman while Basil of Caesarea says Hermogenes of Caesarea in Cappadocia drew up the creed (ibid).
[465] Ibid.

adjudged orthodox,[466] held that Christ was not subordinate to the Father in any way, but that He was co-eternal with him. Arius' interpretation of the scriptures held that the Son was subordinate to and less than the Father because He was created by Him and ascended from grace to grace to become co-equal with Him. Constantine's supposed solution to this acrimonious debate, was to contribute the vague term *homoousios* as a semantic compromise upon which all could agree. While there is disagreement as to what it meant to those attending the council, Constantine asserted that the term meant "of the same essence". He asserted that the term *homoousios* was sufficiently general to accommodate the theological views of both Alexander and Arius.[467] As he had written to them both by Ossius two full years earlier, he expected them to find a solution.[468] Now he was acting as a benevolent but firm mediator.

This word *homoousios* had in fact been agreed between Ossius and Bishop Alexander of Alexandria before the Council at Nicaea was convened,[469] but Grant suggests it would have been very new to most of the other bishops present at the Council. It is also not clear whether the word *homoousios* had been discussed between Constantine and Ossius before the latter departed on his mission to settle the dispute between Alexander and Arius at Alexandria. The term is not mentioned in the letter that Ossius carried to the two men, but the letter is well informed about their argument and direct in its call for an end to their mere

---

[466] Both Hanson and Ayers go to some lengths to suggest the orthodox/unorthodox characterisation of these 3rd and 4th century theological debates are unhelpful. Hanson has written:

> The limits of orthodoxy at the beginning of the fourth century, though more definite than they had been a century earlier, were still loose and unclear. The subject brought to the fore by Arius was one upon which no consensus had yet been reached among the Church's teachers. Each school claimed to represent the true tradition and to know the clearest interpretation of Scripture. No organ for defining universally accepted dogma had yet been devised (above n423), 145).

Ayres notes that we have no primary material from which to assess Arius' theology and he is best seen as "part of a wider theological trajectory". We will understand Nicene theology better if we respect its diversity and interwoven nature. So-called pro-Nicene theology was a culture that developed later (above n451), 1,2, 41-53, 91). Ayres has also confirmed that there was no established orthodoxy in the second and third centuries (ibid 78).

[467] Grant, (above n393), 7.
[468] For the Reverend Daniel R. Jennings' edition of that letter.
[469] Grant, (above n393), 4, 7.

speculation.[470] Grant's account of Ossius' inquiries at Alexandria and Antioch confirm that he raised the 'one essence' idea at those meetings but that it did not solve the argument. That much is clear since one of the Cilician bishops attending the Antioch meeting thought that there was not one essence, or even two (*ousiai*), but three since he considered that God was 'essentially' different from the Son and both were 'essentially' different from man.[471]

Part Five – Consensus?

According to Grant, the term *homoousios* was simply wise because it allowed "a measure of ambiguity" as was appropriate when mortals used their low language to try and express "divine and ineffable" things.[472]

Some of those sympathetic to Arius were able to accept the term as capturing the doctrinal orthodoxy of the majority of the Council, but the final form of the Nicene Creed made it very clear that Arius' views had been rejected. As Grant explains,

> terms acceptable to Arius, such as "Word," "Life," and "First-born of the whole creation"[473]

were deleted even though they came straight out of John's Gospel and the letters written by Paul. As Grant puts it:

> Their final result was very different from what Eusebius [of Caesarea] had proposed. "We believe…in one Lord Jesus Christ the Son of God, begotten from the Father, Only-begotten, that is, from the *ousia* of the Father, God from God, Light from Light, true God from true God,

---

[470] In the Reverend Daniel R. Jennings' edition of that letter, Constantine says that he had hoped for the help of these two in resolving divisions in the African Church but was devastated when he learned they were themselves divided:

> But, O glorious providence of God! how deep a wound did not my ears only but my heart received in the report that divisions existed among yourselves more grievous still than those which existed in that country! so that you, through whose aid I had hoped to procure a remedy for the errors of others, are in a state which needs healing even more that theirs. And yet, having made a careful enquiry into the origin and foundation for those differences, I find the cause to be of a truly insignificant character, and quite unworthy of such fierce contention.

The text of the complete letter may be found in the Appendix.

[471] Grant, (above n393), 4.
[472] Ibid 8.
[473] Ibid

begotten, not made, *homousion* with the Father." The anti-Arian point could hardly be made more clearly. And the addition of "true God from true God" meant that an exegetical distinction proposed by Eusebius of Caesarea had been swept aside.

Finally the victors rushed on to cross 't's and dot 'i's by anathematizing Arian statements. They denounced such expressions as "once he was not" or "before his generation he was not" or "he came into existence from nothing." The Son, they pronounced, could not be described as "of other substance or essence" or "alterable" or "mutable."[474]

Before the Council moved on after June 19th to resolve Christian contention concerning the dating of Easter, Ossius had signed the document along with the Roman representatives and those from Alexandria, although there was some Egyptian and Libyan dissent. The Palestinians and the Bithynians signed, though their bishops from Nicomedia and Nicaea would not sign the anathemas. The result of even this dissent was that "the Egyptian, the Libyan, the two Bithynians, and Arius himself" were also excommunicated.[475]

For a time it seemed that the will of the Council would prevail. Later in the year, Constantine

> wrote letters in support of Nicene decisions….warn[ing] the Church at Nicomedia not to give support to the former bishop, Eusebius, now under sentence of banishment…[and warning] a prominent friend of Arius in Syria…to watch his step. No threats to the new-found unity of the church would be tolerated.[476]

But as later at Versailles, so at Nicaea. The imposed consensus of the victors was soon fractured. The supposed consensus at Nicaea was undone by the failure of the text to explain the theology to the satisfaction of all and because the combinations which had guided its outcomes themselves unravelled. Constantine had trouble at home the following year and executed both his wife and his oldest son for having an affair.[477] His mother Helena, who had apparently uncovered the affair, had also been

---

[474] Ibid. See also Philip Schaff, *Creeds of Christendom, with a History and Critical Notes*, Volume I, 6th ed., (Harper and Brothers, New York, 1931), 46.
[475] Grant, ibid 9.
[476] Ibid.
[477] Ibid 10.

insulted by Eustathius, the bishop of Antioch who had been prominent in the final formulations at Nicaea and in the banishment of Eusebius of Caesarea. Eusebius was restored to favour and to the presidency of a synod of more than thirty eastern bishops many of whom had condemned him along with Arius at Nicaea. Eustathius was himself deposed, and then "Constantine invited Arius to visit him at Nicomedia".[478] Thereafter, Arius was "readmitted to communion" as were the bishops of Nicomedia and Nicaea, and all within the space of eighteen months after the great Council.[479]

Though Alexander and his successor Athanasius at Alexandria in Egypt, were able to avoid implementing Constantine's direction that they reinstate Arius until the wind changed again five years later,[480] the correct answers to theological disputes were clearly not as important to Constantine or his theological understanding as was the political unity which he craved. Robert Grant concludes his article using "[t]he ups and downs of Eusebius of Nicomedia" as a parable:[481]

> First he stood close to Licinius; then Constantine denounced and banished him. Reinstated as bishop, he even served as tutor to the future emperor, Julian, perhaps even teaching him something about survival. Constantine on his deathbed craved spiritual security, and it was Eusebius who baptized him.[482]

Conclusion

Grant says that the large story of Nicaea was "the story of men who tried to achieve final solutions and total victory over their opponents" only to see "their work crumble."[483] Perhaps, Grant counsels, "we can learn from Nicaea, the advisability of pursuing less absolute goals in less totalitarian ways."[484] But this interpretation of the results of the Nicene Council, really responds only to the anathemas which were pronounced against Arius and

---

[478] Ibid 11.
[479] Ibid.
[480] Ibid.
[481] Ibid 12.
[482] Ibid.
[483] Ibid.
[484] Ibid.

his followers and do not form part of the creedal formula itself. Nor does it acknowledge the personal agenda of Constantine who must have watched on in frustration as intolerance drafted the anathemas despite his example of restraint from the opening of Council and in his suggestion of the idea of *homoousios* as a theological compromise that could accommodate everyone. While Grant is correct that "the anti-Arian point" was also made in the Creed by the "God from God, Light from Light, true God from true God, begotten, not made" language,[485] those words were very general in accordance with Constantine's accommodation mandate and contrast with the words of the anathema which led to the short-lived excommunications which followed.[486] What is fascinating per Grant's aspiration, is that the words of anathema have not endured through time as a wiser more distant church has seen them as unbecoming of Christianity. But Constantine's words of generalisation in the Creed itself have lasted, however much later theologians have played with them in the interests of other agendas. That may be a consequence of Constantine's political rehabilitation of all those excommunicated within the eighteen months after the Council closed. Constantine seems to have envisioned a church, and maybe even an empire, which would continue to minister to the disaffected and bring them back to Christ's truth and practice with an increase of love and sincere respect despite the vindictiveness he must have witnessed at the Council.

With this historical and political understanding, we can now review the words of the Nicene Creed itself and do our best to understand what those framers intended in the light of the understanding of God to which they had come in the fourth century A.D.

---

[485] Ibid 8.
[486] In Philip Schaff's 1877 translation, the words of the anathema read:
But those who say: 'There was a time when he was not;' and 'He was not before he was made;' and 'He was made out of nothing,' or 'He is of another substance' or 'essence,' or 'The Son of God is created,' or 'changeable' or 'alterable' – they are condemned by the holy catholic and apostolic Church (Philip Schaff, (above n474), 51).

5

WHAT THE NICENE CREED SAYS AND WHAT IT MEANS

Introduction

In this chapter, I will review the Christological issues that the Nicene Council was convened to resolve, the language the Council used in its attempted resolution and what the words they used likely meant on the floor of the Council assembly in the fourth century A.D. I will do that in three parts. First, I shall review the theological arguments about the nature of Christ which had seen Constantine send Bishop Ossius of Cordoba to Alexandria in Egypt and thereafter to Antioch. The core issue was whether Jesus is subservient to his Father in any way and whether he had a beginning. The nature of God the Father and the Holy Spirit were not issues of debate during the early part of the fourth century. In the second part, I will set out the Creed itself using Philip Schaff's English translation of the original Greek and I will briefly observe how it is different than the later versions which were developed from it. In the third part I will discuss what the language used meant to those who wrote and agreed it. That discussion will necessarily further focus on the word *homoousios* which has been translated as 'substance' in the Schaff translation of the Creed that I have chosen. I will conclude by restating that the word *homoousios* was chosen to be accommodating of diverse beliefs about Christ though the anathema which was appended to the Creed at the Council was used, and has been used subsequently, to divide Christianity despite Constantine's unifying purpose when he convened the Council.

Part One - The Nicene theological argument in its fourth century context

The key theological question at Nicaea

According to Grant, the Council at Nicaea was convened because neither Constantine's previous policy of writing letters to those in dispute, nor Licinius' policy of forbidding independent ecumenical councils without approval, had brought peace and harmony to the Eastern part of the Roman Empire.[487] So after Constantine finally defeated Licinius and united the empire politically, he had sent his customary religious advisor, Bishop Ossius of Cordoba, to Alexandria with a letter addressed to both Alexander and Arius with direction that they must settle their dispute.[488] The letter expressed displeasure because their conflict had seeded dissension over trivialities that should not have been aired in public, if at all. Their public argument had brought the Christian Church into disrepute.[489] It is not clear whether Constantine's "careful enquiry" before he wrote his letter fully comprehended the theology before he prejudged it. Nor is it clear whether his prejudgment continued through the Council meetings and included his contribution of the *homoousios* concept as a theological and a practical solution. But it is clear that Constantine believed he was sufficiently "a servant of God" to engage in the reconciliation process and that the three of them (Constantine, Alexander and Arius) were entitled to the help of a "higher power" as they sought to resolve their "trifling" difference. While we do not know how early Constantine settled on the *homoousios* concept as the solution to 'the Arian contest', Constantine believed that the underlying

---

[487] Grant, (above n393), 3.
[488] For a full copy of the letter, see the Appendix.
[489] In the Reverend Daniel R. Jennings' edition of that letter, Constantine says that he had hoped for the help of these two in resolving divisions in the African Church but was devastated when he learned they were themselves divided:

> But, O glorious providence of God! how deep a wound did not my ears only but my heart received in the report that divisions existed among yourselves more grievous still than those which existed in that country! so that you, through whose aid I had hoped to procure a remedy for the errors of others, are in a state which needs healing even more that theirs. And yet, having made a careful enquiry into the origin and foundation for those differences, I find the cause to be of a truly insignificant character, and quite unworthy of such fierce contention.

argument between Alexander and Arius was a purely "intellectual exercise", and should have been confined "to the region of their own thoughts".[490] For Constantine, the difference between Alexander and Arius did not concern one "of the leading doctrines or precepts of the Divine law".[491]

Constantine's summary and admonition in the letter that Bishop Ossius carried to the disputants in Alexandria did not resolve the matter. Indeed, when Bishop Ossius arrived in Alexandria, he learned that Alexander had been lobbying many of the Eastern bishops for support against Arius.[492] So far as we can determine from the fragmentary evidence that remains, the difference between Alexander and those bishops was whether the Father and the Son were two essences (*ouisia*) or just one (*homoousios*) – was "the Son… essentially different from the Father?"[493] While Grant notes that Ossius sided with Alexander on the 'one substance' idea in the failed Council convened at Antioch before Nicaea,[494] Jorg Ulrich suggests that Ossius pressed the 'one substance' position on Constantine's instructions and that he was engaged as the Emperor's religious affairs legate not because of his theological erudition, but because he was a capable mediator and the Emperor wanted a peaceful unified solution.[495] Ulrich also says Ossius was not renowned as a theologian and was not dogmatic. That his theology was moveable is manifest in the fact that he "put his name to several rather differing creeds"[496] after Nicaea, and after Constantine's death.[497] His legatine mission to Alexandria bore Constantine's purpose of finding peace through doctrinal unity.

Ulrich has also noted considerable academic debate as to whether the *homoousios* idea originated in the East or West (as a latin idea translated into

---

[490] Ibid.
[491] Ibid.
[492] Grant, (above n393), 3-4.
[493] Ibid 4.
[494] Ibid. Ossius was sent to Alexandria as Constantine's imperial legate in late 324 A.D. and convened a Council at Antioch to "close the ranks" (Grant citing Henry Chadwick).
[495] Ulrich, (above n422), 15-16.
[496] Ibid 16.
[497] Ibid.

Greek), but says the Western origin idea must be discounted.[498] What then did the *homoousios* idea favoured by Constantine, mean?

For Ulrich, that meaning is revealed in the story of the West's later reception of and understanding of the Creed formulated at Nicaea. Though the Arian debate raged unabated in the East in the decades after the Nicene Council because of the reinstatement of Arius and his influential supporters, the Nicene Creed made no significant waves in the West for nearly forty years until Gregory of Elvira used the original text of the Nicene Creed in the second edition of his theological work entitled *De fide orthodoxa*.[499] Until then, the West had relied on an interpretation of the Nicene Creed accepted at the Council of Serdica in 341 A.D. even though that interpretation had been supplied by Marcellus of Ancrya who had been deposed from his Eastern see because of his unorthodox doctrinal teaching.[500]

In Ulrich's words, Marcellus "felt that Nicaea had not gone far enough in an anti-arian (and anti-origenistic) direction."[501]

> Marcellus…interpreted the relation between God the Father and God the Son as 'one substance' (*'mia ouisia/hypostasis*)…[which] was more than Nicaea had said.[502]

Ulrich suggests the reason Marcellus succeeded in convincing the West that this more anti-Arian position (which completely omitted reference to the *homoousios*) was the official Nicene position, was because it resonated with Western theological sentiments inherited from Tertullian. That is, "Marcellus' *'mia ousia/hypostasis*' [idea] was the precise equivalent" of

---

[498] Ibid 13-14. RPC Hanson says that the *homoousios* idea was not an importation from Western theology and at Nicaea was intended to have a "looser, more ambiguous sense than has in the past history of scholarship, been attached to it" (above n423), 202). He also adds that while the *homoousios* idea may have been a Greek translation of Tertullian's 'one substance' idea, in his view it was "most unlikely to be a means of ending the Arian Controversy" (ibid 168). Lewis Ayres notes that this term and the *ousia* and *hypostasis* ideas did not have fixed meaning for any of those present at Nicaea and the *homoousios* term had been the subject of earlier theological debate. The most that it meant "was membership of a class, a generic similarity between things that were, in some sense, coordinate" ((above n451), 92-95).
[499] Ibid 20.
[500] Ibid 16-20.
[501] Ibid 17.
[502] Ibid.

Tertullian's *una substantia*.⁵⁰³ But as Ulrich points out, there were important differences between Marcellus and Tertullian since Marcellus did not follow Tertullian's insistence that Father and Son were *distinctio personarum* "and avoided talking about different '*personae*' in God the Father and God the Son."⁵⁰⁴ Marcellus was also strident in claiming that Origen's "three *hypostaseis*" doctrine was Arian,⁵⁰⁵ an extreme position that was not required at Nicaea and again, did not accord with Constantine's accommodationist desire for unity and religious peace in his empire.

Ulrich demonstrates the West's immersion in Marcellus' theology from Leslie Barnard's "thorough study of the Serdican council"⁵⁰⁶ in 343 A.D.⁵⁰⁷ He says that the Western part of the Council

> drew up a creed…[which] emphasized the term '*mia hypostasis*'/Latin: '*una substantia*' and it strictly ruled out any idea of two or three '*hypostaseis*'/Latin: '*substantiae*' as being Arian.⁵⁰⁸

The Western attenders of the Serdican Council held that the difference between the Father and the Son was insignificant. They said that it could be reduced to terminology differences, which were "not far away from Sabellianism, the theological opposite extreme to Arianism."⁵⁰⁹

Marcellus' interpretation of the Nicene Creed which substituted *mia hypostasis* and *una substantia* for *homoousios* was not detected by theologians in the West for forty years⁵¹⁰ after the Nicene Council had been convened and by that time, the Western theological sails had acquired a slightly different trim.

What is the difference between the Greek term *homoousios* and Marcellus' alternative Greek and Latin terms - *mia hypostasis* and *una substantia*?

---

⁵⁰³ Ibid.
⁵⁰⁴ Ibid 18.
⁵⁰⁵ Ibid.
⁵⁰⁶ Ibid referring to Barnard LW, *The Council of Serdica 343 A.D.*, (Sofia 1983). Ulrich also refers to Hess H, *The Canons of Serdica 343 A.D. A Landmark in the Early Development of Canon Law* (Oxford 1958) as authority for Marcellus' influence in the West.
⁵⁰⁷ The writer has here followed Barnard's date for the Council of Serdica. Other authors variously date it to 341 and 342 A.D.
⁵⁰⁸ Ulrich (above n422), 19.
⁵⁰⁹ Ibid.
⁵¹⁰ Ibid 20-21.

The distinction is evident in Tertullian. While he was happy to use the 'one substance' idea with which Marcellus was later to anathematize the Arians, Tertullian would not concede that God the Father and God the Son were one person. Though later critics might suggest that Tertullian's monarchy and sunray analogies were not precise enough for their philosophical/theological purposes, Tertullian did not apologise, qualify or retreat from those analogies. Indeed, they present as the reason why he says that Father and Son were of the same substance, but were not the same person. He sought analogies that enabled him to teach that the unity between Father and Son which can not be understood by mortals, is a unity of purpose. The unity of the Father and Son and which the Son also sought for his Apostles and those who believed their teaching, was much more than the unity that obtains in a board of directors that shares a profit motive. The Father and Son are united as we might say to emphasize the point, 'in every fibre of their beings'. That was the kind of unity that Jesus also sought for his followers. The unity of all these was beyond intent. It was a unity of heart desires; a unity that did not need to be checked or matched because it was innate, guileless and equal.[511] But the unity of the Father and the Son did not combine them into one personal being as Marcellus taught the West.

Part Two – The Nicene Creed

I will now demonstrate that Tertullian's 'oneness beyond intent' accords with the theological settlement achieved at Nicaea; that it is consistent with Constantine's accommodation mandate, and that the words used were general enough to include Arius and his supporters despite the sustained wish of their detractors to anathematize them.

While this analysis does not resolve later theological questions that arose about the nature of the Holy Spirit and which Constantine would likely have said was also unnecessary, the generality of the Nicene words are consistent both with Tertullian's Trinity theology and Constantine's drive

---

[511] Colin Gunton's idea is that the Son's journey into the world shows that mortal unity with the divine is possible and the perfect outcome. But that unity has to transcend contract and become social. Humans are intended for sociality with God (*The One, the Three and the Many: God, Creation and the Culture of Modernity*, (Cambridge University Press, 1993), 220-229).

for unity and the dispute resolution practices he followed in the Nicene Council.[512]

There are many English translations of the original Greek[513] in which the Nicene Creed was written. Some of those translations have been written in the first person singular and others in the first person plural. I have used Philip Schaff's translation below,[514] for five reasons. First, it follows the 325 A.D. text; second it omits the controversial 'filioque clause' language which came later; third, it uses the word 'substance' rather than 'being' which allows Marcellus' interpretation as a good faith argument; fourth, it enables discussion of the Greek word *homoousios* which was a critical part of the compromise that was achieved under Constantine's soft direction; and finally, the plural form captures both the idea that this creed was a joint expression of theological understanding and it captures the idea that future liturgical use was anticipated.

Schaff's 1877 translation reads:

> We believe in one God, the Father Almighty, Maker of all things, visible and invisible.
>
> And in one Lord Jesus Christ, begotten of the Father, Light of Light, very God of very God, begotten, not made, being of one substance with the Father; by whom all things were made; who for us men, and for our salvation, came down and was incarnate and was made man; he suffered, and the third day he rose again, ascended into heaven; from thence he

---

[512] For example, in his letter carried by Ossius to Alexandria (see Appendix), he suggested to both Alexander and Arius that they were arguing about trifles, and after soliciting many personal complaints at Nicaea, he burned them unread to avoid both personality contests and minutiae. I have not discussed the Constantinople Creed of 381 A.D. which was promulgated by the Emperor Theodosius though unlike the Emperor Constantine, he did not attend the Council he convened and was not as visible in his influence. My reason for leaving out that discussion responds primarily to Lewis Ayres observations about the twelve differences Hanson had observed between the Creeds of Nicaea and Constantinople (referring to Hanson, (above n423), 816). Though Ayres said JND Kelly said Constantinople had to be regarded as an entirely new Creed, in fact eight of those differences were not doctrinal, the addition of "and his kingdom shall have no end" was insignificant for Trinitarian review purposes which left three – the addition of an extended statement about the Spirit; the omission of "from the ousia of the Father", and the omission of the Nicene anathemas. Ayres and Hanson were agreed that the intentional generalized ambiguity remained and the Nicene settlement was endorsed (Ayres, (above n451), 255-258). The only thing that had really changed was that some of the debate had subsided for a time, because the original personalities had left the stage.

[513] Compare the variety of translations that Wikipedia has assembled and which it admits is incomplete and insufficiently reviewed.

[514] Philip Schaff, (above n474), 27-29.

shall come to judge the quick and the dead.

And in the Holy Ghost[515]

The anathema, which was omitted from the 381 A.D. Constantinople version, said:

> But those who say: 'There was a time when he was not;' and 'He was not before he was made;' and 'He was made out of nothing,' or 'He is of another substance' or 'essence,' or 'The Son of God is created,' or 'changeable' or 'alterable' – they are condemned by the holy catholic and apostolic Church.[516]

In his published work, Schaff used a variety of parentheses and italics to visually show up the various versions of the creed. He shows how it was enlarged in 381 A.D. at Constantinople. He shows how various Western additions were made at later times, and he provides those versions in parallel columns so that readers may see how the original Nicene Creed compares with Apostles' Creed, the Chalcedon Creed and the Athanasian Creed among others. He also provides theological commentary and explains the later creedal development in the Greek churches. But for my purposes, Schaff's translation of the original Greek version of the Nicene Creed suffices. Schaff's translation is as unadulterated a version of what was agreed in 325 A.D. as I can find.

The three persons of the Godhead or Trinity are dealt with separately. The statements made about the Father and the Holy Ghost present as uncontroversial. The Council expended its energy discussing the nature of the Lord Jesus Christ. Arius suggested that he was subordinate to the Father because he came later. The words issued by the Council are conservative and closely tied to the words of the scriptural canon. For clarity's sake, I now separate and restate them:

> And in one Lord Jesus Christ, begotten of the Father, Light of Light, very God of very God, begotten, not made, being of one substance with the Father; by whom all things were made; who for us men, and for our salvation, came down and was incarnate and was made man; he suffered, and the third day he rose again, ascended into heaven; from thence he shall come to judge the quick and the dead.

---

[515] Ibid 50.
[516] Ibid 51.

In accordance with Tertullian's analogies, the Lord Jesus Christ is a separate person from the Father and the Holy Ghost. He is begotten not made. As is stated in the first chapter of John's Gospel, he existed with the Father before he was begotten and made incarnate, and the text states that he "came down…and was made man". The reference to his suffering, his resurrection, ascension into heaven and future role as judge of the quick and dead were uncontroversial in the dispute with Arius, so I do not propose to discuss them further.[517] The enduring theological debate about who are and who are not Trinitarian Christians may thus be further reduced down to the meaning of the words – "Light of Light, very God of very God, begotten, not made, being of one substance with the Father".

From a Nicene point of view, there is no need for debate about the meaning of the word 'begotten'. Though there is debate between churches professing the divinity of Christ about how he was begotten, it appears that Constantine and his Council did not see any theological argument about the nature of the begetting and respectfully left the words of the scriptural canon to speak for themselves. They were satisfied as we might now say, that the Lord Jesus Christ was begotten as the genetic Son of the Father and the details of how that was done, did not matter. None suggested that the Lord Jesus Christ was not the Father's Son.

The phrases, "Light of Light" and "very God of very God" were intended and remain as repetitive restatements of the Lord Jesus Christ's Godhood. That is, the Nicene composers were affirming as Tertullian before them had done, that just as light begets light, so when a Father begets a Son, he begets that Son with all that Father's characteristics and capacities. As again we might say in the twenty-first century, the Son inherited the characteristics and capacities of his Father genetically and thus he was verily or truly God by virtue of the fact that he was begotten of him.

If that is a fair treatment of the relevant language, all that remains for understanding is the phrase – "and being of one substance with the Father", meaning that the only phrase in the Nicene creed that was or is controversial, is expressed by the original Greek word *homoousios* which

---

[517] I note that there was later controversy in Western teaching as to whether the Father suffered when the Son was in Gethsemane and on the cross if they were one person as Marcellus would have it.

was introduced by either Constantine himself or Bishop Ossius, perhaps with the concurrence of Alexander of Alexandria. Some translations of this Greek word prefer that it be translated as "being" rather than as "substance". If that is so, then those translators would appear to hold that this remaining phrase, like its predecessors in the paragraph, "Light of Lights", "very God of very God" and "begotten", was nothing more than a parallel fourth restatement of the fact that the Lord Jesus Christ was the Father's literal Son.

Another interpretive possibility, is that the word *homoousios*, whether translated as 'substance' or 'being', was intended to mean that the Father and Son were physically one. But despite later theological, epistemological and ontological arguments that have been made to that effect, that is inconsistent with the expressions chosen in the rest of this creedal formula, and the debate that went on during those six weeks at Nicaea. No one suggested that Father, Son and Holy Ghost were other than separate Persons. They used Tertullian's words "God of God" and "light of light", so it is valid to ask why those councillors would have chosen words from Tertullian if they had intended to suggest that the Father, Son and Holy Ghost were merged in a homogenous nirvana? None of the theological discussion leading up to Nicaea in the fourth century had canvassed 'a nirvana interpretation' despite considerable Jewish argument in earlier centuries that a distinction between the persons made these Jewish apostates, polytheists. Christians said they were monotheists because the Father and the Son were unified – one, in the same way that Christ had described in his intercessory prayer as his great suffering for humankind began.

The purpose for which the Nicene Council was convened was not to discuss the nature of their blending; the Nicene Council was convened to answer Arius' argument that Christ was not as fully God as was his Father. The Creed answered that question with four phrases intended to tell believers and non-believers alike, that Christians believed that the Lord Jesus Christ was every bit God. He was not less than the Father in any sense. He had existed with the Father before the world began and was the executive in the creation itself. The Lord Jesus Christ was no mere mortal prophet. He was one with the Father himself, co-equal with him in every respect.

Part Three - What did those attending mean by the words they used?

So what did those framers intend that the *homoousios* phrase in their formula should add to the phraseology that preceded it in their explanation of the nature of the Lord Jesus Christ? I suggest that they were making the same connection as the Apostle John made in the first chapter of his Gospel between the creative work that the Father and Son had done in the beginning as was recorded in the book of Genesis. For when the God persons (*Eloheim* in Genesis 1) had finished their other work of creation, they had said to each other, "let us go down and make man in our image, male and female". That is, let us go down and make man of the same 'god-stuff' of which we are comprised. The Lord Jesus Christ's part of that enduring and unified one-God covenantal mission about which he prayed in the garden of Gethsemane (John 17), was to bring those humans that would be obedient to the same covenant as existed between the god persons in the beginning (the *let us* covenant), into a oneness with the god persons who had made them flesh.

To say more than this was to go beyond scripture, and to speculate. Constantine's original letter to Arius and Athanasius made it clear that he wanted them to avoid the speculation that was dividing his empire. His suggestion that the *homoousios* word generalised back to the words and concepts of the scriptures themselves, was intended to set a formula that could accommodate all the bishops at the Council. To the extent that either side in the Arian dispute would go beyond the words of scripture, was to take interpretive licence that no man was entitled to take.

Conclusion

The words chosen in Greek by the framers of the Nicene Creed were intended to reflect scripture and followed the meaning that Tertullian had given them a century earlier. When Tertullian said that God the Father and God the Son were of the same substance, he was not suggesting they were the same person in any way. He was confirming that they were perfectly unified in purpose, but that their unity transcended any kind of union that mortal men had achieved or could comprehend. Tertullian chose the word 'substance' to explain that even the thoughts, intents and desires of the hearts of the Father and the Son were the same. But that did not make them the same person.

6

HOW THE IDEA OF TRINITY WAS DEVELOPED IN WESTERN CHRISTIAN THEOLOGY AFTER NICAEA UNTIL THE REFORMATION

Introduction

In this chapter I will explain what happened to the Trinity doctrine after the Nicene Council in 325 A.D. I will do that in three parts.

I will first observe that the agreement about theology at Nicaea did not immediately take hold in either the East or the West of Constantine's briefly united empire. That is because Constantine did not support the strict dividing lines between orthodoxy and heresy envisaged by those who drafted the anathemas at Nicaea. Mostly, that was because the anathemas were at odds with Constantine's drive for unity in the empire and saw him insist that the Church readmit all those who had been cut off within the following eighteen months. In Part Two, I will explain that it took forty years before Western Christianity received the theology of Nicaea because they first received a corrupt version through Marcellus, the deposed Bishop of Ancrya. I will explain that though it may seem odd that Marcellus' theology should be accepted as gospel in the West for several decades since he came to Rome as a heretic, until Gregory of Elvira identified the nuanced differences between Marcellus' teaching and the original Nicene Creed, Marcellus' version seemed consistent with what the Western Father Tertullian had taught more than a century earlier. I also discuss briefly the differences between the Nicene Creed promoted by the Emperor after 325 A.D., and that promoted by the Emperor Theodosius after the Constantinople Council in 381 A.D., but I conclude following Ayres that those differences were doctrinally insignificant.

In Part Three, I will discuss Saint Augustine's contributions to the development of the Trinity theology, the sixth century Athanasian Creed and the 'filioque clause' which has divided East and Western Christianity since the eleventh century. The discussion of Augustine's theology is not extended but records his effort to systematize Christian theology and to answer the questions about the nature of God that had not been considered at Nicaea. Mary T. Clark's summary of Augustine's Trinity theology in *The Cambridge Companion to Augustine* is my principal source in that discussion. Augustine's proposition that the Holy Spirit proceeds from both the Father and the Son is accepted in the Athanasian Creed but has troubled Eastern Christianity ever since though officially, only since the eleventh century. My discussion does not take sides in that argument, but I do conclude with observations that Constantine might have made to the disputants if those disputes had arisen during his imperial reign. In particular, I observe that the Nicene Creed was intended to unite fourth century Christianity and retains its uniting power if modern Christians can disavow the sectarian spirit. I will suggest in particular that East and West can still agree on the original language of the 325 A.D. version of the Nicene Creed. The pity is that few of them have any interest in considering the possibilities that such agreement might unfold.

Part One – The immediate aftermath of the Nicene Creed

As discussed in chapter four, some of those sympathetic to Arius were able to accept the term *homoousios* as capturing the doctrinal orthodoxy of the majority of the Council, but the final form of the Nicene Creed including the anathema, confirmed that Arius' views had been rejected.

Bishop Ossius signed the document as did the Roman representatives and those from Alexandria, but there was disquiet in the East which culminated in the excommunication of bishops from Egypt, Libya and

Bithynia along with Arius himself.[518]

But Constantine was not happy with 'the settlement'. Though during the first year afterwards, he wrote letters that supported the decisions taken, Eusebius of Caesarea was returned to favour as the Nicene combinations unraveled. And within eighteen months "Constantine [had] invited Arius to visit him at Nicomedia"[519] and been "readmitted to communion" as were the bishops of Nicomedia and Nicaea.[520] Nor did the anathemas added by others to the Creed at Nicaea hold since they were not a part of the compromise Constantine wanted from the outset.

Though Arius was never reinstated in Alexandria,[521] Constantine's craving for political unity was more important than what he always regarded as 'trivial theological disputes'. The large story of Nicaea was "the story of men who tried to achieve final solutions and total victory over their opponents" only to see "their work crumble." [522] "Perhaps", again as Robert Grant counsels, "we can learn from Nicaea, the advisability of pursuing less absolute goals in less totalitarian ways."[523]

Part Two – The Nicene theology after the Council

Ulrich says that the Western church did not engage theologically at Nicaea because the presybters Victor and Vicentia who represented the Bishop of Rome were not in a position to make much of an impact at a Bishops' Council, and because it was Constantine himself who was responsible for the *homoousios* concept at the Council meeting.[524] Certainly Ossius was aware of the *homoousios* idea since it had come up in his earlier mission to Alexandria and to Antioch, but

> it seems most unlikely that Constantine would rely mainly on a Westerner like Ossius when he had to solve a theological problem that merely

---

[518] Ibid 9.
[519] Ibid 11.
[520] Ibid.
[521] Ibid. Constantine's reiteration of the direction that Arius be readmitted to fellowship after Alexander died was strong. He wrote: If I learn that you have prevented any of them from returning to the church or have impeded their admission, I will immediately send someone to remove you by my authority and depose you from your offices.
[522] Ibid.
[523] Ibid.
[524] Ulrich, (above n422), 14-15.

concerned the bishops of the East...[and] he was obviously not very well informed about how the controversy had developed in the previous seven years.[525]

Ulrich also observed that Ossius had been surprised at Antioch when Narcissus of Neronias had "freely admitted that he believed in three '*ousiai*'",[526] and that Ossius later put his name to three other creeds, the last of which "was almost Arian". For Ulrich, Bishop Ossius was not a significant theological force at any time, including at the Council of Nicaea.[527] Rather, Ulrich points to the observation of Eusebius of Caesarea that Ossius was the peacemaker at Nicaea[528] and concludes that Ossius' presiding role at the Council "does not justify any *theological* conclusions" (italics original).[529]

Ulrich continues that the West remained "blessedly aloof from the [continuing] Arian controversy"[530] until Marcellus of Ancrya and Athanasius of Alexandria came to Rome as outcasts of the Eastern church in 340 A.D. - three years after Constantine's death, and the division of the empire into three new parts. Though Marcellus' detractors suggest that he deceived Bishop Julius of Rome with his version of the Nicene theology, Ulrich doubts that, since Julius consulted Vicentius and Victor who had attended the Nicene Council on behalf of the bishop of Rome before he found that Marcellus' views were "in accordance with the doctrine of the church". Ulrich also observes that "the Roman Synod and 50 bishops" concurred with Bishop Julius in his acceptance of Marcellus and his Trinity teaching.[531]

For Ulrich, this means that Rome's first interaction with the Trinity doctrine from Nicaea was a finding that the ideas of Marcellus of Ancrya were a "correct and orthodox" expression of that doctrine.[532] Rome, he says, did not engage with the doctrine, nor was there any discussion of the *homoousios* idea.[533] The version of the Trinity doctrine they received in 341 A.D. included a version of "the unity of the Trinity that was even stronger

---

[525] Ibid 15.
[526] Ibid.
[527] Ibid 16.
[528] Ibid.
[529] Ibid.
[530] Ibid quoting V. de Clercq, *Ossius of Cordoba*, (Washington, 1954), 290.
[531] Ibid 17.
[532] Ibid.
[533] Ibid 17-18.

than in the Nicene creed itself."⁵³⁴ According to Ulrich, the reason why Marcellus' version was so successful at Rome was because it came so close to Tertullian's *una substantia* idea which was said to be precisely equivalent to *mia ousiai* and *hypostasis*.⁵³⁵ In the early years after Marcellus taught the Trinity doctrine at Rome, there was no engagement with Tertullian's differences, and in particular his idea that Father and Son were *distinctio personarum*.⁵³⁶

When the Council of Serdica convened between the East and Western churches in 342 A.D., the West opted for a version of the Trinity which denied that "ideas of two or three *hypostaseis* [or] *substantiae* [were] Arian". It also held that "the difference between God the Father and God the Son [were] insignificant", though this later finding came very close to "Sabellianism, the theological opposite extreme to Arianism".⁵³⁷ Ulrich underlines that

> it was the Serdican creed, not the Nicene one that was widely spread in the Latin speaking West in the years after 342.⁵³⁸

Ulrich thus affirms that it was the more extreme views of Marcellus and Athanasius which settled the Arian controversy in the West, and that it was not until Gregory of Elvira worked on the issue forty years later, that the differences between *una substantia* and *homoousios* began to be understood. Thereafter, and only when the differences between the Nicene and Serdican creeds were understood, did Augustine of Hippo develop those ideas into a distinctive Western Christian theology.

Part Three – The Trinity doctrine from the Council of Serdica (342 A.D.) to the Protestant Reformation

As Edmund Hill summarizes, the Council of Nicaea

> did not solve the [Trinitarian definitional] problem for the orthodox; it only forced them to realize that there was a problem to solve, by

---

⁵³⁴ Ibid 18 citing W.E.H. Turner, *The Pattern of Christian Truth*, (London 1954), 439 where that author considers Marcellus to have followed an extremist version of the Nicene doctrine.
⁵³⁵ Ibid.
⁵³⁶ Ibid.
⁵³⁷ Ibid 19.
⁵³⁸ Ibid.

affirming that the Arian solution was unacceptable.[539]

It "left the orthodox…two questions to answer" what does *homoousios*/consubstantial mean, and if the Father, Son and Holy Spirit "are one numerically identical substance, in what sense are they distinctly three?"

I have not discussed the Constantinople Creed of 381A.D. in detail even though it was as officially promoted by the Emperor Theodosius as the Nicene Creed had been by Constantine fifty years earlier. That is because I accept Lewis Ayres' view that the Constantinople Creed simply refreshed the Nicene theology.[540] While Ayres' noted that Hanson had found twelve differences between the two,[541] and though JND Kelly considered the Constantinople Creed had to be regarded as an entirely new creation, Ayres found that eight of Hanson's differences were not doctrinal, and the remaining four were not doctrinally significant. That is, the addition of the words - "and his kingdom shall have no end" were insignificant for Trinitarian review purposes. Similarly, the extended statement about the Spirit did not change the underlying Trinitarian view of the Godhead expressed in the Nicene Creed and the omission of the Nicene anathemas made no theological change either. Ayres and Hanson were agreed that the intentional generalized ambiguity remained and the Nicene settlement was essentially endorsed and reiterated. While the omission of the words "from the *ousia* of the Father", has been thought significant by some Trinitarian scholars, "[t]he increasing importance of *homoousios* as" the key to understanding the Nicene Creed, meant that the *ousia* phrase was considered redundant.[542] The only thing that had really changed was that some of the debate had subsided for a time, because the original personalities had left the stage. Hanson's final conclusion was that after all their experimentation, the trial and error of the fourth century theologians led to the truth. In effect, they returned to where Constantine had taken them at Nicaea.[543]

But while Hanson and Ayres thus suggest that the search for the basic truth about the nature of God was over when the First Council

---

[539] Hill E, *Saint Augustine, The Trinity*, (introduction, translation and notes), Rotelle JE, ed., (New City Press, New York, 9th printing, 2010), 46.
[540] Ayres, (above n451), 255-258.
[541] Referring to Hanson, (above n423), 816.
[542] Ayres, above n451, 257 referring in part to Hanson, (above n423), 817.
[543] Hanson, (above n423), 873-875.

of Constantinople in 381A.D. affirmed the Nicene creed and enlarged it to specifically include the Holy Spirit as part of the Christian Triune God,[544] neither Council answered the more detailed doctrinal questions that have arisen since. J. Warren Smith has observed that the Trinity was not the only disputed theological subject at the Councils of Nicaea and Constantinople:[545]

> Rather, the Trinity stood out as the most important subject in a constellation of related theological loci, including epistemology, the Incarnation, and Biblical interpretation.

That was because

> [I]n the fourth century, theology was not broken down into discrete loci. The Son's co-eternal relationship with the Father was inseparable from the Son's salvific work in the Incarnation. Thus there was not one controversy about the Trinity but many controversies, some theological some not.[546]

Mary Clark has similarly noted that the reason Augustine's student friend Nebridius asked him the questions in 389 A.D. that prompted his extended *De Trinitate* treatise, was because the Nicene theology had not answered the more detailed questions that arose from the pronouncements of the fourth century councils.[547] Nebridius wanted to know, for example, how it could be said that the Father and the Holy Spirit were not incarnated if the Son was, and incarnation was essential to his mission of atonement?[548] Neil Ormerod's observation that the Eastern Church never fully accepted Augustine's scripturally framed assertion that the Holy Spirit emanates from the Father and the Son,[549] is another example of Christian doctrinal uncertainty even though the creeds were said to have settled the fundamentals of orthodox Christian theology of God ever after.

For the Western Church, Augustine presents as the primary developer of Trinitarian theology after Nicaea down to Thomas Aquinas in the

---

[544] <https://www.britannica.com/event/Council-of-Constantinople-AD-381>. See also <http://www.theopedia.com/first-council-of-constantinople>.
[545] Smith JW, "The Trinity in the Fourth-Century Fathers" in *The Oxford Handbook of the Trinity*, Emery E and Levering M eds., (Oxford University Press, 2011), 109.
[546] Ibid.
[547] Clark MT, "*De Trinitate*" in *The Cambridge Companion to Augustine*, 91.
[548] Ibid 92.
[549] Ormerod N, *A Trinitarian Primer*, (St Paul's Publications, Australia, 2010), 54.

thirteenth century. Though Augustine's contributions to that theology have filled volumes, for current purposes I have followed Mary Clark in distilling them down to seven relatively simple propositions. Augustine explained:

- Why only the Son became a man;
- Why the Holy Spirit is not an inferior member of the Trinity;
- Why the Son and the Holy Spirit are not inferior to the Father even though they were said to be sent by Him;
- That one could not know the nature of the Trinity and fully be made into that image, without being united with 'it';
- That unlike mortal personhood which arises by virtue of human consciousness, the personhood of the members of the Trinity arises from their relationship to one another since they all have the same nature, and
- That human beings are created in the image of the Trinity rather than any one of its members alone.[550]

Though Mary Clark says Augustine's development of Trinity theology was founded in scriptural exegesis,[551] Edmund Hill says that Augustine's contributions required a "wholesale reinterpretation of scripture",[552] and Neil Ormerod concedes that Augustine is often criticized for being non-scriptural.[553] Others go much further and suggest that because Augustine sought to reconcile Christian theology to Greek philosophy and was followed in that process of reconciliation by Thomas Aquinas, they thoroughly hellenized Christian theology or so syncretized it with Greek philosophy that the simplicity of the original scriptural accounts has been lost.[554]

Ormerod's suggestion that acceptance or rejection of Augustine's teaching that the Holy Spirit emanates from both Father and Son at the

---

[550] See generally, Clark, (above n547), 92-99.
[551] Ibid 92-94.
[552] Hill, (above n539), 48.
[553] Ormerod, (above n549), 72.
[554] For example, Eric Herboso in <http://peopleof.oureverydaylife.com/greek-philosophy-christian-theology-5507.html>, though note the process of hellenization began long before even the birth of St Augustine. See also "St Augustine", *Stanford Encyclopedia of Philosophy*, <https://plato.stanford.edu/entries/augustine/>, and Parsons JJ, "Theology and the Greek mindset, A brief exploration". Note that Ormerod responds by saying that in fact the West christianised the hellenists ((above n549), 48).

same time has differentiated the two great Trinitarian traditions ever since,[555] and is another indicator that the fourth century creeds at Nicaea and Constantinople were never understood as a revelation that bound all of Christendom. For while Ormerod says this Augustinian idea which was accepted universally in the West from the eighth century and can be derived independent of scripture from the Nicene creed itself,[556] Eastern Church believers have always been content with the idea of the Monarchy of the Father and have not found the idea of God as monarch inconsistent with their rejection of the Arian idea that Christ was subservient to the Father at Nicaea.[557]

This core difference in Eastern and Western Christian theology after Nicaea is emblematic of the authority questions that swirl around the fourth century creeds. For some, including Augustine, those creeds set the framework within which the scriptures were to be interpreted.[558] For others, including Ormerod in his primer on Western Trinitarian theology, neither the scriptures nor the creeds alone, are a sufficient foundation from which to understand the theology of the Trinity. The practices of the Church have a legitimate part to play in the interpretive process since those practices reflect the nature of the Christian faith that was developed around the creeds.[559]

In his chapter on "The Three 'Persons' or 'Hypostases'", Gilles Emery respectfully discusses the different Eastern interpretation of various aspects of Trinity theology and summarizes that after 350 A.D. what he calls the "'mature' doctrine of the Fathers of the Church" has three characteristics. There is

> first, a clear version of the distinction between person and nature, entailing the principle that all that is attributed to the divine nature is found in an equal and simple way in each divine person; second, a formulation of the generation of the Son that clearly signifies that this generation occurs within the incomprehensible divine being; [and] third,

---

[555] Ormerod, (above n549) and supporting text. For further discussion of the schism between East and West over the 'filioque clause' in some versions of Nicene creeds see below in the section entitled, "The filioque clause and the schism between East and West".
[556] Ibid, 54.
[557] Ibid 54-57.
[558] Hill, (above n539,) 48.
[559] Ormerod, (above n549), 30-32.

a clear expression of the inseparable action of the divine persons.[560]

Though there is room for debate that the first and third characteristics are clear and simple, even Emery does not make that claim for his second point where the disagreement remains between East and West. When one adds his concession that "dogmatic reflection on the generation of the Son and the procession of the Holy Spirit" alone cannot enable human understanding of these mysteries but that "the revelation of Christ" is required,[561] one senses that more generalization could include others who do not completely accept Emery's three point summary of the Nicene formula. That is because Constantine's purpose in generalizing the Nicene formula enough to enable the unity of his empire, has been forgotten.

That forgetfulness is also evident in Gilles Emery and Matthew Levering as editors of *The Oxford Handbook of The Trinity* in 2011.[562] For though they trace diverse currents in contemporary enquiry about Trinity,[563] and while they concede that their "Handbook is not…theologically neutral", they only "present… contributions from scholars…who *generally agree* in working out their Trinitarian theology in relation to the Nicene faith" (emphasis added).[564] One thing that they do not do in that summary, for example, is recognise that the Nicene formula could easily accommodate the idea that the sameness of the three persons of Godhead is not a sameness of substance, but a complete unity of love and communion and a holding of everything in common. This idea most recently called 'social Trinitarianism', has ideological history as old as Novatian in the third century, St John of Damascus in the eighth, and Richard of St Vector

---

[560] Emery G, *The Trinity, An Introduction to Catholic Doctrine on the Triune God*, translated by Levering M, (The Catholic University of America Press, Washington D.C., 2011), 90. Note however, that Gilles Emery seems to have reconsidered this statement that the Trinity theology was mature midway through the fourth century when he wrote in the same year about twenty-first century Trinity theology and said:

> it is probably too early to speak of a 'maturity': the enquiry continues to feel its way forward, and has not yet born full fruit ("Introduction", *The Oxford Handbook of the Trinity*, Emery G and Levering M eds., (Oxford University Press, 2011), 1).

[561] Ibid 97 and 99.
[562] Emery and Levering eds., *The Oxford Handbook of the Trinity*, (above n560).
[563] Ibid, Introduction, 1.
[564] Ibid 4-5.

in the twelfth.⁵⁶⁵ The most Emery and Levering will concede in favour of contemporary social Trinitarianism is that it provides "a resource for combating individualism, patriarchy and oppressive forms of political and ecclesiastical organization".⁵⁶⁶

While the editorial policy that Emery and Levering followed in their *Handbook* suggests that post-Nicene Christian orthodoxy still seeks to control the interpretation of Christian scripture in a manner that accords with the established liturgies of mainstream Christian denominations, it does not explain the reason why scripture should be interpreted in a manner consistent with those mainstream conventions. However, Emery's acknowledgement that "the revelation of Christ" is necessary if one is to understand the mysteries of the Trinity in his *Introduction to Catholic Doctrine,*⁵⁶⁷ does present more ecumenical possibilities.

What Emery means by this "revelation of Christ" phrase is set out in his opening chapter entitled "Entering into Trinitarian Faith". There "[t]he liturgy of the Church" and particularly its sacraments of baptism, confirmation and the Eucharist⁵⁶⁸ provide the key. These sacraments reveal "the Trinitarian mystery" to believers. They enable the beginning of a "new creation" for sincere believers who are enabled through Christ and the Holy Spirit to "enter into divine life".⁵⁶⁹ The "revelation of Christ" that Emery speaks of was enabled when God the Father sent Christ as the Word of truth and the Spirit of sanctification into the world for those who would confess and accept them.⁵⁷⁰ The Word manifests and reveals "the true face of God" and that knowledge "transforms hearts" which are then sanctified by "the outpouring of the Holy Spirit".⁵⁷¹

---

⁵⁶⁵ Daniel C. Peterson discusses the idea of social Trinitarianism more fully together with criticisms of the theory in his 2017 article entitled "Notes on Mormonism and the Trinity" in *To Seek the Law of the Lord, Essays in Honor of John W. Welch*, Paul Y. Hoskisson and Daniel C. Peterson, (The Interpreter Foundation, Orem Utah), 267, 287-298.

⁵⁶⁶ Rowland T, "Globalization, Postmodern Theories of Culture and the Trinity" in *The Oxford Handbook of the Trinity*, Giles Emery and Matthew Levering eds., Oxford University Press, 2011, 586 quoting Kilby, K "Perichoresis and Porjection: Problems with Social Doctrines of the Trinity", *New Blackfriars*, 81: 432-44 (438). See also *The Oxford Handbook of the Trinity*, Giles Emery and Matthew Levering eds., Oxford University Press, 2011, 342, 422-5, 534-5, 554, and 586-7.

⁵⁶⁷ Above nn560-561 and supporting text.

⁵⁶⁸ Emery, *The Trinity, An Introduction to Catholic Doctrine on the Triune God*, (above n560), 2.

⁵⁶⁹ Ibid 3-4.

⁵⁷⁰ Ibid 4.

⁵⁷¹ Ibid 4-5.

But Emery also speaks of a form of revelation which comes by reflection. The same

> God who inspires holy Scripture…can help us understand better the meaning of scripture, to know better God the Trinity and to love him more

by casting light on his image in the human mind.[572] "[B]y catching the light that comes from God's action…the human mind becomes to some extent luminous by reflection."[573] This kind of revelation is an expression of the way the Holy Spirit "dwells in the heart of believers… [and] reveals who he is".[574]

This personal kind of revelation which comes to the spiritually focused human mind by reflection as well as that which Emery says comes by sincere participation in Christian liturgy, appears to be the same kind of revelation of which Christ taught when he said that "eternal life was to know God the Father and Jesus Christ whom he had sent."[575]

Catholic Western Christianity is not alone in its claim that believers can receive both of these kinds of revelation – that is, that they can understand Christ through the liturgy and ordinances of Christian faith, and that they can receive profound further spiritual insights by sincere reflection on sacred experiences and scripture. Despite the inference in orthodox Christianity, that such insights only come to those who hold to what is now supposed to be, the Nicene Christian faith, there is abundant testimony outside so-called orthodoxy, that suggests otherwise. And that testimony frequently points to Christ's teaching that the Father answers prayers, and that those who do miracles in Christ's name cannot lightly speak evil of him, or otherwise work against his divine purposes.[576]

Despite Emery's acceptance that some understanding of the Trinity

---

[572] Ibid 138.
[573] Ibid.
[574] Ibid 138-139.
[575] John 17:3.
[576] Matthew 7: 7-11; Luke 11: 1-13; Mark 9:38-39; Luke 9: 49-50. See also the following examples: Varghese P, "5 Keys to Receiving a Revelation From God", <https://pastorpriji.com/blog/life-principles/revelation-from-god/>, Johnson B, "How do I receive a revelation?", <http://bjm.org/qa/how-do-i-receive-revelation/>, Burton J, "Try This: Revelation-Driven Prayer", <http://www.charismamag.com/spirit/prayer/23637-try-this-revelation-driven-prayer> and The Church of Jesus Christ of Latter-day Saints, "Prayer and Personal Revelation", <https://www.churchofjesuschrist.org/youth/topic/prayer-and-personal-revelation?lang=eng>.

comes by revelation, there was no such suggestion at the Councils of Nicaea and Constantinople during the fourth century. Though the resulting theology may be described as the product of collective reflection including a revelatory element, all of the history is more consistent with negotiation following a conflict that results in an accord – an agreement that all the participants can live with, though largely ignoring the views of the vanquished. Absent from those fourth century councils, was either a prophetic or apostolic voice of authority competent and confident enough to proclaim the truth in the manner that Peter described in his second epistle,[577] or a unanimous council that was able to declare the future practice of the church without dissent as was the result of the Jerusalem Council concerning gentile converts around 50 A.D.[578]

So how did the orthodox theology of the Trinity develop after the Councils of Nicaea and Constantinople in the fourth century? The answer is, that it was largely developed through additions to fourth century creeds and the first and arguably most influential of those, was the creed named for Athanasius.

The Athanasian creed

Though this creed bears the name of the famous Bishop of Alexandria,[579] modern Christian scholars are now almost universally agreed that Athanasius did not write it.[580] That agreement credits the scholarship of Gerard Voss in 1644[581] who showed that no writer contemporary with Athanasius credited him with the composition and that its latinate origin was unlikely from an

---

[577] 2 Peter 1:16-21.
[578] Acts 15:6-29.
[579] Note that the dispute between Athanasius and Arius predated Athanasius' appointment as bishop of Alexandria. The Council of Nicaea was convened in 325 A.D. and Athanasius attended as a Deacon from Alexandria. He succeeded Alexander as Archbishop of Alexandria three years later.
[580] For an example of contemporary Catholic scholarship agreeing that Athanasius did not author the creed that bears his name see Sullivan J, "The Athanasian Creed." The Catholic Encyclopedia. Vol. 2. New York: Robert Appleton Company, 1907.21 Jun. 2019 <http://www.newadvent.org/cathen/02033b.htm>. For a Lutheran view, Living Hope (Lutheran) Church, "Athanasian Creed", < https://livinghopeomaha.com/about-living-hope/about-living-hope/athanasian-creed/>.
[581] Rowland Williams dates the Voss scholarship to 1642 (*Essays and Reviews, The 1860 Text and its Readings*, Victor Shea and William Whitla eds., (University of Virginia Press, Charlottesville and London, 2000), 229, fn 138.)

Eastern bishop whose primary language was Greek.[582]

The Catholic Encyclopedia nonetheless attributes its authorship to Athanasian influences, probably in the fifth century shortly after Athanasius' death since it so accurately reflects his theological views.[583] In particular, the Athanasian Creed "states and restates in terse and varied forms… the trinity of the Persons of God, and the twofold nature of the Divine Person of Jesus Christ."[584] Generally known as the "Quicumque vult" (in English, "Whosover wishes") because of its opening words, it has been considered by some church historians to be a liturgical work composed to assist in the teaching of Trinitarian theology by virtue of its mnemonic rhetorical devices.[585] Even though its theology is attributed to Athanasius, it never gained acceptance in Eastern churches because of its inclusion of the 'filioque' language used in Western Christianity which holds that the Holy Spirit proceeds forth from both Father and Son and not just the Father.[586] Accordingly, the *Oxford Dictionary of the Christian Church* says that it probably originated in Gaul in the 420s.[587]

Today it is rarely used even in Western Churches because its clauses damning non-adherents have not resonated with Christian toleration since the late eighteenth century.[588] If its damnatory or anathemic clauses are ignored, Western Christianity is inclined to see the Athanasian creed as presenting a very clear, albeit repetitive statement of orthodox Trinitarian

---

[582] *The Oxford Dictionary of the Christian Church* (Cross FL and Livingstone EA eds., (Oxford University Press, 2005), 120) states that attribution to Athanasius was abandoned "on the ground that the Creed contains doctrinal expressions which arose only in later controversies."

[583] Sullivan J, "The Athanasian Creed." The Catholic Encyclopedia. Vol. 2. New York: Robert Appleton Company, 1907. See also Victor Shea and William Whitla (above n581), 229, fn 138.

[584] Sullivan, Catholic Encyclopedia, ibid.

[585] Some historians suggest without authority, that it may originally have been intended to be sung. See for example Prayer Book Society, "The Creed Sung as a Psalm", <http://www.pbsusa.org/wp-content/uploads/2016/07/2004-09-10.pdf> and *The Encyclopedia of Early Christianity*, 2nd ed., Ferguson E, (Garland Publishing, New York and London, 1998), 428.

[586] The debate between Eastern and Western churches as to whether the Holy Spirit proceeds from both Father and Son (Western Church) or from the Father through the Son (Eastern Church), and whether the Eastern Church position denies the consubstantiality of the Son, is discussed below in the section entitled, "The filioque clause and the schism between East and West".

[587] Cross and Livingstone (above n582), 120.

[588] Shea and Whitla (above n581), 229, fn 138.

theology. But its repetitive insistence on the equality of the Persons in the Trinity in the face of Eastern acceptance of the Fatherhood or Monarchy of the Father, focuses the theological debate which underlies the schism between Eastern and Western Christianity.

The filioque clause and the schism between East and West

Although the schism between East and West has multiple causes,[589] for the purposes of this book, I shall only discuss those that concern Trinitarian doctrine. As indicated above, the Eastern Church has never accepted that the Holy Spirit proceeds both from the Father and the Son. In Eastern theology, the Son is not diminished by conceding that the Holy Spirit proceeds from the Father alone, because the Son is not diminished when it is accepted that the Son was begotten by the Father alone. Indeed, traditional Eastern theology holds that Western insistence on 'dual procession' misunderstands and diminishes the role of the Holy Spirit as a member of the Holy Trinity. From an orthodox Western perspective, the Eastern denial of 'dual procession' makes the Son less than consubstantial with the Father. Others, Constantine-like, think these are merely semantic differences and that it is time to heal the one thousand year old rift. And there is some hope since the Pope and the Ecumenical Patriarch have been meeting regularly in a symbolic effort to heal these enduring differences since the 1960s.[590]

The question of when the 'filioque' words were added to fourth century creeds however is moot. No scholar is certain, though there is little question that the words were originally added as a belt and braces effort to more authoritatively rebut the Arian heresy in the West. Scholars are also able to point to many Western examples where the filioque clause

---

[589] Other differences concern the kind of bread that should be used in the Eucharist, whether the Catholic Pope has universal jurisdiction, and where the most prominent eastern dioceses are placed in the overall hierarchy of Christian dioceses.

[590] Note the BBC expressed view that the Greek word for 'procedure' does not include a starting point within something suggesting that the whole argument is the result of a linguistic misunderstanding (<http://www.bbc.co.uk/religion/religions/christianity/beliefs/trinity_1.shtml>). This BBC site also notes that the first steps towards such reconciliation were taken by Pope Paul VI and Patriarch Athenagoras of Constantinople in 1965 when they revoked the reciprocal excommunications of 1054 (referred to below) and declared their intention to pursue mutual understanding.

has been used in Western rites beginning in the fifth century.[591] However, the conflict did not really crystallize until the end of the eighth century when the then Frankish king, Charlemagne, accused the Eastern Patriarch Tarasios, of heresy in connection with the Trinity doctrine. History records that Charlemagne would not back off even though Pope Hadrian rejected the heresy accusations and suggested that the theology did not lend itself to identical expression in the Latin and Greek languages.[592] When Charlemagne became Emperor in 800 A.D., he pressed the point over the objections of Pope Leo III.[593] Since that time, the difference has proven irreversible even though the formal schism dates to 1054 A.D. when the Pope and Ecumenical Patriarch of the day, reciprocally excommunicated one another.[594]

Despite the suggestion of Earl Morse Wilbur that Protestantism might have disavowed Trinitarianism altogether if Servetus had not challenged its leaders at a critical time,[595] most Protestant churches have followed the West in the 'filioque' argument. Nick Needham summarizes why very well:

> When the Reformation brought about the secession of half Western Europe from its papal allegiance in the sixteenth century, one might have thought that the Reformers would look again at the *Filioque* debate. After all, they were not bound by what Rome had done in 1054, and Eastern Orthodoxy was a potential ally in the struggle against the papacy. Amazingly, however, the Reformers did not re-examine this issue. They took over, lock, stock and barrel, the pre-Reformation Western concept of the Trinity, and reproduced it. This can perhaps be explained by the Reformers' loyalty to Augustine, who was the fountainhead of Filioquism.

---

[591] Greg Uttinger suggests that the latin phrase 'filioque' was first used in Spain the 6th century when the 589 Council of Toledo denounced Arianism anew, issued 23 anathemas, and added the 'filioque' phrase into its version of the Nicene creed (<http://chalcedon.edu/research/articles/christianity-101-the-theology-of-the-ancient-creeds-the-procession-of-the-spirit/>). As noted above from Ormerod, Augustine's detailed theology is probably the philosophical genesis of the schism, though Nick Needham is more specific in his article, "The *Filioque* clause: East or West?" in the *Scottish Bulletin of Evangelical Theology* (15/2 (Autumn1997) 142), and asserts directly that Augustine was the author of "Filioquism". That is because "Augustine is happy…to separate out the divine essence from the Person of the Father". The shift is from Person to essence (Uttinger, op cit, 142-143).
[592] Ferguson E (above n585), 428.
[593] Ibid.
[594] "Great Schism", <https://www.theopedia.com/great-schism>.
[595] See below, Chapter Seven, Part Two.

In the *Institutes*, Calvin simply says, as though it were virtually self-evident, 'The Son is said to come forth from the Father alone; the Spirit, from the Father and the Son at the same time' (*Institutes* 1:13:18). By and large, this Protestant acceptance of Filioquism has remained the case to the present day; with rare exceptions, Protestant theologians have championed the *Filioque* clause and its underlying concept of the Trinity (apart, of course, from those who have stopped believing in the Trinity altogether). All you have to do is look at almost any Protestant systematic theology. For all his defects, Karl Barth was the greatest Protestant theologian of the twentieth century, and he zealously defended the *Filioque* clause. So does Wayne Grudem in his recent systematic tome of *Systematic Theology*.[596]

Conclusion

As observed from Gilles Emery and Matthew Levering above, and save for the schism between East and West, the rudiments of Trinitarian theology were settled in the creeds that were formulated by the end of the fourth century. All that has happened since is commentary coupled with a continuing search for reflective understanding of the nature of God. In the West, the Church has accepted that most of that reflection was done by Augustine as he strove to answer the questions I have summarized from Mary Clark above. Whether an understanding of the nature of God is now enhanced or impeded by understanding the Nicene Creed, is a moot question in the wider Christian community. However, understanding the nature of God as set forth in the Nicene Creed, has been complicated by the contributions made to Trinitarian theology by Protestant churches and more particularly by Thomas Cranmer who was installed as Archbishop of Canterbury in England by Henry VIII on October 1, 1532.

---

[596] Needham N, "The *Filioque* clause: East or West?" in the *Scottish Bulletin of Evangelical Theology* 15/2 (Autumn1997) 142, 151-152. See also Uttinger, (above n591). Note however the more detailed discussion of Calvin's consideration of the Trinity doctrine which follows in Chapter Seven, Part Two.

7

How Protestant Christianity contributed to the theology of the Trinity

Introduction

In this chapter, I observe that although the Protestant Reformers accepted the theology of God received from the Western Catholic Church, there were some innovations. Earl Morse Wilbur has suggested that Calvin might have reviewed Western Trinity theology more closely if he had not been so directly challenged by Michael Servetus. While he and the other Reformers in Europe took no issue with the orthodox Western Trinity theology received from the Catholic Church, things were different in England perhaps because early on during the Reformation, some consideration was given to Eastern alliances. Though Henry VIII was reluctant to approve any of the evangelical theological changes proposed by Thomas Cranmer as his Archbishop of Canterbury, during the reign of Edward VI, Cranmer developed an expanded Protestant reform agenda and set it out in the Forty-Two Articles issued early in 1553, the year when he was executed following Mary's accession to the throne. Though the Forty-Two Articles were never implemented, the Thirty-Nine Articles were implemented with only minor adjustments in 1571 and formed the theological foundation of the Westminster Confession of Faith in 1646.

Like the preceding chapters, this one is also divided into parts. In Part One, I detail the treatment of the Trinity doctrine under the Protestant Reformation in England. I note Cranmer's initial Ten Article proposal that was reduced to Six with minimal theological change during the reign of Henry VIII. I then discuss the Trinity theology in Cranmer's Forty-Two Articles propounded during Edward VI's reign. That discussion will note that Cranmer's Forty-Two Articles were the word-for-word foundation of the Thirty-Nine Articles that were first published as the orthodox doctrine of the Anglican Church in 1571. I note that those Thirty-Nine Articles were in their turn followed without adjustment in the Westminster Confession of Faith in 1646 and have subsequently been influential in Presbyterianism and Methodism. This discussion of Protestant theology identifies significant departures from Nicene theology.

In Part Two, I discuss the life and Trinity teaching of the Spanish polymath, Michael Servetus who was famously martyred as a heretic in Geneva during the ministry of John Calvin in 1553. Though Servetus' theology is hard to follow, it is surprising that his assertion that the very idea of the Trinity was without scriptural foundation did not resonate with at least some of the European Protestants since their Reformation was founded in theology that held that Catholic theology could not be followed to the extent it could be shown to depart from the scriptures – the *sola scriptura* idea. I also note Servetus' popularity with traditional Unitarians as a foundation for further discussion of their theology in Chapter Eight.

I conclude that the Protestant theology that descends from Cranmer's Articles through the Westminster Confession of Faith in 1646, is significantly different than what was generalised at Nicaea in 325 A.D. under the soft guidance of Constantine.

Part One - The Protestant Reformation in England

Though King Henry VIII wanted his divorces whether the Pope would grant them or not, and though he claimed with some precedential authority that the English Church was independent of Rome,[597] the 'Defender of the Faith'[598] was conservative when it came to theology.[599] Thus though he trusted Thomas Cranmer as his Archbishop of Canterbury completely[600] and toyed with his reformist theological ideas, there was no Anglican canon law till the end of the reign of his daughter Elizabeth[601] and Henry only ever passed the Six Articles of Faith[602] that retreated from Cranmer's slightly more reformist Ten Article proposal.[603] While Henry VIII's son Edward was more Protestant minded in theology, or more susceptible to advice, Cranmer's Forty-Two articles propounded during Edward's reign had not been legislated by the time Mary came to power on Edward's death,[604] but later provided the foundation for Elizabeth's Thirty-Nine Articles.[605]

Those numbered I, II, IV, V and VIII are Archbishop Thomas Cranmer's expression of the Trinitarian theology in 1553 that was accepted

---

[597] Henry sketched his theory in his preamble to the *Statute of Appeals 1533* (24 Henry VIII c 12). His theory held that the English King held plenary power over church and state. Marius explained that this theory was supported by the ecclesiastical idea that "the church was inspired in the whole body by the Holy Spirit and that the pope was unnecessary to the unity of Catholic doctrine" (Marius R, *Thomas More, A Biography*, (Harvard University Press, Cambridge Massachussetts and London England, 1984), 433). Holdsworth has observed that Henry was supported in his theorizing by lawyers and ecclesiastics who "had…a professional interest in maintaining this thesis" and that its "historical worthlessness" was not demonstrated until the dissenting historian Maitland took the matter in hand in the nineteenth century (Holdsworth WS, *A History of English Law*, 2nd ed., (Little Brown and Co, Boston), 1923, Vol I, 591 referring to FW Maitland whom he there called "the greatest historian of this century").

[598] This title was conferred upon Henry VIII by the Pope in 1521 as a reward for his "blast against Luther", *The Assertion of the Seven Sacraments*, which was prepared for him by redactors including Thomas More (Richard Marius, (above n597), 203, 276).

[599] MacCulloch D, *Thomas Cranmer*, (Yale University Press, New Haven and London, 1998), chapters 6-7, but particularly 212, 216, 220, 223, 229, 237-238, 243-244, 246-247, 251-254, 428.

[600] Ibid, 252, 280.

[601] *The constitutions and canons ecclesiastical 1603* published 1900 <https://archive.org/details/constitutionscan00lond>.

[602] 31 Henry VIII c 14 (1539).

[603] MacCulloch, (above n599), chapter 7 but particularly 243-247.

[604] Ibid, chapters 11-14, but particularly 528-529, 536-538, 541, 567 and 618. For detail of the Forty-Two Articles and the subsequent amendments, see *Documents of the English Reformation*, Bray GL ed., (James Clark & Co, Cambridge, 1994) (<http://www.davidscottgehring.com/his361/fortytwoarticles.pdf>). Note that while the Forty-Two Articles were never legislated into effect as were the Six Articles, they were promulgated on 19 June 1553 with clergy instructed to implement them. But that instruction was never enforced because of King Edward VI's death less than three weeks later on 6 July. The Forty-Two Articles were eventually dropped.

[605] Ibid 621-622.

by the Anglican Church in 1571 and remain an accurate statement of its theology. I have set out those articles below along with Gerald Lewis Bray's style adjustments showing the minor amendments[606] that were made to Cranmer's original draft promulgated in June 1553.

Article I – *Of Faith in the Holy Trinity*

There is but one living and true God, everlasting, without body, parts or passions, of infinite power, wisdom and goodness, the maker and preserver of all things both visible and invisible. And in Unity of this Godhead there be three persons, of one substance, power and eternity, the Father, the Son and the Holy Ghost.

Article II – *That (Of) the Word or Son of God, which was made Very Man*

The Son, which is the Word of the Father, (begotten from everlasting of the Father, the very and eternal God, of one substance with the Father), took man's nature in the womb of the Blessed Virgin, of her substance: so that two whole and perfect natures, that is to say the Godhead and manhood, were joined together in one Person, never to be divided, whereof is one Christ, very God and very Man, who truly suffered, was crucified, dead and buried, to reconcile his Father to us and to be a sacrifice **for all sin of man, both original and actual** (not only for original guilt but also for all actual sins of men).

Article IV – *(Of) the Resurrection of Christ*

Christ did truly rise again from death, and took again his body, with flesh, bones and all things appertaining to the perfection of man's nature, wherewith he ascended into heaven, and there sitteth, until he return to judge (all) men at the last day.

Article V – *(Of the Holy Ghost)*

(The Holy Ghost, proceeding from the Father and the Son, is of one substance, majesty and glory with the Father and the Son, very and eternal God).

Article VIII – *(08) (Of) the Three Creeds*

The three Creeds, Nicene Creed, Athanasius' Creed, and that which is

---

[606] The portions of the 1553 text that were deleted in 1563 and 1571 are indicated in bold type. The additions that were made to the 1563 and 1571 texts are indicated in parentheses. Where the numbering of the Articles differs in 1563 and/or 1571, this is indicated in parentheses.

commonly called the Apostles' Creed, ought thoroughly to be received (and believed), for they may be proved by most certain warrants of Holy Scripture.[607]

Professor Terryl Givens has commented further upon these English doctrinal innovations in his 2015 book, *Wrestling the Angel*.[608] He wrote:

> In 1563, building upon the Augsburg Confession, the Anglican Thirty-Nine Articles added "passions" to the attributes God did not possess, thus turning the inherited tradition of impassibility into an explicit creedal statement. "There is but one living and true God, everlasting without body, parts or passions" affirmed the first article. The Westminster Confession of Faith, approved by the English Parliament in 1648, established the basis of Reformed theology, embraced by the Puritans and the Presbyterians. This document, which served as the basis of Baptist and Congregationalist theology as well, confirmed the impassibility of God and added the phrase "a most pure spirit, invisible" to the formula of the Articles.
>
> When Methodists broke with the Anglican creed, Wesley's 1784 Articles of Religion affirmed belief in the "one true and living God, everlasting, without body or parts" omitting the "passions". But the Methodists were clearly unsure about the passibility of God. The 1801 Book of Common Prayer restored the term "passions," and then the American branch of Methodism (the Protestant Episcopal Church of America) also reaffirmed the precise, earlier language in its 1801 Articles of Religion. "There is but one living and true God, everlasting, without body, parts *or passions*." However, the Methodist Book of Discipline of 1808 again omitted passions, describing "one living and true God, everlasting, without body or parts, of infinite power, wisdom and goodness." Then the *Methodist Magazine* reverted to the older form (God is "without body, parts or passions), and the formula persisted into the twentieth century.[609]

---

[607] *Documents of the English Reformation*, Bray GL ed., (James Clark & Co, Cambridge, 1994), 'Cranmer's Reformation: The Reign of Edward VI", 285-290.

[608] Oxford University Press.

[609] Ibid 85-86, citations omitted. The Augsburg Confession dates to 25 June 1530 and was essentially the Lutheran response to the Holy Roman Emperor Charles V's call for an explanation of the European Protestant Church's beliefs. It's 28 Articles were drafted by Philip Melanchthon, but drew upon the Articles of Schwabach that he had drafted with Martin Luther and Justus Jonas the previous year. Note that Professor Givens and his wife Fiona, have written more about the emotions of God in their book *The God Who Weeps*, (Crawfordsville, Indiana, Ensign Peak, 2012).

To more easily enable comparison of the Anglican Trinity theology with the fourth century source, I now provide translations of the original text of the original Nicene Creed from 325 A.D. and the version agreed at Constantinople in 381 A.D. Those 325 and 381 A.D. versions both predate the addition of the 'filioque' clause in the 8th century.[610] The Athanasian creed from the 5th century,[611] and the Apostles' Creed[612] are also reproduced below so that readers can understand the discussion of the theological development which then follows:

The Nicene Creed – Original 325 A.D. version

We believe in one God, the Father Almighty, Maker of all things, visible and invisible.

And in one Lord Jesus Christ, begotten of the Father, Light of Light, very God of very God, begotten, not made, being of one substance with the Father; by whom all things were made; who for us men, and for our salvation, came down and was incarnate and was made man; he suffered, and the third day he rose again, ascended into heaven; from thence he shall come to judge the quick and the dead.

And in the Holy Ghost.[613]

The Nicene Creed – Constantinople 381 A.D. version

We believe in one God,
the Father almighty,
maker of heaven and earth,
of all things visible and invisible;
And in one Lord, Jesus Christ,
the only begotten Son of God,
begotten from the Father before all ages,
light from light,
true God from true God,
begotten not made,
of one substance with the Father,

---

[610] See Chapter Six, Part Three above and particularly nn579-596 and supporting text.
[611] See above (nn579-588) and supporting text.
[612] The earliest known version has been dated to a letter written by the Council of Milan to Pope Siricius around 390 A. D. (Thurston H, "Apostles' Creed." *The Catholic Encyclopedia*. Vol. 1. New York: Robert Appleton Company, 1907).
[613] Translation by Philip Shaff (Philip Schaff, *Creeds of Christendom, with a History and Critical Notes*, Volume I, Harper and Brothers, New York, 1877, 27-29).

through Whom all things came into existence,
Who because of us men and because of our salvation came down from the heavens,
and was incarnate from the Holy Spirit and the Virgin Mary
and became man,
and was crucified for us under Pontius Pilate,
and suffered and was buried,
and rose again on the third day according to the Scriptures
and ascended to heaven, and sits on the right hand of the Father,
and will come again with glory to judge living and dead,
of Whose kingdom there will be no end;
And in the Holy Spirit, the Lord and life-giver,
Who proceeds from the Father,[614]
Who with the Father and the Son is together worshipped and together glorified,
Who spoke through the prophets;
in one holy Catholic and apostolic Church.
We confess one baptism to the remission of sins;
we look forward to the resurrection of the dead and the life of the world to come. Amen.[615]

The Athanasian Creed

Whosoever will be saved, before all things it is necessary that he hold the catholic faith. Which faith except everyone do keep whole and undefiled, without doubt he shall perish everlastingly. And the catholic faith is this: That we worship one God in Trinity, and Trinity in Unity, neither confounding the persons, nor dividing the substance.

For there is one Person of the Father, another of the Son, and another of the Holy Spirit. But the godhead of the Father, of the Son, and of the Holy Spirit, is all one, the glory equal, the majesty co-eternal.

Such as the Father is, such is the Son, and such is the Holy Spirit. The Father uncreated, the Son uncreated, and the Holy Spirit uncreated. The Father incomprehensible, the Son incomprehensible, and the Holy Spirit incomprehensible.

---

[614] The 'filioque' clause is added here by Western Christianity so that the line reads with the addition – "Who proceeds from the Father [and the Son],".
[615] "Nicene Creed", <http://www.earlychurchtexts.com/public/nicene_creed.htm>.

The Father eternal, the Son eternal, and the Holy Spirit eternal. And yet they are not three eternals, but one Eternal.

As also there are not three incomprehensibles, nor three uncreated, but one Uncreated, and one Incomprehensible. So likewise the Father is Almighty, the Son Almighty, and the Holy Spirit Almighty. And yet they are not three almighties, but one Almighty.

So the Father is God, the Son is God, and the Holy Spirit is God. And yet they are not three gods, but one God.

So likewise the Father is Lord, the Son Lord, and the Holy Spirit Lord. And yet not three lords, but one Lord.

For as we are compelled by the Christian verity to acknowledge each Person by Himself to be both God and Lord, so we are also forbidden by the catholic religion to say that there are three gods or three lords.

The Father is made of none, neither created, nor begotten. The Son is of the Father alone, not made, nor created, but begotten. The Holy Spirit is of the Father, neither made, nor created, nor begotten, but proceeding.

So there is one Father, not three fathers; one Son, not three sons; one Holy Spirit, not three holy spirits.

And in **Trinity** none is before or after another; none is greater or less than another, but all three Persons are co-eternal together and co-equal. So that in all things, as is aforesaid, the Unity in Trinity and the Trinity in Unity is to be worshipped.

He therefore that will be saved must think thus of the Trinity.

Furthermore, it is necessary to everlasting salvation that he also believe rightly the Incarnation of our Lord Jesus Christ. For the right faith is, that we believe and confess, that our Lord Jesus Christ, the Son of God, is God and man; God, of the substance of the Father, begotten before the worlds; and man of the substance of his mother, born in the world; perfect God and perfect man, of a rational soul and human flesh subsisting. Equal to the Father, as touching His godhead; and inferior to the Father, as touching His manhood; who, although He is God and man, yet he is not two, but one Christ; one, not by conversion of the godhead into flesh but by taking of the manhood into God; one altogether; not by confusion of substance, but by unity of person. For as the rational soul and flesh is one man, so God and man is one Christ; who suffered for our salvation, descended into hell, rose again the third day from the dead. He ascended into heaven, He sits at the right hand of the Father, God Almighty, from whence He will come to judge the quick and the dead. At His coming all men will rise again with their bodies and shall give account for their own works. And they that have done good shall go into life everlasting; and they that have done evil into everlasting fire.

This is the catholic faith, which except a man believe faithfully, he cannot be saved.[616]

The Apostles' Creed

I believe in God the Father Almighty, Maker of heaven and earth.

And in Jesus Christ his only Son our Lord; who was conceived by the Holy Ghost, born of the Virgin Mary, suffered under Pontius Pilate, was crucified, dead, and buried; he <u>descended</u> into hell; the third day he rose again from the dead; he ascended into heaven, and sitteth on the right hand of God the Father Almighty; from thence he shall come to judge the quick and the dead.

I believe in the Holy Ghost; the holy catholic Church; the communion of saints; the forgiveness of sins; the resurrection of the body; and the life everlasting. AMEN.[617]

I have set out these texts in full so that Cranmer's modifications can be more simply observed. The most significant theological additions are the words "without body, parts or passions" in Article I. These words raise a number of theological issues that do not obviously flow from the text of the Nicene, Athanasian or Apostolic creeds however much they may reflect orthodox Christian theology in the Twenty-First century. Though I have noted above[618] that the Catholic and Anglican Churches among other major branches of Western Christianity do not

---

[616] "Athanasian Creed", <http://www.theopedia.com/athanasian-creed>.
[617] "Apostles Creed", <https://www.creeds.net/ancient/apostles.htm>.
[618] Chapter Six, n559 and supporting text referring to Ormerod, (above n549), 30-32.

subscribe to *sola scriptura* interpretational methodology[619] in that they believe that established church traditions and liturgy are a valid aid in scriptural interpretation, these Anglican additions present significant hurdles for many other Christians and raise conflicts that are not easily resolved. Without wishing to trivialize the underlying theology, it is difficult to accept that the Trinitarian God does not have a body in accordance with Article I of these Anglican articles when Article IV asserts that Christ was resurrected with a body of flesh and bone. And it is also difficult to comprehend how the Trinitarian God including Jesus Christ could not have passions in Article I when he "was made very man" but with two natures so that he might suffer and reconcile man to God in Article II.[620]

While Cranmer's denial that the resurrected anthropomorphic Christ is an enduring part of the Trinitarian God is a more recent theological addition than the 'filioque' clause which Cranmer accepted in Article V, it identifies more diversity in Christianity than was evident at Nicaea if the Creed there issued indicates what was orthodox till 1553. For while Cranmer's summary of the Trinity doctrine in the Westminster Confession of Faith in 1646[621] may have been accepted without demur[622] by many Protestants at the time, it is unclear how

---

[619] *Sola scriptura* is one of five '*solae*' said to capture the difference between most of Protestantism and the Western Catholic Church. The other *solae* are *sola fide* (by faith alone), *sola gratia* (by grace alone), *solus Christus* (by Christ alone), and *soli Deo gloria* (glory to God alone). However, not all Protestant churches subscribe to these *solae* or have reservations about some of them. Anglicanism and Methodism for example, in a manner close to Roman Catholicism, accept that faith and scriptural interpretation, can be illuminated by tradition, reason and even by experience.

[620] See also Hebrews 2:9-18.

[621] For a brief history of the Westminster Confession of Faith in 1646, see Marlowe MD, "The Westminster Confession of Faith", <http://www.bible-researcher.com/wescon01.html> and "Reformation History, The Westminster Assembly", <http://reformationhistory.org/westminsterassembly.html>.

[622] There was significant division over other content in the Westminster Confession of Faith before it can be said that it was the settled doctrine of the Church of England. But though the Westminster Confession became law by Act of Cromwell's Parliament in 1648 (*Articles of Christian Religion* passed 27 June 1648) and was restated by the Parliament of William of Orange in 1690 since the restored British Monarchy had nullified it in 1660, the divisions never focused on Cromwell's "without body, parts and passions" formula from 1553.

that happened since it is not accepted in Catholicism.[623] There are also questions as to whether all of the Christian churches which profess to follow the original Nicene Creed, recognize the difference between that Creed and Cranmer's version of the underlying theology.[624]

But Cranmer was not the only Christian theologian who complicated understanding of the Trinity during the Reformation. Michael Servetus appears to have considered John Calvin responsible for Protestantism's failure to correct the unscriptural nature of Trinity doctrine in Roman Catholic orthodoxy. Coincidentally Cranmer and Servetus were both executed as heretics in the same year, 1553.

Part Two - Michael Servetus

Servetus was executed under the direction of John Calvin in Geneva at the age of forty-two for heresy and blasphemy because he had published books that denied the Trinity doctrine and the necessity of infant baptism. Questions remain about the court's jurisdiction and process and Calvin's

---

[623] Article XXV(VI) anathematized the Pope and Article XXIX(VI) declared that the mass was a form of idolatry (<http://emp.byui.edu/marrottr/westminsterconf-hist-wikip.pdf>). Note that a number of churches which otherwise subscribe to the Westminster Confession have since repudiated these clauses. Note further that though the *Toleration Act 1689* (1 William and Mary c 18) put an end to the persecution of non-Anglican Christians in England, it did not apply to Catholics. Legislation tolerating Catholicism was not passed until the 19th century (*The Roman Catholic Relief Act 1829*).

[624] For example, consider this statement from the website of St Michael's Church in North Carlton, Melbourne Australia, which confuses the Nicene Creed with Cranmer's expression of theology originally expressed in the 1553 Forty-two Articles:

> Emerging from the English Reformation Article I of the Anglican statement of faith, translated from the latin of the 16th century, emphasizes the distinctiveness [sic] of the Christian view of God as we say in the Nicene Creed: "There is but one living and true God, everlasting, without body, parts, or passions; of infinite power, wisdom and goodness; the Maker and Preserver of all things both visible and invisible. And in unity of this Godhead, there be three Persons, of one, power, and eternity; the Father, the Son, and the Holy Ghost." (<http://www.stmichaelsnc.org.au/Nicene%20Creed%201.pdf>).

involvement in the process.[625] By the time Servetus turned twenty-one, he had published theological texts entitled *On the Errors of the Trinity* (*Errors*), *Dialogues on the Trinity* (*Dialogues*) and *On the Justice of Christ's Reign*. But then he went to ground to avoid persecution, assumed a new name and became expert in editing and translating the classics, in mathematics, geography and medicine which he practised for twelve years in Vienne, France after attending medical school in Paris and Marseille.[626] Why he returned to theology is not entirely clear, but his magnum opus entitled *The Restitution of Christianity* (*Restitution*), was not confined to theology. In the words of Richard Muller,

> it is a significant source for Servetus's understandings of substance; the natural order and the elements; and human physiology including his revolutionary understanding of circulation of the blood in advance of William Harvey.[627]

It may be that Servetus had established such authority in science that he believed his religious heterodoxy would now be forgiven. It is also likely that he would have survived if he had not purposely gone to Geneva perhaps to provoke Calvin. Whether that ill-fated stop-over at Geneva during his flight from France to Italy was motivated by hubris or vanity, a wish to seal his theological testament with his blood, or whether it was

---

[625] Kermit Zaley, *The Restitution of Jesus Christ: Servetus the Evangelical*, 2008, fn 8 cites Hillar M and Allen CS, (*Michael Servetus: Intellectual Giant, Humanist and Martyr*, (University Press of America, Lanham Maryland, 2002), 187-188) as his authority for the following irregularities at Servetus' trial:

> Servetus was refused counsel without reason, despite requesting it twice and being guaranteed by law; (2) he was tried for his book on the Trinity despite it being published twenty-three years prior and in another state; (3) he never published of dogmatized in Geneva; (4) the accusation that *The Restitution of Christianity* corrupted Christians was baseless since it had just been published and not one copy had been sold.

As a corrective, this author observes that there is some anachronistic modernism in Zaley's irregularity charges. For example he observes that an expectation that an accused person would be entitled to legal representation is out of place anywhere in Europe in the 16th century. In England for example, prisoners were not "allowed counsel at the trial itself….until 1696 in cases of treason, [and] until 1836 in cases of felony" (Milsom, SFC, *Historical Foundations of the Common Law*, (London, Butterworths, 1969), 30). Even in the 20th century, criminal defendants were not entitled to counsel in criminal cases (O'Brien FW, "Why Not Appoint Counsel in Civil Cases? The Swiss Approach", 28 *Ohio State Law Journal* (1967) 1. Similarly modern American expectations enlightened by constitutional and procedural protections that were developed much later, have no place in the discussion of Swiss criminal procedure in the 16th century.

[626] Zaley, (above n625), 2.
[627] Muller RA, Book Review < https://muse.jhu.edu/article/261905>.

simply poor judgment, cannot be settled with certainty.[628] Richard Muller suggests that "his understanding of the traditions that he attacked" was "deficient".[629] Others may be similarly satisfied that poor judgment explains much that Servetus did in his life despite his erudition. However, since he is recognized as being ahead of his time in every other field he surveyed, I here set out his contribution to the story of the Trinity doctrine and the nature of the Christian God.

Servetus on the Trinity

Servetus' theological writings proceeded from a *sola scriptura* position[630] that invited conflict with the Roman Catholic tradition in which he was born despite his immersion in that faith. For the purposes of this book, it is not necessary to unpick that conflict save to observe that Servetus did not accept as Emery does above,[631] that the established Church traditions and liturgy were a valid aid in discerning the correct interpretation of passages of scripture that did not readily yield a doctrinal conclusion. Nor did Servetus accept that tradition attributed to the same apostles who wrote many of the New Testament books should be a factor in their interpretation. Like Martin Luther, he considered himself as competent to read and understand the scriptures as any priest or theologian. Servetus denied that there was any trace of the Trinity doctrine in the scriptures and he asserted that the church creeds from Nicaea onwards were an impediment to the evangelizing mission of the Christian church because they complicated human understanding of Jesus Christ. Servetus denied that Jesus Christ existed before he was born and he asserted that God became Jesus Christ from the moment of his conception. Richard Muller is not alone in his suggestion that Servetus is a challenging read in *Errors*.

---

[628] Gordon FB has written that Servetus desire "to make contact with Calvin bordered on obsession. His arrival in Geneva was a provocation shaped by an apocalyptic view" that he was the Michael spoken of in the bible books of Daniel and Revelations. In this view, Servetus had come to make a final stand against evil and die as a martyr (*Calvin*, (Yale University Press, 2009), 218-219).

[629] Ibid. Note that Muller suggests that Servetus did not understand the differences drawn between *hypostasis* and *ousia* in the development of Trinitarian theology when he equated "substance, essence and person" in his criticism. But that apologetic view ignores Servetus' point about the underlying theology.

[630] For furhter commentary of the five *'solae'* said to capture the difference between most of Protestantism and the Western Catholic Church, see above n619.

[631] Emery, Chapter Six above (nn567-571) and supporting text.

Dibb also says the book is "difficult to follow" though there is a rough "progression of ideas...under the paradigm that Christ is a man, Christ is the Son of God, [and] Christ is God."[632]

Servetus considered he had a mission to return the church to its pre-Nicene four gospels simplicity. For Servetus, admixture with Greek philosophy was the moving cause of the Trinitarian corruption. And yet in Earl Morse Wilbur's summary, "Servetus asserted that the Father, Son and Holy Spirit were dispositions of God, and not separate and distinct beings"[633] which comes close to Sabellianism and modalism and is also subject to his own non-scriptural argument.

Other critics have categorized Servetus as following various of the heresies that were decried by Catholic orthodoxy. Servetus rejected all of these charges in *Restitution* - Adoptionism because it denied Christ's divinity; Arianism because it conceded there was more than one God and that there was a ranking between those Gods; and Sabellianism mostly because it was confusing to say that the Father and the Son were the same person. Wilbur however, as a passionate Unitarian, was quite happy to categorise Servetus as a modalist meaning like the Sabellians, that Servetus saw only one God but considered that he operated in three different modes or ways.[634]

One can interpret Servetus' execution as the product of his own obsession rather than as the pure consequence of his theology. That is because Servetus seems to have singled out John Calvin as the devil's tool and then went out of his way to provoke him. Certainly Calvin's declaration in 1546 seven years before the execution that Servetus would not leave alive if he ever came to Geneva, does not accord with the ethical expectations that

---

[632] Dibb AMT, *Servetus, Swedenborg and the Nature of God*, (University Press of American, Lanham Maryland, 2005), 67.

[633] Goldstone L and Goldstone NB, *Out of the flames: the remarkable story of a fearless scholar, a fatal heresy, and one of the rarest books in the world*, (Broadway Books, New York, 2002), 72 citing Earl Morse Wilbur, the Unitarian Scholar and former Dean of the Pacific Unitarian School for Ministry, Berkeley, California, 1904-1910.

[634] Servetus is said to have rejected each of these heresy charges in his *Christianismi Restitution* (1553). In the Spanish, these rejections are at pages 137, 148, 168 and 169.

modern Christians impose upon their leaders.[635] But those expectations are anachronistic in an age where heretical teaching was analogous to advocating terrorism in the twenty-first century. Calvin believed that Europe needed to be rid of this intelligent criminal and he had no misgivings about his part in the execution despite the international disgust that followed.[636] But when it is reviewed dispassionately, Servetus' theology does not advance Christian understanding of the nature of God and arguably presents as a storm in a teacup because the difference is only about terminology. For even though many interpreters including Tertullian, have insisted on the separate identity of the three different persons who comprise the Trinity, Constantine's *homoousios* compromise formula seems to have been designed broadly enough that even Servetus' views could be accommodated. That Calvin and Servetus could not agree was not for any want of effort on the part of Constantine and those who advised him at Nicaea. One senses that Constantine would have sought a compromise between these two opinionated and forceful men since he hoped that the Nicene Creed might unite Christianity. That irony is the stronger in the light of Earl Morse Wilbur's belief that Servetus forced Protestant theology in Europe to

---

[635] Calvin wrote to Guillaume Farel on 13 February 1546:

> Servetus has just sent me a long volume of his ravings. If I consent, he will come here, but I will not give my word; for if he comes here, if my authority is worth anything, I will never permit him to depart alive.

This has led many to question whether Calvin is guilty of murder. That is a stretch since despite his influence, Servetus did pass through an established legal process and despite his considerable influence, Calvin was not one of his judges (see for example, Rives S, *Did Calvin murder Servetus*, (BookSurge Publishers, Charleston, South Carolina, 2008), 291 citing various authorities for the letter at fns 542 and 543). See also chapter 4 of Peter Zagorin's book *How the Idea of Religious Toleration Came to the West*, (Princeton University Press, 2003), where Zagorin discusses Sebastian Castellio's criticism of Servetus' execution in light of contemporary standards of tolerance and his previous closeness to Calvin.

[636] There was no disgust from contemporary Christian leaders. Zaley says that all the Reformers approved in perfect harmony with the intolerant spirit of the age (above n625, 8). But later historians have been unanimous in their disagreement and on the 350th anniversary of Servetus' death, descendants of Calvin "assembled at the site of [the] execution to ceremoniously denounce their forebear's role in the Spanish martyr's death." He continues that the reverse side of the monument bears the following inscription:

> As reverent and grateful sons of Calvin, our great Reformer, repudiating his mistake, which was the mistake of his age, and according to the true principles of the Reformation and Gospel, holding fast to the freedom of conscience, we erect this monument of reconciliation on 28 October 1903 (ibid).

prematurely decide where it stood on Trinitarian theology and prodded it in favour of Nicene orthodoxy despite the *sola scriptura* probabilities. While that interpretation serves Wilbur's Unitarian purpose, the idea that without Servetus, "the Reformers might have more critically examined the Trinitarian teaching and dismissed it as biblically unsound"[637] is consistent with the *sola scriptura* approach of Protestant Christianity to the other doctrinal questions that arose out of orthodox Roman Catholic theology.

One of the reasons why Wilbur argued that Servetus' anti-Trinitarian dogma had hardened Protestantism in favour of the Trinity doctrine so as not to unnecessarily rile the Catholic Church,[638] was his idea that John Calvin did not support the Athanasian creed. Though Wilbur's reasoning as to why Calvin subsequently affirmed the orthodox Roman Catholic position on the Trinity is far from well established,[639] his argument has drawn attention to Benjamin Breckenridge Warfield's 1909 earlier insight that Calvin had not wholeheartedly support the Athanasian Creed.[640] But in Warfield's less partisan analysis, Calvin had simply rejected Peter Caroli's[641] pressure to take a technical theological position on the Trinity. For Warfield, Calvin preferred simpler declarations of the divinity of Christ to the idea that any technical theological statement could resolve the issue. In that respect, Calvin's approach accords with Constantine's wish before 325 A.D. that those called to lead God's people should forbear from "trivial" and "idle"

---

[637] Zaley, (above n625), 8 summarizing Wilbur in "The Two Treatises of Servetus on the Trinity" in *The Harvard Theological Studies* translated by Earl Morse Wilbur 1932 (reprinted Kraus, New York 1969) xvi-xvii, and Wilbur EM, *Our Unitarian Heritage: An Introduction to the History of the Unitarian Movement*, (Beacon, Boston, 1925), 40-42.

[638] Ibid 7-8.

[639] Warfield BB, "Calvin's Doctrine of the Trinity", *Princeton Theological Review*, vii (1909) 553-562. See also more recently that Stephen Wedgeworth has doubted the argument that Calvin ever broke ranks with mainstream Trinitarian doctrine in his 2012 article in *The Calvinist International*. Wedgeworth also notes Beckwith's criticism of Calvin's "negative development" of Trinitarian theology. For the Beckwith article see "The Calvinist Doctrine of the Trinity", *Churchman* 115/4 (2001) 308.

[640] Warfield, ibid.

[641] Warfield says it is unjust to call Peter Caroli a "theological adventurer" as some have (Warfield, ibid). It is probably fairer to describe him as a theological critic. Other sources suggest that though he was a Dr of ecclesiastical law, he was an outcast from the Sorbonne perhaps on account of his vitriol which had seen him charged with defamation. The "theological adventurer" tag which Warfield picks up, was apparently coined by Philip Schaff.

questions not "enjoined by the force of [any] law".[642]

Conclusion

Though Peter Caroli dared John Calvin to conduct a technical review of the accuracy of the Trinity theology Protestantism received from the Roman Catholic Church, Calvin never obliged. Constantine-like, Calvin preferred so-called generality over the uncertain detail later theologians had added to the Nicene summary of theology about God. The point for Calvin, as for the bishops and Constantine at Nicaea, was that Jesus was fully God, that he had redeemed mankind and that he had been resurrected. It was not essential to the salvific power of Christian faith to say or write any more than that. But Michael Servetus was not satisfied with such a soft position from the de facto leader of the Reformation in sixteenth century Europe. Even more than Caroli, Servetus wanted Calvin to make error in the Trinity theology of the Catholic Church, a cornerstone of the Reformation's development in its second century. Calvin never took the bait because that theology was correct enough for his purposes.

Thomas Cranmer in England may have approached the matter differently than Calvin because he was not being openly provoked by critics like Servetus and Caroli but also because he was not as physically safe in England as Calvin was in Geneva. Cranmer believed in reforming the Church but had to preserve Henry VIII's good will at the same time as he staved off the anti-evangelical criticism of conservatives. But when Henry VIII died, and while Cranmer had no inkling that his young son Edward VI would die prematurely of tuberculosis, he wrote and published the Forty-Two Articles which provided the theology behind the Westminster Confession of Faith. That document set the theological sails of the English Reformation and has carried with it Presbyterianism and Methodism. But it has also confused many other Protestants about what the Nicene Creed said. That much is evident when one examines many of the liturgical statements Protestant churches make about God believing that they are quoting the Nicene original. Cranmer's most significant innovation must surely have been his statement that the triune Christian God is "without body, parts and passions" despite the Nicene doctrine that

---

[642] Constantine's letter to Alexander and Arius in 323 or 324 A.D. preserved in Eusebius of Caesarea's *Life of Constantine* 2:64-72, Gelasius of Cyzicus 2:4, Socrates Scholasticus' Ecclesiastical History 1:7. See also in the Appendix.

Jesus was bodily resurrected from the dead – a fact he made clear to his disciples by eating human food in front of them. Cranmer's "without body parts and passions" innovation has been a wedge that has further divided Christianity ever since. Cranmer's wedge would have grieved Constantine before and at Nicaea since he admonished the clergy not to dilute the unifying redemptive message of the one true faith with trivial speculations that should have remained in their own minds.

This identification of 'Cranmer's wedge' provides a segue into chapter eight where I discuss several representative Christian traditions that have rejected Trinitarian theology. While there are various reasons for that rejection, many focused on what Michael Servetus might have said was the Trinity's inconsistency with a *sola scriptura* approach to theological accuracy. And for the members of the Church of Jesus Christ of Latter-day Saints at least, Cranmer's wedge has been the main problem.

8

NON-TRINITARIAN CHRISTIANS IN THE TWENTY-FIRST CENTURY?

Introduction

While there has been Christian teaching that challenged the orthodoxy of Nicene Trinity theology since it was first formulated in the fourth century,[643] with the exception of the schism following the Western canonisation of the filioque clause in the eleventh century, those challenges have readily been dismissed and extinguished as heresy until the nineteenth century.[644] While the effectiveness of those dismissals is ironic given that Jewish Rabbis did not succeed in extinguishing Christianity by labelling its teaching as heretical polytheism, some more recent opposition to Trinitarian orthodoxy has not been as easily dismissed. While it may be too early to confirm this conclusion since classical Unitarian teaching has arguably died out and the teaching of The Church of Jesus Christ of Latter-day Saints (Latter-day Saint) and of the Jehovah's Witnesses is not yet 250 years old, if Rodney Stark's sociological predictions are accurate in any measure,[645] their

---

[643] Arius' challenge to Alexander's teaching about Christ in the Eastern Roman empire in the fourth century was discussed above in Chapters Four and Five.

[644] For example, and as discussed in Chapters Seven and Eight, Michael Servetus' challenge did not change the theology at all, though his martyrdom has become a badge of dishonour for Calvinist Protestant Christianity.

[645] Rodney Stark predicted in the early twenty-first century that Mormonism would be the next major world religion. Though the growth rate he relied on for his prediction has slowed, the LDS Church is still growing and is now established in 184 of the earth's 220 countries. More recently Stark has made similar predictions about the growth of the Jehovah's Witness ("Why the Jehovah's Witnesses Grow *so* Rapidly: A Theoretical Application", *Journal of Contemporary Religion*, Vol. 12, No. 2, 1997, 133).

challenge to Trinitarian teaching is not receding. The theological success of both Latter-day Saint and Jehovah's Witness teaching in the face of 'orthodox Christian' criticism, may also be sourced in the independent origins of these two faiths meaning that it is challenges from within that have not fared so well.

In this chapter I discuss these modern challenges to Nicene theology in three parts. In the first I discuss modern Christian disagreement with the Nicene Creed generally before specifically addressing the Unitarian challenge to the Trinitarian idea of God that was strongest in the nineteenth century. While that challenge has fallen away more recently, I identify its source in the *sola scriptura* idea that Trinitarian teaching is inconsistent with Christian scripture.

In Part Two, I discuss the Latter-day Saint theology of God and conclude that there is not much difference between that teaching and Trinitarian orthodoxy. In part that is because the Latter-day Saint Book of Mormon features some very Trinitarian passages, but the 'not much difference' conclusion also flows from orthodox Christianity's confusion about the nature of God since the Westminster Confession of Faith was first drafted in 1646.

In Part Three, I observe that while it is difficult to identify Jehovah's Witness teaching about the nature of God, their official website statements are not as far from the original Nicene formula as their comments about Trinitarian doctrine there suggest.

I conclude with the suggestion that because Unitarians, Latter-day Saints and Jehovah's Witnesses all believe in the personal example, teaching and redeeming mission of Jesus Christ, it ought not surprise any of them, that their differences concerning the nature of God can be circumscribed within a very small compass. This conclusion introduces the final chapter of the book where I suggest that common teaching about Jesus provides room for improved interfaith cooperation between all the churches that seek to follow him. While Latter-day Saints and Jehovah's Witnesses are unlikely to compromise the detail of their teaching about the nature of God absent direction from Jesus Christ himself, they have more theology in common than divides them.

Part One - Modern criticisms of Nicene theology

Though some Unitarians claim Michael Servetus as their theological ancestor,[646] not all do. That is because Michael Servetus believed that Jesus Christ became the Son of God when Mary conceived him,[647] but that he was not God before that date. Other Unitarians believe that Jesus Christ was a great man and a prophet but that he was a finite human being and never God.[648] Historical Unitarian criticism of Trinitarian theology was premised in scriptural interpretation. For while *sola scriptura* Protestant Christians believe that they can demonstrate the Trinity from the scriptures without reference to established ritual or tradition, the original Unitarians interpreted the same biblical passages to different conclusions.[649] In the twenty-first century however, the 'Unitarian' label includes a variety of Christian believers,[650] some of whom are quite happy to be labelled 'non-Christian'[651] by evangelical Christians who deny the 'Christian' label to believers in Jesus Christ who do not subscribe to their version and interpretation of the Nicene creed.[652]

---

[646] For example, Marilyn Sewell a Unitarian Universalist Minister has written:

> The Unitarian scholar Servetus, who wrote *On the Errors of the Trinity*, was burned in effigy by the Catholics and then burned in fact by Calvin, with a copy of his book strapped to his thigh. It is said that if he had been willing to change just one word of his book — to change "Jesus is a son of God" to "Jesus is the son of God" — he could have saved his life.
>
> So this is our heritage — or at least a little taste of it (<http://www.huffingtonpost.com/marilyn-sewell/unitarian-universalist-theology_b_870528.html>).

[647] Servetus M, *De Trinitatis Erroribus*, Book VII.
[648] Miano DR, "An Explanation of Unitarian Christianity", Article VI.
[649] See for example, Tuggy D, "Unitarianism", *Stanford Encyclopedia of Philosophy*
[650] For example, the Unitarian Universalist Association which sets out its seven principles in the liberal Christian tradition on its website but "believe more than one thing" (Unitarian Universalist Association, "The Seven Principles").
[651] Note that this BBC view that many North-American Unitarians do not identify themselves as Christians (<BBC, "Religions – God", <http://www.bbc.co.uk/religion/religions/unitarianism/beliefs/god.shtml>)
contrasts with Miano's more official statement that Unitarians are Christians since they believe in Jesus Christ (Miano DR, "An Explanation of Unitarian Christianity", Article VI. Article II/7.
[652] Dale Tuggy sets out the development and diversity of contemporary Unitarian belief (Tuggy D, "Unitarianism", *Stanford Encyclopedia of Philosophy* <https://plato.stanford.edu/entries/trinity/unitarianism.html>). Note that there is irony in the denial of the 'Christian' label to believers in Jesus Christ who do not subscribe to the Nicene creed since the label was originally a term of derision in which some of the early Christians took no pleasure (Keating D, *Catholic Commentary on Sacred Scripture, First and Second Peter, Jude*, (Baker Academic, 2011), 108-109).

The core of the original anti-Trinitarian teaching of the Unitarians was "virtually defined" in "an 1819 sermon" by William Ellery Channing which "la[id]out [its]'distinguishing opinions'".[653] In that sermon, Channing set out the principles the Unitarians followed in interpreting the scriptures, followed by "[s]ome of the doctrines, which the Scriptures, so interpreted, seem to us clearly to express."[654] In Givens' summary, Channing insisted "that 'the Father alone is God' and that the doctrine of the Trinity was 'irrational and unscriptural.'"[655] For Channing,

> the doctrine of the Trinity…subverts…the unity of God…[While each of the] three infinite and equal persons…has his own particular consciousness, will and perceptions…[t]hey perform different parts in man's redemption…neither doing the work of the other.…[I]f these things do not imply and constitute three minds or beings, we are utterly at a loss to know how three minds or beings are to be formed.

Channing continued:

> "To us," as to the Apostle and the primitive Christians, "there is one God, even the Father." With Jesus, we worship the Father, as the only living and true God.…We find the Father continually distinguished by this title. "God sent his Son." "God anointed Jesus." Now, how singular and inexplicable is this phraseology, which fills the New Testament, if this title belongs equally to Jesus[?][656]

Dale Tuggy in the *Stanford Encyclopedia of Philosophy*, agrees that like the English Unitarians before them, Channing's American Unitarians "argued at length that the Bible supports Unitarianism and human christology over trinitarianism", but says that the American organisation was

> transformed…towards Transcendentalism and universalism…by an increasing focus on political causes [and internal movements over the course of the mid 19th century].[657]

The upshot is that while still "anti-creedal, anti-Calvinist and dedicated

---

[653] Givens T, *Wrestling the Angel*, (Oxford University Press, 2015), 72.
[654] Channing WE, "Unitarian Christianity", delivered at the ordination of Rev. Jared Sparks in the First Independent Church of Baltimore on May 5, 1819 (<http://www.transcendentalists.com/unitarian_christianity.htm>).
[655] Givens, (above n653), 72.
[656] Channing, (above n654).
[657] Dale Tuggy, "Unitarianism", *Stanford Encyclopedia of Philosophy* <https://plato.stanford.edu/entries/trinity/unitarianism.html>.

to 'freedom of conscience', American Unitarianism" is now "a theism-optional religion" which most Christian theologians consider irrelevant enough to ignore.[658] Tuggy categorises the Jehovah's Witnesses as subordinationist unitarians because they believe that

> the Son was created before the Cosmos…was the agent through which God created the Cosmos…[and that t]he Holy Spirit is simply the power of God, the Father

even though other Trinitarian Christians have disparaged Jehovah's Witnesses as "Arians" in the absence of significant scholarly literature.[659]

Givens says the Latter-day Saints present an entirely different case. Though they are strident in their rejection of Trinitarian thought and "the Nicene solution"[660] since

> 'the Book of Mormon is even more express than the Bible in teaching that the Father, Son and Holy Spirit are one God'…Mormons actually 'face the same original puzzle as traditional Christians of explaining how that is.'[661]

Rather than "reduc[e] the Trinity to one, Mormons expand…the 'Unity in Trinity' to three physically distinct, fully individuated persons."[662] And while Huff has observed that the Mormons thus face the traditional Christian puzzle of explaining how three gods can be one, they have not solved the problem with a mystery.[663] Nor have they fully recoiled from the 'polytheism' charge levelled at the early Christians by their Jewish critics.[664] In fact, they replicate the 'unity in Trinity' idea from the top to the bottom of their church organizational structure with three person Presidencies, Bishoprics and Auxiliary leadership teams that can only make decisions unanimously.[665] There is also a significant degree of 'arianness' about the

---

[658] Ibid.
[659] Ibid.
[660] Givens, (above n653), 72.
[661] Ibid 73 quoting Benjamin Huff, "Unity in Action and the Unity of God", *Element* 2.1 (Spring 2006): 17-18.
[662] Ibid 72.
[663] *Catechism of the Catholic Church*, 234..
[664] Above Chapter Three, Part One.
[665] The most obvious example is the Church's First Presidency which is comprised of three presiding high priests, but the Presidency of every Stake (Diocese) in the world is similarly constituted as are the Bishoprics of every Ward (Parish) and the presidencies of every auxiliary organization, whether male or female.

unity Latter-day Saints see in the Godhead, their First Presidency and their local leadership. For there is always one who presides and who is sustained by the others, but whose final decision is respected and implemented after counsel has been duly taken from the two subordinates.

There are ironies here that I will develop in the discussion of increased interfaith cooperation that follows in Chapter Nine. The first is that the 'arianness' of the Latter-day Saint theology of the Godhead coincides with the Eastern interpretation of the Nicene creed before the 'filioque' clause was added in the West. That is because Eastern Orthodox Christians do not think that conceiving of the Father as a Monarch within the Trinity is inconsistent with the Nicene Creed. The second is that the Latter-day Saint explanation of Trinity in unity potentially answers Channing's Unitarian concern that the Trinity fails to differentiate Father, Son and Holy Ghost.[666] And third, while The Church of Jesus Christ of Latter-day Saints would not accept Cranmer's assertion that the Trinitarian God has no "body, parts or passions" since they insist that God the Father and Jesus Christ are separate anthropomorphic beings, the original Nicene formulation is general enough to accommodate both positions.

The Unitarian view of Christ

As discussed above,[667] there is no longer a single and unified view of Christ among those who espouse Unitarian belief. That may be demonstrated in the internet statement of the Unitarian Universalist Association, which states that their "seven Principles and six Sources grew out of [their].... grassroots...were affirmed democratically and are now part of who we are."[668] Neither those Principles nor Sources say anything about the Lord Jesus Christ.

To understand the traditional Unitarian objections to the Trinity doctrine, we must thus refer to their earlier teaching, and the definitive

---

[666] Note that Channing may have misunderstood the Nicene Creed at this point if it is accurate to say that the Nicene Creed replicated Tertullian's understanding which was that while Father, Son and Holy Ghost were of the same substance, yet they remained separate personalities.

[667] Chapter Eight Part one but more particularly nn646-658 and supporting text.

[668] Unitarian Universalist Association, "The Seven Principles", <http://www.uua.org/beliefs/what-we-believe>.

speech of William Ellery Channing referred to above,[669] suffices for that purpose. While his concern that the Trinity doctrine denied separate minds to "the three infinite and equal persons"[670] appears to misunderstand the original Nicene Creed, the Nicene insistence that Jesus was God in his own right does collide with Channing's insistence that "the Father alone is God".[671] Thus the Nicene generalization cannot accommodate Channing's Unitarianism no matter how much we stretch it. And it also seems clear that Channing would not want to be accommodated. Though Channing is correct that the early Christians worshipped God the Father and that the scriptures repeatedly affirm the Lord Jesus Christ's identity as God's Son rather than God, it is not clear how Channing interpreted John's scriptural references to the pre-existence of Jesus Christ or his role in the creation as the Word of God.[672] Because the Nicene Creed cannot accommodate traditional Unitarians, there is no need to take the analysis or the scriptural interpretation argument any further. The Unitarians cannot meaningfully be included within the 'Nicene Christian' category, but what of the Latter-day Saints?

Part Two - The Latter-day Saint view of Christ

I noted above Givens' observation that the Latter-day Saints reject "the Nicene solution" because they teach that the Godhead is comprised of "three physically distinct, fully individuated persons".[673] But I also observed his disquiet that the rejection of the Nicene teaching may not be completely just since "the Book of Mormon is even more express than

---

[669] Channing WE (above n654).
[670] Ibid
[671] Channing, (above nn655-656) and supporting text.
[672] John 1:1-3, 14.
[673] Givens, (above n660), 72. See particularly n18 above and supporting text.

the Bible in teaching that the Father, Son and Holy Spirit are one God".[674]

Givens' disquiet is easily demonstrated with a number of Book of Mormon quotations. There are many but the following three examples will suffice.

Abinadi is one of the most memorable prophets in the Book of Mormon. Circa 150 B.C, he came among a group of descendants of the Egyptian Joseph who professed to live according to the Law of Moses. He declared that they were apostate and, Paul-like, taught that the Law of Moses was a schoolmaster to prepare them to worship the Messiah when he should come in the flesh as their Saviour. For this teaching he was scourged to death with faggots as a heretic. Part of his teaching has a striking Nicene flavour. It reads:

> And now Abinadi said unto them: I would that ye should understand that God himself shall come down among the children of men, and shall redeem his people.
>
> And because he dwelleth in flesh, he shall be called the Son of God, and having subjected the flesh to the will of the Father, being the Father and the Son –
>
> The Father because he was conceived by the power of God; and the Son, because of the flesh; thus becoming the Father and Son –
>
> And they are one God, yea, the very Eternal Father of heaven and of earth.
>
> And thus the flesh becoming subject to the Spirit, or the Son to the Father, being one God, suffereth temptation, and yieldeth not to temptation, but suffereth himself to be mocked, and scourged, and cast out, and disowned by his people.[675]

---

[674] Givens, (above n660), 73 quoting Benjamin Huff, "Unity in Action and the Unity of God", *Element* 2.1 (Spring 2006): 17-18. Givens is not the only Latter-day Saint scholar to have engaged with the detail of Trinity theology in the recent past. Professor Daniel C. Peterson has observed that the Latter-day Saint theology of God has much in common with social trinitarianism – the idea that God, Jesus Christ and the Holy Ghost are not united in substance but in love and perfect communion. Peterson explains that the Greek term *perichoresis* (the mutual indwelling, coherence and interpenetration of the divine persons) also teaches advocates of social trinitarianism how Christian communities should live together on earth (Hoskisson PY and Peterson DC eds., "Notes on Mormonism and the Trinity" in *To Seek the Law of the Lord*, (The Interpreter Foundation, Orem, Utah, 2017)).

[675] *Book of Mormon*, Mosiah 15:1-5.

Perhaps sixty years later, two missionaries were similarly preaching this gospel to another group of descendants of apostates. One of them, named Amulek, was challenged by a lawyer named Zeezrom. His cross-examination was apparently preparatory to similar charges of blasphemy or heresy. Part of the dialogue follows:

> Now Zeezrom said: Is there more than one God?
>
> And he answered, No....
>
> And Zeezrom said again: Who is he that shall come? Is it the Son of God?
>
> And he said unto him, Yea.
>
> And Zeezrom said again, Shall he save his people in their sins? And Amulek answered and said unto him: I say unto you he shall not, for it is impossible for him to deny his word.
>
> Now Zeezrom said unto the people: See that ye remember these things; for he said there is but one God; yet he saith that the Son of God shall come, but he shall not save his people – as though he had authority to command God...
>
> Now Zeezrom saith again unto him: Is the Son of God the very Eternal Father?
>
> And Amulek said unto him: Yea, he is the very Eternal Father of heaven and of earth, and all things which in them are; he is the beginning and the end, the first and the last;
>
> And he shall come into the world to redeem his people; and he shall take upon him the transgressions of those who believe on his name; and these are they that shall have eternal life, and salvation cometh to none else.
>
> ...and the death of Christ shall loose the bands of this temporal death, that all shall be raised from this temporal death...and we shall be brought to stand before God, knowing as we know now, and have a bright recollection of all our guilt.
>
> Now, this restoration shall come to all...[who] shall be brought and arraigned before the bar of Christ the Son, and God the Father, and the Holy Spirit, which is one Eternal God, to be judged according to their works, whether they be good or whether they be evil.[676]

---

[676] *Book of Mormon*, Alma 11: 28-44.

The statement of the Three Witnesses to the Book of Mormon also concludes with a statement of "honor…to the Father, and to the Son, and to the Holy Ghost, which is one God, Amen".[677] These three men provided their testimony to confirm that they had seen the plates from which Smith translated the record, and that they had heard the voice of the Father declaring that the translation had been enabled by his gift and power.

The Trinitarian language in all three of these excerpts justifies Givens' observation, quoting Huff, that the Mormons face the traditional Christian puzzle of explaining how three Gods can be one. But it is not necessary for the purposes of present analysis, to discuss Givens' further observation that the only real difference between the Mormons and the rest of Trinitarian Christianity, is that the Mormons solve that puzzle without a mystery. The analysis required here is to determine whether what Givens calls "the Nicene solution" extends to include Mormon teaching about Father, Son and Holy Ghost as perhaps Constantine might have intended.

Again, the Nicene creedal formula contributes very little to Christian understanding of the nature of the Father and the Holy Ghost. It is the references to the Son in this Latter-day Saint literature which we must review against the Nicene coordinates.

Abinadi is explicit that "God himself shall come down among the children of men…[and] shall be called the Son of God…[and be both] the Father and the Son". Even Abinadi's more detailed explanation of how the Son of God will be both Father and Son accords with the original exposition at Nicaea, as well as with John's expression in the first chapter of his Gospel from which the Nicene language was drawn. Abinadi also prophesied the divine birth and suffering of the Son in the manner in which it is expressed in the Creed.

Similarly, Amulek's affirmation under cross-examination, that "the Son of God [is] the very Eternal Father of heaven and earth", resonates explicitly with the Nicene creedal language right down to the use of the adverbial qualifier, "very".[678] Amulek's focus on the mission of the Son to

---

[677] *Book of Mormon*, The Testimony of Three Witnesses.
[678] Note that in Philip Schaff's translation of the original Nicene Creed language used elsewhere in this book, Jesus Christ is described in the opening four lines as "Light of Light, very God of very God, begotten, not made".

redeem mankind, to be resurrected and then to judge "the quick and the dead" also coincides with the Nicene expression.

What are we to conclude from this analysis? At least, save for misunderstanding that may arise from the "of one substance" phrase if it is read out of its Nicene context,[679] that the exposition of the nature of God in the Book of Mormon and by its most prominent witnesses, accords with the original formulation of the Nicene Creed. Even the first Latter-day Saint Article of Faith[680] and the statement of God the Father's anthropomorphism in the Doctrine and Covenants[681] are consistent with the Nicene formula though they discord with Cranmer's 1553 doctrinal expression in the Forty-Two Articles that was canonized for the Church of England in the Westminster Confession of 1646.

The conclusion from these sources is that while Latter-day Saint theology differs from the theology of Catholicism and Protestantism that was developed in the West by Augustine and later, it is not correct to assert that Latter-day Saint theology is inconsistent with the Nicene Creed.

Part Three - The Jehovah's Witness view of Christ

Like both Latter-day Saints and Unitarians, the Jehovah's Witnesses consider themselves to be Christians,[682] however much other Christian believers may wish to deny them access to that name.[683] The Jehovah's Witnesses believe they are Christians because they "believe that Jesus is the key to salvation", "try to follow closely [his] teachings", "are baptized… and offer [their] prayers" in his name, and believe that "Jesus is the head,

---

[679] See above Chapter Three Part Three and Chapter Five Part Two.
[680] The First Article of Faith written by Joseph Smith in response to a question from John Wentworth's inquiry for the *Chicago Democrat* newspaper in 1842 says:
We believe in God, the Eternal Father, and in His Son, Jesus Christ, and in the Holy Ghost.
[681] *Doctrine and Covenants* 130:22 reads:
The Father has a body of flesh and bones as tangible as man's; the Son also; but the Holy Ghost has not a body of flesh and bones, but is a personage of Spirit. Were it not so, the Holy Ghost could dwell in us.
[682] For example, see the Jehovah's Witness official website where it is stated that they are proud to call themselves Christians ("Jehovah's Witnesses – Who Are We?").
[683] For example, see Slick M, Christian Apologetics and Research Ministry (CARM), "Is the Jehovah's Witness religion Christian?", Morton C, "Are Jehovah's Witnesses Christian?" and Dave, "How do Christians and Jehova's witness differ?".

or the one appointed to have authority, over every man".[684] However, while they believe "that Jesus is the Son of God", they do not believe that he is "part of a Trinity."[685] For the purposes of this chapter, the question is whether Jehovah's Witnesses' theology about God can objectively fit within the bounds set by Constantine's Council at Nicaea in 325 A.D. That is a more challenging question because, as Andrew Holden has observed, the Jehovah's Witnesses have written very little theologically and little has been written about them.[686] It is also challenging since "they refuse all ecumenical relations with other religious denominations".[687]

However, their official website eases this difficulty from a Nicene comparison point of view. In answer to the question – "Do Jehovah's Witnesses Believe in Jesus?", they have responded:

> Yes. We believe in Jesus, who said: "I am the way and the truth and the life. No one comes to the Father except through me." (John 14:6) We have faith that Jesus came to earth from heaven and gave his perfect human life as a ransom sacrifice. (Matthew 20:28) His death and resurrection make it possible for those exercising faith in him to gain everlasting life. (John 3:16) We also believe that Jesus is now ruling as King of God's heavenly Kingdom, which will soon bring peace to the entire earth. (Revelation 11:15) However, we take Jesus at his word when he said: "The Father is greater than I am." (John 14:28) So we do not worship Jesus, as we do not believe that he is Almighty God.[688]

In answer to their further Frequently Asked Question – "In What Way are Jesus and His Father One?",[689] the Church's official website response focuses on conceptions of the Christian God which hold that the Father and Son are the same person, though as we have seen above, that conception of the Trinitarian God is different than what was expressed at Nicaea. The official Jehovah's Witness statement says:

> "I and the Father are one," said Jesus. (John 10:30) Some quote this text to prove that Jesus and his Father are two parts of a triune God. Is that

---

[684] Jehovah's Witnesses, "Are Jehovah's Witnesses Christians?".
[685] Ibid.
[686] Holden A, *Jehovah's Witnesses: Portrait of a Contemporary Religious Movement*, (Routledge, London and New York, 2002), 2-3.
[687] Ibid 1.
[688] Jehovah's Witnesses, "Do Jehovah's Witnesses Believe in Jesus?".
[689] Jehovah's Witnesses, "In What Way Are Jesus and His Father One?".

what Jesus meant by this statement?

Let us take a look at the context. In verse 25, Jesus stated that he did works *in the name of his Father*. From verses 27 to 29, he talked about symbolic sheep whom *his Father had given him*. Both statements by Jesus would have made little sense to his listeners if he and his Father were one and the same person. Instead, Jesus said, in effect, 'My Father and I are so close-knit that no one can take away the sheep from me, just as no one can take them away from my Father.' It is much like a son saying to his father's enemy, 'If you attack my father, you attack me.' No one would conclude that this son and his father were the same person. But all could perceive the strong bond of unity between them.

Jesus and his Father, Jehovah God, are also "one" in the sense that they are in complete agreement as to intentions, standards and values. In contrast with Satan the Devil and the first human couple, Adam and Eve, Jesus never wanted to become independent of God. "The Son cannot do a single thing of his own initiative, but only what he beholds the Father doing," Jesus explained. "For whatsoever things that One does, these things the Son also does in like manner." – John 5:19; 14:10; 17:8.

This strong bond of unity, however, does not make God and his Son, Jesus, indistinguishable from each other. They are two individuals. Each one has his own distinct personality. Jesus has his own feelings, thoughts, experiences, and free will. Nevertheless, he chose to submit his will to that of his Father. According to Luke 22:42, Jesus said: "Let, not my will, but yours take place." These words would have been meaningless if his will could not differ from his Father's. If Jesus and his Father were really one person, why did Jesus pray to God and humbly admit to not knowing things only his Father knew? – Matthew 24:36.

Members of many religions worship gods that are depicted as quarreling and fighting with their own family members. In Greek mythology, for example, Cronus overthrew his father, Uranus, and devoured his own children. How different this is from the oneness based on true love between Jehovah God and his Son, Jesus! And how this unity endears them to us! In fact, we have the incomparable privilege of being in union with these two highest Persons in the universe. Regarding his followers, Jesus prayed: "I make request…that they may all be one, just as you, Father, are in union with me and I in union with you, that they may also be in union with us." – John 17:20,21.

Thus, when Jesus said, "I am my Father are one," he was speaking not of a mysterious Trinity, but of a wonderful unity – the closest bond possible between two persons.[690]

For clarity's sake, I again separate out the Nicene explanation of Jesus Christ. It reads –

> And in one Lord Jesus Christ, begotten of the Father, Light of Light, very God of very God, begotten, not made, being of one substance with the Father; by whom all things were made; who for us men, and for our salvation, came down and was incarnate and was made man; he suffered, and the third day he rose again, ascended into heaven; from thence he shall come to judge the quick and the dead.

When these Jehovah's Witness explanations of the nature and mission of Jesus as the Son of the Father are compared with the Nicene expression, there is less conflict than either the critics or the Jehovah's Witnesses themselves infer. For though like Latter-day Saints, Jehovah's Witnesses would have difficulty with a non-contextual reading of the "one substance" phrase discussed above, and because they do not worship Jesus as Almighty God, Jehovah's Witnesses do believe that Jesus Christ is the ruler of God's Kingdom in the heavens. Jehovah's Witnesses also believe that Jesus is the key to human salvation; that he came to earth from heaven, suffered for man, was resurrected and will come again to judge mankind consistent with the will of his Father. To the extent that there is conflict between Jehovah's Witness theology and Trinitarian Christian theology, it is not conflict with the expression of that theology at Nicaea. Rather, it is conflict with the expression of Trinitarian theology as it was developed after Nicaea and particularly as it was expressed by Thomas Cranmer in 1553. As in the discussion above concerning Latter-day Saint theology, the conflict arising out of the "one substance" phrase, can be resolved by the Nicene context since that phrase was included to parallel the explanations of the separate personalities of the Father and the Son which precede it.[691] That is because Constantine intended the Nicene formula to generalise its description of Jesus' nature so that it could encompass Arian believers in Christ's divinity as well as those who had opposed them.

---

[690] Ibid.

[691] For more detail, see the discussion of the 'one substance' phrase as first used by Tertullian in Chapter Five.

This limited discussion of the Unitarian, Latter-day Saint and Jehovah's Witness' theology of Jesus Christ, has asked whether these faiths are properly dismissed as non-Christian because they either do not subscribe to or follow beliefs about Christ that are not consistent with the Nicene Creed. The conclusion that flows from a sensitive analysis, despite rejection of the Trinitarian label by most adherents of these faiths, is that save for the interpretive confusion which surrounds the "one substance" phrase, the Nicene formulation of Christian belief concerning the Father, the Son and the Holy Ghost is broad enough to accommodate Latter-day Saints and Jehovah's Witnesses though not nineteenth century Unitarians. Nineteenth century Unitarians but not their twenty-first century descendants, may be labelled as non-Nicene Christians since they denied the divinity of Christ holding that "the Father alone is God",[692] but it is still semantically unreasonable to suggest they are not Christians – followers of Christ in accordance with the original use of the label in Acts[693] – because they do not subscribe to a formula defining belief nearly three hundred years after the label was coined.

Conclusion

Despite the anathemas, for reasons explained in Chapter Five, the Nicene creed was formulated in broad terms consistent with Constantine's wish that it accommodate as many views of the underlying theology as it could in the interests of unity in the Empire and also because the details about the nature of God were matters of speculation. While the Unitarians attacked the Nicene Creed head on in the nineteenth century suggesting that it was incomprehensible, irrational and unscriptural, their underlying criticism was that the normal explanations of the Trinity did not make sense to them. However, even though I have asserted that the Nicene Creed was intended to accommodate a variety of belief about the nature of the Christian God, even a sensitive reading of traditional Unitarian teaching about Christ cannot be squared with the Nicene formula since nineteenth century Unitarians did not accept that Jesus Christ was God or equal with him.

---

[692] See above nn655-656 and supporting text.
[693] Acts 11:26.

On the other hand, Latter-day Saints and Jehovah's Witnesses teaching can be squared with the original Nicene Creed even though that would be a surprise to most of their adherents. That surprise is not because Latter-day Saints and Jehovah's Witnesses are unfamiliar with their own theology, but because like many mainstream Christians, they do not know what the original Nicene Creed says. The Book of Mormon is completely consistent with the final language chosen by Constantine and the Bishops at Nicaea. Even the Nicene anathemas are consistent with Latter-day Saint teaching if they are interpreted in the same way as the biblical anathemas in Deuteronomy and Revelations.[694] But Latter-day Saint theology cannot accept Cranmer's sixteenth century assertion that the triune God of Christianity is "without body parts or passions". That is because Latter-day Saints hold that the resurrected Jesus Christ is an anthropomorphic being and the Father must be the same since Jesus Christ and all human beings were formed in the image of the Father. For Latter-day Saints, Cranmer's additions would deservedly invoke the anathemas pronounced by the fourth century bishops at Nicaea.

The coincidence between Jehovah's Witness teaching and the Nicene creedal formula is not as striking as in the Trinitarian Book of Mormon passages considered in this chapter. But despite official Jehovah's Witness website denials of consistency premised as I have suggested in their misunderstanding of what the Nicene Creed actually says, there is more alignment than Jehovah's Witness believers or their mainstream Christians detractors would expect. That is ultimately because Jehovah's Witnesses believe that Jesus Christ rules God's kingdom in heaven. As we have seen, the separate personalities of God and Jesus Christ asserted by Tertullian despite their unity in substance, were preserved at Nicaea. Jehovah's Witness teaching that Jesus became God presents as a Nicene inconsistency if one believes that the Nicene Creed was intended to outlaw the Arian idea that Christ was less than God. But if the language chosen at Nicaea was consistent with Constantine's unity agenda and is also consistent with the Greek Orthodox belief that it does not subordinate Christ to hold that the

---

[694] Deuteronomy 4:2 and Revelations 22:18-19. Latter-day Saints interpret these anathema passages to proscribe interference with the text of the individual books concerned long before they were collected into the Biblical library. If the Nicene Creed anathemas are interpreted in the same way, then the subsequent interpretive work of St Augustine and the addition of the filioque clause which causesd the schism between East and West in the eleventh century invoke those anathemas.

Father is still the ultimate King of heaven, then Jehovah's Witness teaching is not inconsistent with the Nicene Creed.

In the final chapter of this book, I draw together the different threads of Trinitarian doctrine that have been identified through the book and weigh them against Constantine's unity agenda at and after Nicaea. I observe in particular that the human habit of categorizing those we do not know as others and then treating them with less respect than we accord to more familiar kinship and social groups, is a failing in human behaviour that Christian teaching was intended to overcome.

9

WHAT CAN CONSTANTINE'S ENCOMPASSING THEOLOGICAL VISION TEACH MODERN CHRISTIANITY?

Introduction

In this concluding discussion, I review the doctrine about Christ that was agreed at Nicaea and the steps that Constantine took there to unify the church in 325A.D. I suggest that his effort to unite the Christian church, is something that would benefit the world today. While I would like to suggest that physical merger of all Christian churches is possible, I do not believe that can happen without the personal leadership of Jesus Christ himself. Given that it is unlikely that Christianity can achieve physical unity before he comes again in accordance with traditional Christian doctrine, my purpose in this book has been to more fully unfold the politics and theology at Nicaea so that the simplicity of the resulting formula might be better understood. I believe that better understanding can enable deeper and more respectful inter-Christian dialogue. I further believe that the soft leadership of Constantine and Bishop Ossius at Nicaea was intended to enable unity rather than cries of heresy, apostasy and other labels of human otherness. That is not to say that it is not important to get our doctrine about Christ right, or that there was not a forceful movement at Nicaea that wanted to 'otherize' Arius and his supporters. But if the anathemas that were there pronounced by the will of the majority are laid to one side as they later were at Constantinople and the theology of Christ agreed at Nicaea is examined, it is difficult for most Christians to disagree with it.

In this concluding chapter, I therefore review the preceding chapters and explain how the Jewish idea of monotheism produced the Christian doctrine of the Trinity. I do that in five parts. In Part One, I explain where the idea of monotheism came from. I remind readers that the word monotheism is a seventeenth century construct and does not perfectly capture the diversity of historical Israelite, Jewish, or Christian belief. But my purpose in tracing the origin of Jewish monotheism has been to demonstrate that until at least the Babylonian captivity, Israelite religion was not monotheistic in the modern sense of that term. Rather, Jewry developed the One God idea as a defensive strategy to protect its theology from syncretism as superpowers dictated and otherwise introduced new beliefs about additional gods. However ironic or even hypocritical that makes subsequent Jewish persecution of Christian belief including belief in the Trinity, there has always been more that united Judaism and Christianity than divided them. Though they fought about their understanding of the One True God through at least the first and second centuries A.D., both faiths originally believed that there was more to heaven than their One God.

In Part Two, I remind readers how the Christians responded to Jewish criticism in the first two centuries of the common era. That response is the story of the origin of the Christian doctrine of the Trinity. The essence of that story was the Christian search for a way to tell Jews that Christians believed in the same God as they did because the Messiah was so united with the Father and the Holy Ghost as to be one with them in a way that human beings could not comprehend. Tertullian's best effort to explain that celestial oneness, was to say that they were one in substance though they retained their separate personalities. Part II continues with a summary of the Nicene Council and its Creed, a Creed which simply confirmed that Jesus Christ was one with God and not some lesser being.

In Part Three, I explain the origins of the schism between Eastern and Western Christianity in the filioque clause before I identify the innovations of the Protestant Reformers which emphasis on Thomas Cranmer in the sixteenth century. In Part Four, I return to Constantine's unity agenda in the fourth century and observe his patience with religious dissent as he sought a path of unity for his empire and in his church. Though his post Nicene Council efforts to reach out and include Arius and his sympathizers in the Church may be interpreted as vacillation or as proof of his thin Christian commitment, I suggest those efforts are consistent with the unity agenda that he sincerely followed until his death twelve years later. I identify his destruction of the written complaints he solicited during the first days of the Council as a Christ-like symbol of forgiveness and new beginning. I further suggest that when he introduced the *homoousios* idea at the Council, he was pointing to the futility of the underlying argument between Arius, Alexander and Athanasius. As when he originally wrote his letter of disapproval to Arius and Alexander by Bishop Ossius, at Nicaea, Constantine was also directing Christian clergy not to argue about things that would not save souls. Following such counsel today would open doors to increased ecumenical dialogue and cooperation between Christian churches.

In Part Five, I discuss human 'otherness' in sociology as the reason why such dialogue and cooperation have not occurred despite Christ's vision of unity for his disciples.

I conclude the book with the hope that such dialogue and cooperation can unfold in the future as Christians learn to strengthen one another rather than to sift one another as wheat and tares.

Part One - Monotheism and Judaism

In the first chapter I challenged some paradigms of thinking about Judeo-Christian theology. The first was the idea of monotheism itself. I explained that the modern word was not coined until the 17th century and the idea that 'One God' worship began with the ancient Hebrews is wrong. While I did not elaborate, the first humans to dabble with the idea of 'one God' worship were the Egyptians during the twenty year reign of the Pharoah, Amenophis IV in the 14th century B.C. The modern idea of monotheism must be distinguished from many other ideas including henotheism where a believer worships one God without denying that others exist, and monolatry, where a believer recognizes the existence of many gods, but worships only one. The Judeo-Christian and Islamic idea that there is only one God and that no others exist, was developed in Judaism in the first millennium B.C., but it is not an idea with a long Israelite history.

The second Judeo-Christian thought paradigm that I challenged was the idea that the ancient Israelites believed that their God was an ineffable spiritual being. With Benjamin Sommer as primary guide, I explained that the Israelite God was completely anthropomorphic and communicated with their ancient prophets as a 'human' being, sometimes from within a cloud, but sometimes face to face. That understanding is also challenging in Christianity where God is perceived as a spiritual being despite the fact that the resurrected Christ appeared to his disciples on multiple occasions and went to some lengths to demonstrate his resurrected corporeality as when he ate broiled fish and honeycomb before them and when he insisted Thomas feel the wounds in his hands, feet and side.

The third Judeo-Christian thought paradigm that I challenged was the idea that the Jews of the Judeo-Christian tradition, always believed in only one God. Before they were dominated by the superpowers of the ancient world, the ancient Israelites believed in as many four levels of divine 'human' beings presided over by a Divine Council chaired by Elohim, possibly with his consort Asherah and their seventy sons. That belief was not so much suppressed during the periods when Israel was subject to Assyrian, Babylonian, Greek and Roman rule and influence, as it was hidden to prevent it being misunderstood, admixed or confused with other systems of belief particularly when the superficially similar ideas of the Greek and Roman god pantheons came to the fore. But by the time of the advent of Christianity, these hidden traditional Israelite beliefs had been totally eclipsed by worship of Yahweh as the one true God of rabbinical Judaism.

The aniconic idea is that the rabbinic ban on the use of anthropomorphic, theriomorphic, or physiomorphic images to represent or house the deity, may have originated in the first two commandments given to Moses on Sinai. But in the context of earlier Israelite belief in the Divine Council, it is unlikely these commandments were interpreted aniconically at the beginning. However, by the time their Babylonian and Jerusalem Talmuds were compiled, the Jews were thoroughly monotheistic. For in those texts, some time between 500 B.C and 500 A.D., the God who always presided over the Divine Council in heaven for the Israelites had become the solitary Lord or King of the Universe, the Father of mankind in heaven, the Most High, the Living God, the Author of Creation, the Rock of the World, the Eternal God of Truth, the Creator and the Almighty. And though both Talmuds acknowledge theological criticism of the duality of God as for example in the Genesis account of the creation, that duality is thoroughly rebutted by the Rabbis.

Part Two - Jewish doctrinal criticism of Christianity and the Christian response

The Christian view that Jesus of Nazareth was the Jewish Messiah and was to be worshipped as the Son of God, was blasphemous polytheism. The members of this Jewish splinter group were not only breaking the first two commandments given by Moses, they were crediting Jews who did not believe in Jesus Christ, with the crime of deicide.

In this battle to reclaim and then to discredit the Christian apostates, the chief Jewish intellectual weapon was the charge of polytheism since by the time of the advent of Christianity, every Jew had been indoctrinated in the one true God theology. And the charge of polytheism stung the early Christians. That much is clear from the burden of their defensive ante-Nicene literature. In Justin Martyr's *Dialogue with Trypho*, Jesus Christ's oneness with and subordination to God, rebuts the Jewish charge of polytheism because the one true God they both worship is the same.

But by the time of Tertullian and Origen, the theological idea of Trinity first coined in writings attributed to Theophilus and Clement of Alexandria, is used to explain a unity between God and Christ that humans cannot comprehend or explain. In Tertullian's analogies, it is as if God and Christ are united in their very substance though they remain separate and distinct persons. Origen's additional insight is that the Son and the Holy Spirit are co-eternal with the Father, but they are still subordinate to him. But these ideas began to fracture early Christianity. Even though the theological charge of polytheism by the Jews subsided in importance, the Trinitarian ideas of unity and co-eternality most prominent from Tertullian and Origen spawned many diverse views within Christianity as sincere thinkers continued to try and understand the true nature of God.

By the beginning of the fourth century, Christian theology was a tinderbox waiting to explode. Hanson and Ayres see Arius as a prominent example of a controversial school of thought that was opposed by powerful forces in the see of Alexandria where he began his ministry. But they do not see him as a profound thinker because he did not leave a significant literature that would enable that assessment. Nonetheless, Arius' views so exercised some of the great religious minds of his age that they required correction at the highest levels in the Empire and attracted Constantine's personal intervention. Not only did Constantine dispatch his favourite Christian advisor, Ossius of Cordoba, to settle this dispute in the see of Alexandria, but he wrote a personal letter to the two primary combatants and told them to cease exciting debate about trifles they could not possibly answer. Constantine wanted Christianity to be the glue that unified his empire.

The upshot of Ossius of Cordoba's unsuccessful mission to Alexandria was Constantine's convention of a council of all the bishops of his Empire at Nicaea near his summer residence so that he could personally attend and participate. Not only did he participate, but significant scholarly opinion accepts that the *homoousios* idea in the final Creed composed by the mostly Eastern bishops in attendance, was Constantine's personal compromise recommendation. Constantine saw to it that the resulting creed was ambiguous - abstracted to a level of generality that would allow agreement by all those in attendance. Schaff's 1877 translation of the resulting Creed reads:

> We believe in one God, the Father Almighty, Maker of all things, visible and invisible.
>
> And in one Lord Jesus Christ, begotten of the Father, Light of Light, very God of very God, begotten, not made, being of one substance with the Father; by whom all things were made; who for us men, and for our salvation, came down and was incarnate and was made man; he suffered, and the third day he rose again, ascended into heaven; from thence he shall come to judge the quick and the dead.
>
> And in the Holy Ghost.

The anathema omitted from the 381 A.D. Constantinople version which originally followed, said:

> But those who say: 'There was a time when he was not;' and 'He was not before he was made;' and 'He was made out of nothing,' or 'He is of another substance' or 'essence,' or 'The Son of God is created,' or 'changeable' or 'alterable' – they are condemned by the holy catholic and apostolic Church.

That omission, under the direction of the Emperor Theodosius, is in keeping with Constantine's intent in 325A.D. at Nicaea. Constantine's wish to resolve the dispute and use the Christian religion and its message of love as glue to keep his empire together, was also manifest in his efforts during the eighteen months after the Nicene Council adjourned to restore those who had been anathematized to a place of accommodation within the Church. While he did not interfere with the Church autonomy that was demonstrated in the addition of the anathemas to the Creed, he worked promptly to render the anathemas practically meaningless as quickly as he could.

Part Three - Trinitarian theology after Nicaea, the 'schism' and modern challenges to Trinitarian 'orthodoxy'

Because the Western Church was barely present at Nicaea, it is not surprising that the resulting Creed did not feature in Western theological discussion till some time afterwards. In the East, despite Constantine's best efforts to reinstate those anathematized at Nicaea, the politicization of Christian theology continued and did not abate with his death. Gregory of Elvira eventually 'corrected' the corrupted version of Nicene theology which the West had received from Marcellus of Ancrya, the Nicene anthemas were removed at Constantinople in 381 A.D., and Augustine began to write. But the Eastern Church never fully accepted Augustine's scripturally framed assertion that the Holy Spirit emanates from the Father 'and the Son' (the filioque clause that featured in later Western creedal expression). Eastern theology did not accept that the Holy Spirit's origin in the Father diminished the Son's status in any way because they held that the Father was always the Sovereign in the Godhead. While there were other political and personality reasons for the deepening rift between East and West from the 8th and 11th centuries, the filioque clause was the focus of the formal excommunications and so-called 'schism' of 1054 A.D.

Western Protestant Reformers did not challenge the Western version of Trinitarian theology either. Indeed, they championed the Roman version after the Reformation even though some analyses of early Reformation politics suggest it would have been very easy for those reformers to lean Eastward for theological support.

But the Western version of Trinitarian theology hardened under the influence of Thomas Cranmer who became King Henry VIII's Archbishop of Canterbury in 1532. While Cranmer's theology was initially tempered by Henry's conservative wish to avoid more changes than were necessary to secure his divorce and the break with Rome, Cranmer manifested his enthusiastic Protestantism in the Forty-Two Articles which he prepared during the reign of Edward VI in 1553. While in some respects he simply recorded Western Christian practice, Cranmer's Articles also anathematized unpopular Catholic doctrines and adjusted foundational Trinitarian theology.

In due course the Thirty-Nine Articles (which were an edited versions of Cranmer's 1553 draft) were accepted by the English Church and became the foundation for the Westminster Confession of Faith in 1646. Terryl Givens has detailed Cranmer's doctrinal innovations in *Wrestling the Angel* in 2015. Though Cranmer had started with the Protestant Augsburg Confession from 1530 when asserting that the Trinitarian Christian God lacked a body and parts, Cranmer's Articles also added that the Christian God lacked passions.

This document eventually became the basis of Baptist, Congregationalist and Methodist theology despite the efforts of the polymath Michael Servetus on the European Continent to make the Reformers reconsider Trinitarian theology more thoroughly. His death for heresy at the instigation of John Calvin caused scarcely a ripple perhaps because he was only ever arguing about terminology.

Part Four - Constantine's unity agenda

I suggest that Constantine's generosity in the face of petty religious difference is an example of the tolerance of doctrinal difference that is possible in post-Nicene Christianity.

When he wrote to Alexander and Arius before the Nicene Council was convened, he said their differences were of a "truly insignificant character and quite unworthy of…fierce contention."[695] And he doubted than anyone was able to "accurately…comprehend, or…adequately explain subjects so sublime and abstruse" as they were arguing about.[696]

He later demonstrated his view that theological disputes should be laid aside in the interests of enduring fellowship when he burned the complaints he had received as the Council opened. But his consistent unity argument is also set out in the letter which he earlier sent by Ossius of Cordoba to Alexander and Arius and in his efforts to reclaim those cut up by the anathemas imposed by the majority at Nicaea.

In his letter to Alexander and Arius, he said that he felt it was his duty to work towards a uniformity in matters of religion that could help the overall unity of his empire. He said that Alexander and Arius had provoked unnecessary contention in the Synod at Alexandria and as their fellowservant, he was enjoining them to avoid such provocation in the future since their action and the universal difficulty in understanding the matters they had been arguing about, tended to blasphemy and schism. Since philosophers were able to heal their internal rifts by retreat to common doctrines, he expected no less of Alexander and Arius as ministers of Christ.

While he did not want to force them to unity, in the spirit of various of Paul's letters and particularly that written to Philemon concerning the slave Onesimus, he pled that they exert all their efforts to return to a common faith and understanding.

After the Nicene Council concluded, Constantine went to extended further effort to reclaim those who had been anathematized at its

---

[695] See Appendix.
[696] Ibid.

conclusion.[697]

The main focus of this book is the suggestion that the differences between the Christians who claim allegiance to the Nicene Creed and the Christians who do not, are not as large as may appear. My premise is that Constantine did a much better job of generalizing agreement about the nature of God than most Christians have appreciated. For not only did his Council write in Greek using 'proceed' language which allowed the eternity of both Christ and the Holy Spirit, but the Nicene Creed did not deny the anthropomorphism or emotion in the Godhead that Thomas Cranmer summarized in 1553 when he wrote his Forty-two Articles of Christian belief.

While those who deny the godhood of Jesus Christ will not be able to agree with the Nicene Creed, if they examine it closely, they will be able to agree with more its original expression than they may expect. While traditional Unitarians who deny the divinity of Christ cannot agree with the formula expressed at Nicaea, modern Unitarians will not have a problem. And thoughtful Jehovah's Witnesses and Latter-day Saints may not find as much to argue with as they have been conditioned to expect. That is because Constantine's goal at Nicaea in 325 A.D. was to express a creed as general and as inclusive as he could make it. That is not to suggest that any of these faiths should compromise their beliefs or submit to the theology or direction of any other Church. My purpose here is only to enable more reciprocal understanding and enlightenment in the future.

Constantine was not a theological ogre. While we may be glad that we were not members of his immediate family or one of his enemies in war, his wisdom in soliciting and then tearing up the grievances of all who surrounded his Nicene Council tables, was a farsighted and remarkably modern alternate dispute resolution tool. Modern believers in Jesus would do well to learn from his example and find even better ways to talk to one another.

---

[697] Hanson says the only bishops anathematized at the Council were Secundus of Ptolemais and Theonas of Marmarike (Hanson, (above n423), 162). But both of these were restored to their bishoprics and even Arius' exile was lifted within eightenn months though he was never accepted back into the see of Alexandria (ibid 178; see also Smedley E, Rose HJ and Rose HJ eds., *Encyclopedia Metropolitana*, (Rest Fenner, 1822-1845), Volume 11, 327).

Part V - Religious 'otherness'

Sociologically, "'otherness' is central to...analyses of how majority and minority identities are constructed."[698] Groups with more power use their identity as a way of consolidating and retaining power, often by marginalizing other individuals and minority groups. Ideas of difference promoted to enable the power of majoritarian groups, are a part of how human beings "achieve a sense of identity and social belonging",[699] but the resulting social identities are not natural. They are socially constructed and regularly interfere with the different choices that human individuals would like to make about the world and their place in it. Quoting Andrew Okolie, Zevallos says that

> Social identities are relational; groups typically define themselves in relation to others. This is because identity has little meaning without "the other". So by defining itself a group defines others. Identity is rarely claimed or assigned for its own sake. These definitions of self and others have purposes and consequences. They are tied to rewards and punishment, which may be material or symbolic. There is usually an expectation of gain or loss as a consequence of identity claims. This is why identities are contested. Power is implicated here, and because groups do not have equal powers to define both *self* and the *other*, the consequences reflect these power differentials. Often notions of superiority and inferiority are embedded in particular identities.[700]

Religious groups follow these sociological templates to the letter. For example, John Shook has observed quoting Welch, Sikkink and Loveland that

> inside a church...trust drops towards unfamiliar people. If the cause for this decrease in trust is just the prior social familiarity, and not any religious factor, then all religious and nonreligious groups would roughly display the same pattern, but they don't. Conservative Protestants are more distrusting of strangers than nonreligious groups or Mainline Protestants, and Catholics are even more distrusting.[701]

---

[698] Zevallos, Z. (2011) 'What is Otherness?,' *The Other Sociologist*, 14 October.
[699] Ibid.
[700] Ibid quoting Okolie A C, "Introduction" to the Special Issue of *Identity*, "Now You Don't see It; Now You Do", 2.
[701] Shook J quoting "The Radius of Trust: Religion, Social Embeddedness and Trust in Strangers", Welch MR, Sikkink D, and Loveland MT, (2007) *Social Forces* 86(1), 23-46.

Shook also quotes Rees, LaBouff, Rowatt, Johnson and Finkle as authority for his conclusion that religion seems to increase distrust and hostility "towards all sorts of social groups" and that "conservative religion does not succeed in teaching its "love thy neighbour" principle unless one's neighbour belongs to the same church, though the research he cites does not support such a generalized conclusion.[702]

However, while the Nicene Creed is used to 'otherize' people who lead lives of faith and virtue in different belief systems,[703] it is also sometimes used to marginalize people of faith who do not subscribe to the Creed though they do believe in the divinity of Jesus Christ.[704] The discussion that follows therefore discusses the original words of the Nicene Creed to identify whether those who have faith in the atoning mission of Jesus Christ really are 'others' under the rubric that it sets forth. Those from Christian faith systems for whom liturgy and practice has become an interpretive device, may find this discussion challenging. This discussion may also seem futile to those who do not believe that there is a transcendent world. It may also prove difficult for those who do not accept any of the precepts of

---

[702] Ibid quoting "Differences in Attitudes Toward Outgroups in Religious and Nonreligious Contexts in a Multinational Sample: A Situational Context Priming Study", Labouff J., Rowatt W., Johnson M and Finkle C., *International Journal for the Psychology of Religion*, 22 (1) 1-9. Note however, that there is a considerable literature that demonstrates that "religion is largely the force behind performing good deeds and living healthier lifestyles." In a literature review provided to Deloitte Access Economics at the request of the LDS Church, Professor Ram Cnaan of the University of Pennsylvania provided a list of more than 100 studies collected during the last thirty years confirming that finding in Preventing Suicide, Helping People Find Employment, Job Training, Crime Prevention, Supporting Prisoners Re-entry, Ending Alcohol and Drug Abuse, Enhancing Health and Reducing the Cost of Illness, Caring for the Elderly while the Families Work, Helping Immigrants get Green Cards/Naturalisation, Helping People Find Relationships and Networks, Preventing Divorce, Ending Abusive Relationships, Teaching Pro-Social Values to Children, Teaching Youth Civic Behaviour, Providing Social Services to Religious Congregations, Taxpaying and Religions Involvement and Giving and Volunteering. The full literature review is in the writer's possession and is available on request.

[703] For example, in Grondelski's introduction to Scott Hahn's book entitled *The Creed, Professing The Faith Through The Ages*, he says that "the Nicene-Constantinopolitan Creed...sets Christianity apart from...the other major world religions: Hinduism, Buddhism, Shintoism, Confucianism [and] even...Judaism. It clearly contradicts Islam, in which God is exclusively transcendent" rather than a parent which makes men slaves rather than sons (referring to the Scott Hahn book, (Emmaus Road Publishing, 2016)).

[704] For example, "Why Mormons aren't Christians"; Miller JJ, "Why Mormons aren't Christians"; Harmon SR, "Do Real Baptists Recite Creeds?", ; Van Zuiden J, "Why so many Protestants do not consider Catholics Christian", and Chellew-Hodge C, "Why LBGT-friendly Church is not Christian enough".

Christianity or believe that the nature of God has any consequence in time or eternity. However, the idea that some believers in Jesus Christ may have been excluded from fellowship on false grounds may be transformative for some.

Conclusion

I began this concluding chapter with the observation that "our human tendency to characterize those we do not know as 'others', can be separated from the truth claims we make about each others' beliefs." It is a difficult process because of human nature and emotion, but it is possible. I also stated that my purpose in pursuing that separation was to seek a way around "the human tendency to mistreat others who [we] do not know and who do not belong to [our] clan or kinship group."

In this conclusion, I have suggested that religious liberty, tolerance and respect coupled with the history I have outlined, provide the framework from which greater unity among Christians can be found. Though there are important differences in what Christians believe, I suggest that the traditional issues that have divided Christianity need never have divided it at all. I explain that suggestion by summarizing how monotheism developed in Judaism and how it was transported into Christianity. I then discuss how the Nicene expression of the Trinity doctrine that was developed by Christians to defend against Jewish claims of apostasy, was intended by Constantine and the Bishops at Nicaea to unite the church rather than to divide it.

All of that is prelude to the assertion that modern believers in the atoning mission of Jesus Christ, like Constantine and the bishops who surrounded his Council tables at Nicaea, can find ways to celebrate what they have in common. That is because Jesus Christ's example of sacrifice, ministry and service still present as the only way to save the human race in time or eternity.

APPENDIX

CONSTANTINE'S LETTER TO ALEXANDER, BISHOP OF ALEXANDRIA AND ARIUS, ONE OF HIS PRESBYTERS[705]

LETTERS, BOOK 2 (In Chronological Order)

Edited By Rev. Daniel R. Jennings

(323 or 324AD) Letter of Constantine to Alexander the Bishop and Arius the Presbyter.

Synopsis: Expresses his desire for peace, his hope that they might have helped him in the Donatist troubles, his distress at finding that they, too, were in a broil, his opinion that the matters under discussion are of little moment, and what he thinks they are. He exhorts to unanimity, repeats his opinion that the matters are of little moment, mentions his "copious and constant tears," and finally gets through.

VICTOR CONSTANTINUS, MAXIMUS AUGUSTUS, to Alexander and Arius. "I call that God to witness, as well I may, who is the helper of my endeavors, and the Preserver of all men, that I had a twofold reason for undertaking that duty which I have now performed. "MY design then was, first, to bring the diverse judgments formed by all nations respecting the Deity to a condition, as it were, of settled uniformity; and, secondly, to restore to

---

[705] See http://www.constantinethegreatcoins.com/Constantine/Book2.html.

health the system of the world, then suffering under the malignant power of a grievous distemper. Keeping these objects in view, I sought to accomplish the one by the secret eye of thought, while the other I tried to rectify by the power of military authority. For I was aware that, if I should succeed in establishing, according to my hopes, a common harmony of sentiment among all the servants of God, the general course of affairs would also experience a change correspondent to the pious desires of them all. "Finding, then, that the whole of Africa was pervaded by an intolerable spirit of mad folly, through the influence of those who with heedless frivolity had presumed to rend the religion of the people into diverse sects; I was anxious to check this disorder, and could discover no other remedy equal to the occasion, except in sending some of yourselves to aid in restoring mutual harmony among the disputants, after I had removed that common enemy of mankind who had interposed his lawless sentence for the prohibition of your holy synods. "For since the power of Divine light, and the law of sacred worship, which, proceeding in the first instance, through the favor of God, from the bosom, as it were, of the East, have illumined the world, by their sacred radiance, I naturally believed that you would be the first to promote the salvation of other nations, and resolved with all energy of thought and diligence of enquiry to seek your aid. As soon, therefore, as I had secured my decisive victory and unquestionable triumph over my enemies, my first enquiry was concerning that object which I felt to be of paramount interest and importance. "BUT, O glorious Providence of God! how deep a wound did not my ears only, but my very heart receive in the report that divisions existed among yourselves more grievous still than those which continued in that country! so that you, through whose aid I had hoped to procure a remedy for the errors of others, are in a state which needs healing even more than theirs. And yet, having made a careful enquiry into the origin and foundation of these differences, I find the cause to be of a truly insignificant character, and quite unworthy of such fierce contention. Feeling myself, therefore, compelled to address you in this letter, and to appeal at the same time to your unanimity and sagacity, I call on Divine Providence to assist me in the task, while I interrupt your dissension in the character of a minister of peace. And with reason: for if I might expect, with the help of a higher Power, to be able without difficulty, by a judicious appeal to the pious feelings of those who heard me, to recall them to a better spirit, even though the occasion of the disagreement were a greater one, how can I refrain from promising myself a far easier and more speedy adjustment of this difference, when the cause which hinders general harmony of sentiment is intrinsically trifling and of little moment? "I UNDERSTAND, then, that the origin of the present controversy is this. When you, Alexander, demanded of the presbyters what opinion they severally maintained respecting a certain passage in the Divine law, or rather, I should say, that you asked them something connected with an unprofitable question, then you, Arius, inconsiderately insisted on what ought never to have been conceived at all, or if conceived, should have been buried in profound silence. Hence it was that a dissension arose between you, fellowship was withdrawn, and the holy people, rent into diverse parties, no longer preserved the unity of the one body. Now, therefore, do ye both exhibit an equal degree of forbearance, and receive the advice which your fellow-servant righteously gives. What then is this advice? It was wrong in the first instance to propose such questions as these, or to reply to them when propounded. For those points of discussion which are enjoined by the authority of no law, but rather suggested by the contentious spirit which is fostered by misused leisure, even though they may be intended merely as an intellectual exercise, ought certainly to be confined to the region of our own thoughts, and not hastily produced in the popular assemblies, nor unadvisedly intrusted to the general ear. For how very few are there able either accurately to comprehend, or adequately to explain subjects so sublime and abstruse in their nature? Or, granting that one were fully competent for this, how many people will he convince? Or, who, again, in dealing with questions of such subtle nicety as these, can secure himself against a dangerous declension from the truth? It is incumbent therefore on us in these cases to be sparing of our words, lest, in case we ourselves are unable, through the feebleness of our natural faculties, to give a clear explanation of the subject before us, or, on the other hand, in case the slowness of our hearers' understandings disables them from arriving at an accurate apprehension of what we say, from one or other of these causes the people be reduced to the alternative either of blasphemy or schism. "LET therefore both the unguarded question and the inconsiderate answer receive your mutual forgiveness. For the cause of your difference has not been any of the leading doctrines or precepts of the Divine law, nor has any new heresy respecting the worship of God arisen among you. You are in truth of one and the same judgment: you may therefore well join in communion and fellowship. "For as long as you continue to contend about these small and very insignificant questions, it is not fitting that so large a portion of God's people should be under the direction of your judgment, since you are thus divided between yourselves. I believe it indeed to be not merely unbecoming, but positively evil, that such should be the case. But I will refresh your minds by a little illustration, as follows. You know that philosophers, though they all adhere to one system, are yet frequently at issue on certain points, and differ, perhaps, in their degree of knowledge: yet they are recalled to harmony of sentiment by the uniting power of their common doctrines. If this be true, is it not far more reasonable that you, who are the ministers of the Supreme God, should be of one mind respecting the profession of the same religion? But let us still more thoughtfully and with closer attention examine what I have said, and see whether it be right that, on the ground of some trifling and foolish verbal difference between ourselves, brethren should assume towards each other the attitude of enemies, and the august meeting of the Synod be rent by profane disunion, because of you who wrangle together on points so trivial and altogether unessential? This is vulgar, and rather characteristic of childish ignorance, than consistent I with the wisdom of priests and men of sense. Let us withdraw ourselves with a good will from these temptations of the devil. Our great God and common Saviour of all has granted the same light to us all. Permit me, who am his servant, to bring my task to a successful issue, under the direction of his Providence, that I may be enabled, through my exhortations, and diligence, and earnest admonition, to recall his people to communion and fellowship. For since you have, as I said, but one faith, and one sentiment respecting our religion, and since the Divine commandment in all its parts enjoins on us all the duty of maintaining a spirit of concord, let not the circumstance which has led to a slight difference between you, since it does not affect the validity of the whole, cause any division or schism among you. And this I say without in any way desiring to force you to entire unity of judgment in regard to this truly idle question, whatever its real nature may be. For the dignity of your synod may be preserved, and the communion of your whole body maintained unbroken, however wide a difference may exist among you as to unimportant matters. For we are not all of us like-minded on every subject, nor is there such a thing as one disposition and judgment common to all alike. As far, then, as regards the Divine Providence, let there be one faith, and one understanding among you, one united judgment in reference to God. But as to your subtle disputations on questions of little or no significance, though you may be unable to harmonize in sentiment, such differences should be consigned to the secret custody of your own minds and thoughts. And now, let the preciousness of common affection, let faith in the truth, let the honor due to God and to the observance of his law continue immovably among you. Resume, then, your mutual feelings of friendship, love, and regard: restore to the people their wonted embracings; and do ye yourselves, having purified your souls, as it were, once more acknowledge one another. For it often happens that when a reconciliation is effected by the removal of the causes of enmity, friendship becomes even sweeter than it was before. "RESTORE me then my quiet days, and untroubled nights, that the joy of undimmed light, the delight of a tranquil life, may henceforth be my portion. Else must I needs mourn, with constant tears, nor shall I be able to pass the residue of my days in peace. For while the people of God, whose fellow-servant I am, are thus divided amongst themselves by an unreasonable and pernicious spirit of contention, how is it possible that I shall be able to maintain tranquillity of mind? And I will give you a proof how great my sorrow has been on this behalf. Not long since I had visited Nicomedia, and intended forthwith to proceed from that city to the East. It was while I was hastening towards you, and had already accomplished the greater part of the distance, that the news of this matter reversed my plan, that I might not be compelled to see with my own eyes that which I felt myself scarcely able even to hear. Open then for me henceforward by your unity of judgment that road to the regions of the East which your dissensions have closed against me, and permit me speedily to see yourselves and all other peoples rejoicing together, and render due acknowledgment to God in the language of praise and thanksgiving for the restoration of general concord and liberty to all.

(Preserved in Eusebius of Caesarea's Life of Constantine 2:64–72, Gelasius of Cyzicus, 2:4, Socrates Scholasticus' Ecclesiastical History 1:7).

BIBLIOGRAPHY

Articles

Barr J, "The Question of Religious Influence: The Case of Zoroastrianism, Judaism and Christianity", *Journal of the American Academy of Religion*, Vol. 53, No. 2 (June 1985) 201.

Betten FC, "The Milan Decree of A.D. 313: Translation and Comment", *The Catholic Historical Review*, Vol. 6, No. 2, (July 1922), 191

Cnaan RA, (June 2013) Literature Review on the Impact of Religion on Quality of Life (in the possession of the author).

Cross FM Jr., "Yahweh and the God of the Patriarchs", *Harvard Theological Review* 55, 1962, 240

Grant RM, "Religion and Politics at the Council at Nicaea", *The Journal of Religion*, Vol. 55, No. 1 (January 1975), University of Chicago Press, 1

Heiser M, "Deuteronomy 32:8 and the Sons of God", *BibSac* 158, 2001.

Heiser M, "Israel's Divine Council, Mormonism and Evangelism: Clarifying the Issues and Directions for Future Study", *The FARMS Review* 19/1, 2007.

Heiser M, "You've seen on Elohim, You've seen them all? A Critique of Mormonism's Use of Psalm 82", *The FARMS review*, 19/1, 2007.

Huff B, "Unity in Action and the Unity of God", *Element* 2.1 (Spring 2006): 17.

Kasher R, "Anthropomorphism, Holiness, and Cult: A New Look at Ezekiel 40-48", Zeitschrift für die alttestamentliche Wissenschaft (*ZAW*), 1995.

Kilby K, "Perichoresis and Porjection: Problems with Social Doctrines of the Trinity", *New Blackfriars*, 81: 432 (2000)

Labouff J, Rowatt W, Johnson M and Finkle C, Differences in Attitudes Toward Outgroups in Religious and Nonreligious Contexts in a Multinational Sample: A Situational Context Priming Study", *International Journal for the Psychology of Religion*, 22 (1) 1.

Lemaire A, "Who or What was Yahweh's Asherah", *Biblical Archaeology Review* 10/6, 1984, 46.

Needham N, "The *Filioque* clause: East or West?" in the *Scottish Bulletin of Evangelical Theology* 15/2 (Autumn1997) 142.

Peterson DC, "Nephi and His Asherah", *Journal of Book of Mormon Studies*, 9/2,

2000, 16.

Stark R, "Why the Jehovah's Witnesses Grow *so* Rapidly: A Theoretical Application", *Journal of Contemporary Religion*, Vol. 12, No. 2, 1997, 133.

Ulrich J, "Nicaea and the West", *Vigiliae Christianae*, Vol. 51, No. 1 (March 1997) 10.

Welch M R, Sikkink D, and Loveland MT, "The Radius of Trust: Religion, Social Embeddedness and Trust in Strangers", (2007) *Social Forces* 86(1), 23.

Whyshogrod M, "A Jewish Perspective on Incarnation", *Modern Theology* 12, 1996, 195.

Book Chapters

Bolin TM, "The Temple of [the Jews] at Elephantine and Persian Religious Policy" in *The Triumph of Elohim, From Yahwishm to Judaisms*, Edelman DK ed., (William B. Eerdmans Publishing Company, Grand Rapids, Michigan, 1996).

Davies PR, "Scenes from the Early History of Judaism", in *The Triumph of Elohim, From Yahwishm to Judaisms*, Edelman DK ed., (William B. Eerdmans Publishing Company, Grand Rapids, Michigan, 1996).

Edelman DV, "Tracking Observance of the Aniconic Tradition Through Numismatics" in *The Triumph of Elohim, From Yahwishm to Judaisms*, Edelman DK ed., (William B. Eerdmans Publishing Company, Grand Rapids, Michigan, 1996).

Handy LK, "The Appearance of the Pantheon in Judah" in *The Triumph of Elohim, From Yahwishm to Judaisms*, Edelman DK ed., (William B. Eerdmans Publishing Company, Grand Rapids, Michigan, 1996).

Heiser M, "Yahweh and his Asherah? Epigraphic Evidence for Religious Pluralism in Old Testament Times", in Clarke AD & Winter BW, *One God, One Lord in a World of Religious Pluralism*, (Tyndale House, Cambridge, 1991).

Niehr H, "The Ride of YHWH in Judahite and Israelite Religion: Methodological and Religio-Historical Aspects" in *The Triumph of Elohim, From Yahwishm to Judaisms*, Edelman DK ed., (William B. Eerdmans Publishing Company, Grand Rapids, Michigan, 1996).

Peterson DC, "Notes on Mormonism and the Trinity" in *To Seek the Law of the Lord*, Hoskisson PY and

Peterson DC eds., (The Interpreter Foundation, Orem, Utah, 2017).

Rowland T, "Globalization, Postmodern Theories of Culture and the Trinity" in *The Oxford Handbook of the Trinity*, Emery G and Levering M eds., (Oxford University Press, 2011).

Schmidt BB, "The Aniconic Tradition on Reading Images and Views Texts" in *The Triumph of Elohim, From Yahwishm to Judaisms*, Edelman DK ed., (William B. Eerdmans Publishing Company, Grand Rapids, Michigan, 1996).

Smith IG, "Alexander of Byzantium" in Wace H, and Piercy, WC, *Dictionary of Christian Biography and Literature to the End of the Sixth Century*, 3rd ed., (London, John Murray, 1911).

Smith JW, "The Trinity in the Fourth-Century Fathers" in *The Oxford Handbook of the Trinity*, Emery G and Levering M eds., (Oxford University Press, 2011).

Thompson TL, "The Intellectual Matrix of Early Biblical Narrative: Inclusive Monotheism in Persion Period Palestine" in *The Triumph of Elohim, From Yahwishm to Judaisms*, Edelman DK ed., (William B. Eerdmans Publishing Company, Grand Rapids, Michigan, 1996).

Williams R in *Essays and Reviews, The 1860 Text and its Readings*, Shea V and Whitla W eds., (University of Virginia Press, Charlottesville and London, 2000).

Books

Assmann J, *Moses the Egyptian, The Memory of Egypt in Western Monotheism*, (Harvard University Press, Cambridge Massachusetts and London, 1997).

Auerbach L ed., *The Babylonian Talmud*, (Philosophical Library, New York, 1944).

Ayres L, *Nicaea and its legacy*, (Oxford University Press, 2004).

Barnard LW, *The Council of Serdica 343 A.D.*, (Synodal Publication House, Sofia 1983).

Brand P, *The Origins of the English Legal Profession*, (Blackwell, Oxford, UK and Cambridge, USA, 1992).

Carroll WH, *The Building of Christendom*, (Christendom Press, 1987).

Canduci A, *Triumph & Tragedy: The Rise and Fall of Rome's Immortal Emperors*, (Pier 9, 2010).

Chazan R, *Fashioning Jewish Identity in Medieval Western Christendom*, (Cambridge University Press, 2004).

Cook SL, *The Social Roots of Biblical Yahwism*, (Brill, Leiden and Boston, 2004).

Cross FL and Livingstone EA eds., *The Oxford Dictionary of the Christian Church* (Oxford University Press, 2005).

De Clercq VC, *Ossius of Cordoba: a contribution to the history of the Constantine period*, (Catholic University of America Press, Washington, 1954).

De Moor JC, *The Rise of Yahwism, The Roots of Israelite Monotheism*, 2nd ed., (Leuven University Press, 1997).

Dibb AMT, *Servetus, Swedenborg and the Nature of God*, (University Press of America, Lanham Maryland, 2005).

Edelman DK ed., *The Triumph of Elohim, From Yahwishm to Judaisms*, (William B. Eerdmans Publishing Company, Grand Rapids, Michigan, 1996).

Eichrodt W, *Theology of the Old Testament*, 6th ed., (The Westminster Press, Philadelphia, 1959).

Emery G, *The Trinity, An Introduction to Catholic Doctrine on the Triune God*, translated by Levering M, (The Catholic University of America Press, Washington D.C., 2011).

Emery G and Levering M eds., *The Oxford Handbook of the Trinity*, Oxford University Press, 2011).

Eusebius of Caesarea's *Life of Constantine* (incomplete, 4th century A.D.).

Ferguson E, *The Encyclopedia of Early Christianity*, 2nd ed., (Garland Publishing, New York and London, 1998).

Gerstenberger E, *Theologies of the Old Testament*, (T & T Clark, London, New York, 2002).

Givens TL, *Wrestling the Angel*, (Oxford University Press, 2015).

Givens TL and F, *The God Who Weeps*, (Crawfordsville, Indiana, Ensign Peak, 2012).

Goldstone L and Goldstone NB, *Out of the flames: the remarkable story of a fearless scholar, a fatal heresy, and one of the rarest books in the world*, (Broadway Books, New York, 2002).

Gordon FB, *Calvin*, (Yale University Press, 2009).

Guggenheimer HW ed., *Jerusalem Talmud* (Walter de Gruyter, Berlin and New York, 2000).

Gunton C, *The One, the Three and the Many: God, Creation and the Culture of Modernity*,

(Cambridge University Press, 1993).

Hahn S, *The Creed, Professing the Faith Through the Ages*, (Emmaus Road, Steubenville, Ohio, 2016).

Hanson RPC, *The Search for the Christian Doctrine of God*, (T & T Clark, Edinburgh, 1987).

Haram M, *Temples and Temple Service in Ancient Israel*, (Eisenbrauns, Winona Lake, Indiana, 1985).

Hess H, *The Canons of Serdica 343 A.D. A Landmark in the Early Development of Canon Law* (Clarendon Press, Oxford 1958)

Helmholz RH, *Canon Law and the Law of England*, (Hambledon Press, London, 1987).

Hillar M and Allen CS, *Michael Servetus: Intellectual Giant, Humanist and Martyr*, (University Press of America, Lanham Maryland, 2002).

Holden A, *Jehovah's Witnesses: Portrait of a Contemporary Religious Movement*, (Routledge, London and New York, 2002).

Holdsworth WS, *A History of English Law*, 2nd ed., (Little Brown and Co., Boston, 1923).

Keating D, *Catholic Commentary on Sacred Scripture, First and Second Peter, Jude*, (Baker Academic, 2011).

Lasker DJ, *Jewish Philosophical Polemics against Christianity in the Middle Ages*, (Littman, Portland, Oregon, 1977).

Leithart PJ, *Defending Constantine: The Twilight of an Empire and the Dawn of Christendom*, (Intervarsity Press, Downers Grove, IL, 2010).

MacCulloch D, *Thomas Cranmer*, Yale University Press, (New Haven and London, 1998).

Maimonides, *Mishnet Torah* (12th century).

Marius R, *Thomas More, A Biography*, Harvard University Press, (Cambridge Massachussetts and London England, 1984).

Milsom SFC, *Historical Foundations of the Common Law*, (Butterworths, London, 1969).

More H, *An Explanation of the Grand Mystery of Godliness*, (Flesher and Morden, London, 1660).

Ochs C, *Matthaeus Adversos Christianos: The Use of the Gospel of Matthew in Jewish*

Polemics Against the Divinity of Jesus, (Mohr Siebeck e-book, 2013).

Ormerod N, *A Trinitarian Primer,* (St Paul's Publications, Australia, 2010).

Pate CM, *From Plato to Jesus: What Does Philosophy Have to Do with Theology",* (Kregel Academic and Professional, Grand Rapids, Michigan, 2011).

Plucknett TFT, *A Concise History of the Common Law,* 5th ed., (Butterworths, London, 1956).

Pollock Sir F & Maitland FM, *The History of English Law,* 2nd ed., (Cambridge University Press, 1968).

Rives S, *Did Calvin murder Servetus,* (BookSurge Publishers, Charleston, South Carolina, 2008).

Roberts A and Donaldson J eds., American edition arranged and referenced by Coxe AC, *Ante-Nicene Fathers, The Writings of the Fathers Down to 325AD,* (Hendrickson Publishers, 2004).

Rodkinson ML transl., *The Babylonian Talmud,* (1918).

Rotelle JE ed., introduction, translation and notes, Hill E, *The Works of Saint Augustione, The Trinity,* (New City Press, New York, 1991).

Scarry E, *The Body in Pain,* (Oxford University Press, 1985).

Schwab M transl, *The Talmud of Jerusalem,* (Williams and Norgate, Covent Garden, England 1886).

Schaff P, *Creeds of Christendom, with a History and Critical Notes,* (Harper and Brothers, New York, 6th ed., 1931).

Schaff P, ed., *Nicene and Post-Nicene Fathers: Series II, Volume XIV (The Seven Ecumenical Councils),* Hendrickson Publishers, Peabody, Massachusetts, 1994).

Servetus, M, *Christianismi Restitution,* 1553

Setzer C, *Jewish Responses to Early Christians* (Minneapolis: Fortress Press, 1994).

Smedley E, Rose HJ and Rose HJ eds., *Encyclopedia Metropolitana,* (Rest Fenner, 1822-1845).

Smith, Mark S., *God in Translation: Deities in Cross-Cultural Discourse in the Biblical World,* (William. B. Eerdmans, Grand Rapids, Michigan, 2010).

Smith MS and Miller PD, *The Early History of God: Yahweh and the Other Deities in Ancient Israel,* (Wm. B. Eerdmans Publishing, 2002).

Sommer BD, *The Bodies of God and the World of Ancient Israel,* (Cambridge University Press, 2009).

Tacitus, *Germania*.

The Church of Jesus Christ of Latter-day Saints, *The Book of Mormon: Another Testament of Jesus Christ*, (Salt Lake City, Utah, 1981, originally published, EB Grandin, Palmyra, New York, 1830).

The Church of Jesus Christ of Latter-day Saints, *The Doctrine and Covenants*, (Salt Lake City, Utah, 1981).

Turner WEH, *The Pattern of Christian Truth*, (London, 1954).

Whitehead KD, *A Short Guide to Ancient Heresies* (e-book < http://www.ignatiusinsight.com/features2005/kwhthd_ancntheresies_july05.asp>).

Wilbur EM, *Our Unitarian Heritage: An Introduction to the History of the Unitarian Movement*, (Beacon, Boston, 1925).

Zagorin P, *How the Idea of Religious Toleration Came to the West*, (Princeton University Press, 2003).

Internet Sources

Aish Rabbi, <http://www.aish.com/atr/Let-Us-Make-Man.html>.

Anglican Church of Canada, "The Athanasian Creed", <http://www.anglican.ca/about/beliefs/athanasian-creed/>.

"Apostles Creed", <https://www.creeds.net/ancient/apostles.htm>.

"Athanasian Creed", <http://www.theopedia.com/athanasian-creed>.

BBC, "Religions – God", <http://www.bbc.co.uk/religion/religions/unitarianism/beliefs/god.shtml>.

BBC, "Introduction to the Trinity", <http://www.bbc.co.uk/religion/religions/christianity/beliefs/trinity_1.shtml>.

Bray GL ed., *Documents of the English Reformation*, James Clark & Co, Cambridge, 1994 (<http://www.davidscottgehring.com/his361/fortytwoarticles.pdf>

Burton J, "Try This: Revelation-Driven Prayer", <http://www.charismamag.com/spirit/prayer/23637-try-this-revelation-driven-prayer>.

Constitutions and canons ecclesiastical 1603 published 1900 <https://archive.org/details/constitutionscan00lond>.

Carr KE, "Constantine's Conversion", < http://quatr.us/religion/christians/constantine.htm>.

Catechism of the Catholic Church, <http://www.vatican.va/archive/ccc_css/

archive/catechism/p1s2c1p2.htm>.

Channing WE, "Unitarian Christianity", <http://www.transcendentalists.com/unitarian_christianity.htm>.

Chapman J, "Eusebius of Nicomedia." The Catholic Encyclopedia. Vol. 5. New York: Robert Appleton Company, 1909.21 Jun. 2019 <http://www.newadvent.org/cathen/05623b.htm>.

Chellew-Hodge C, "Why LBGT-friendly Church is not Christian enough", <http://religiondispatches.org/lgbt-friendly-church-is-not-christian-enough/>.

Christianity Today, "Constantine" <http://www.christianitytoday.com/history/people/rulers/constantine.html>.

Clark MT, *"De Trinitate"* in *The Cambridge Companion to Augustine*, <https://www2.bc.edu/~blackta/Master's%20Comps/DeTrinitateSummary.pdf>.

Dave, "How do Christians and Jehova's witness differ?", <http://christianity.net.au/questions/how_do_christians_and_jehovas_witness_differ>.

DiMaio M Jr., "Licinius (308-324 A.D.)", *De Imperatoribus Romanis*, 1997, < https://www.roman-emperors.org/licinius.htm>.

Encyclopedia Britannica eds., <https://www.britannica.com/biography/Licinius>.

Gelasius of Cyzicus <https://www.catholic.org/encyclopedia/view.php?id=5037>.

"Great Schism", <https://www.theopedia.com/great-schism>.

Grondelksi JM, "Scott Hahn Explains the Creed" <http://m.ncregister.com/daily-news/scott-hahn-explains-the-creed#.WHGL_rGr1sN>.

Hagen JR Jr, <http://americamagazine.org/issue/575/article/real-story-council-nicea>.

Harmon SR, "Do Real Baptists Recite Creeds?", <http://ecclesialtheology.blogspot.com/2010/10/do-real-baptists-recite-creeds.html>.

Herboso E in < http://peopleof.oureverydaylife.com/greek-philosophy-christian-theology-5507.html>.

Heiser M, < https://www.logos.com/academic/bio/heiser>.

Heiser M, < http://www.thedivinecouncil.com>.

Heiser M, < http://www.twopowersinheaven.com>.

Heiser M, < http://drmsh.com/the-naked-bible/>.

Heiser M, <http://lehislibrary.files.wordpress.com/2009/08/divinecouncil-1.pdf>.

Jehovah's Witnesses, "Are Jehovah's Witnesses Christians?", <https://www.jw.org/en/jehovahs-witnesses/faq/are-jehovahs-witnesses-christians/>.

Jehovah's Witnesses, "Do Jehovah's Witnesses Believe in Jesus?", <https://www.jw.org/en/jehovahs-witnesses/faq/believe-in-jesus/#?insight[search_id]=bd6ff6da-cc34-4415-9eac-6a6d88a93805&insight[search_result_index]=1>.

Jehovah's Witnesses, "In What Way Are Jesus and His Father One?", <https://www.jw.org/en/publications/magazines/wp20090901/way-jesus-and-father-one/>.

Jehovah's Witnesses, "Jehovah's Witnesses – Who Are We?", <https://www.jw.org/en/>.

Jennings DR, "Constantine the Great, Letters in chronological order", <http://www.constantinethegreatcoins.com/Constantine/Book2.html>.

Johnson B, "How do I receive a revelation?", <http://bjm.org/qa/how-do-i-receive-revelation/>.

Kiefer JE, <http://justus.anglican.org/resources/bio/175.html>.

Lebreton, Jules. "St. Justin Martyr." The Catholic Encyclopedia. Vol. 8. (New York: Robert Appleton Company, 1910), 21 Jun. 2019 <http://www.newadvent.org/cathen/08580c.htm>.

Living Hope (Lutheran) Church, "Athanasian Creed", < https://livinghopeomaha.com/about-living-hope/about-living-hope/athanasian-creed/>.

Marlowe MD, "The Westminster Confession of Faith", <http://www.bible-researcher.com/wescon01.html>.

Miano DR, "An Explanation of Unitarian Christianity", Article VI <http://americanunitarian.org/explanation.htm>.

Miller JJ, "Why Mormons aren't Christians", < https://www.patheos.com/blogs/joeljmiller/2011/10/why-mormons-arent-christians/?repeat=w3tc%3E;%20%3C%20http://www.kencollins.com/explanations/why-07.htm>.

Morton C, "Are Jehovah's Witnesses Christian?", <https://www.exploregod.com/are-jehovahs-witnesses-christian>.

Muller RA, Book Review < https://muse.jhu.edu/article/261905>.

Nathan NA, "The Trinity according to Origen" < http://dlibrary.acu.edu.au/research/theology/gus_nathan.htm>.

New World Encyclopedia eds, <http://www.newworldencyclopedia.org/entry/First_Council_of_Nicaea>.

"Nicene Creed", <http://www.earlychurchtexts.com/public/nicene_creed.htm>.

O'Brien FW, "Why Not Appoint Counsel in Civil Cases? The Swiss Approach", 28 *Ohio State Law Journal* (1967) 1 < https://kb.osu.edu/dspace/bitstream/handle/1811/68838/OSLJ_V28N1_0001.pdf>.

Okolie AC, "Introduction" to the Special Issue of *Identity*, "Now You Don't see It; Now You Do" < http://dx.doi.org/10.1207/S1532706XID0301_01>.

Parsons JJ, "Theology and the Greek mindset, A brief exploration", < http://www.hebrew4christians.com/Articles/Hellenism/hellenism.html>.

Prayer Book Society, "The Creed Sung as a Psalm", <http://www.pbsusa.org/wp-content/uploads/2016/07/2004-09-10.pdf>.

"Reformation History, The Westminster Assembly" <http://reformationhistory.org/westminsterassembly.html>.

Roberts RE, *The Theology of Tertullian*, 1924, 22-23 < http://www.tertullian.org/articles/roberts_theology/roberts_01.htm>.

Servetus M, *De Trinitatis Erroribus*, Book VII <http://godglorified.com/errors_of_the_trinity.htm>.

Sewell M, "The Theology of Unitarian Universalists", <https://www.huffpost.com>.

Shook J, "Religion and Xenophobia", < https://centerforinquiry.org/blog/religion_and_xenophobia/>.

Slick M, Christian Apologetics and Research Ministry (CARM), "Is the Jehovah's Witness religion Christian?", < https://carm.org/is-the-jehovahs-witness-religion-christian>.

Socrates Scholasticus' Ecclesiastical History, <http://www.documentacatholicaomnia.eu/03d/0380-0440,_Socrates_Scholasticus,_Historia_ecclesiastica_[Schaff],_EN.pdf>.

Stanford Encyclopedia of Philosophy, "St Augustine", < https://plato.stanford.edu/entries/augustine/>.

Sullivan J, "The Athanasian Creed." The Catholic Encyclopedia. Vol. 2. New York: Robert Appleton Company, 1907. 21 Jun. 2019 <http://www.newadvent.org/cathen/02033b.htm>.

The Church of Jesus Christ of Latter-day Saints, "Global Church Benefits All People and Nations", <https://www.churchofjesuschrist.org/prophets-and-apostles/unto-all-the-world/global-church-benefits-all-people-and-nations?lang=eng&_r=1>.

The Church of Jesus Christ of Latter-day Saints, "Prayer and Personal Revelation", < https://www.churchofjesuschrist.org/youth/topic/prayer-and-personal-revelation?lang=eng>.

Thurston H, "Apostles' Creed." The Catholic Encyclopedia. Vol. 1. New York: Robert Appleton Company, 1907. 21 Jun. 2019 <http://www.newadvent.org/cathen/01629a.htm>.

Tuggy D, "Unitarianism", *Stanford Encyclopedia of Philosophy* <https://plato.stanford.edu/entries/trinity/unitarianism.html>.

Unitarian Universalist Association, "The Seven Principles", <http://www.uua.org/beliefs/what-we-believe>.

Uttinger G, <http://chalcedon.edu/research/articles/christianity-101-the-theology-of-the-ancient-creeds-the-procession-of-the-spirit/>.

Van Zuiden J, "Why so many Protestants do not consider Catholics Christian", <https://streetevangelization.com/blog/2013/03/03/why-so-many-protestants-do-not-consider-catholics-christian/>.

Varghese P, "5 Keys to Receiving a Revelation From God", <https://pastorpriji.com/blog/life-principles/revelation-from-god/>.

Warfield BB, "Calvin's Doctrine of the Trinity", *Princeton Theological Review,* vii (1909) 553, < https://www.monergism.com/thethreshold/sdg/warfield/warfield_calvintrinity.html>.

Wedgeworth S, *The Calvinist International* < https://calvinistinternational.com/2012/05/02/is-there-a-calvinist-doctrine-of-the-trinity/>.

White JR, < http://www.equip.org/article/what-really-happened-at-nicea/>.

Wiki, "English versions of the Nicene Creed", <https://en.wikipedia.org/wiki/English_versions_of_the_Nicene_Creed>.

Zaley K, *The Restitution of Jesus Christ: Servetus the Evangelical,* 2008 <http://servetustheevangelical.com/doc/ServetusFromBook.pdf>.

Zevallos, Z. (2011) 'What is Otherness?,' *The Other Sociologist*, 14 Oct, <https://othersociologist.com/otherness-resources/>.

Zwinglius Redivivus, "Peter Caroli: Everyone has one", <https://zwingliusredivivus.wordpress.com/2010/12/28/peter-caroli-everyone-has-one/>.

INDEX

Abinadi – 160, 162

Abraham – 20, 21, 27, 50, 52-54, 59, 60, 77, 91

Adoptionism – 70, 148

Ahura Mazda – 29, 32, 34

Alexander, Bishop of Alexandria – 87-89, 92, 97, 99, 102, 106, 107, 111. 114, 119, 150, 153, 173, 179, 185, 187, 193

Amenophis IV, Pharoah – 2, 3, 173

Amulek – 161, 162

anachronism – 58, 60

Anglican Church – 4, 8, 136-139, 143-145, 147

aniconism – 27, 30, 31

anthropomorphism – 3, 14017, 20, 22, 26, 27, 29-31, 42, 144, 158, 163, 168, 174, 180, 181

Apostles' Creed – 112, 139, 140, 143

Aquinas, Thomas – 123, 124

Aristeas – 36

Arianism – 70, 88, 89, 94-97, 100-103, 107-111, 115, 119-122, 125

Arius – 81, 84, 88, 94, 95, 99-102, 106-108, 110-115, 118, 119, 129, 150, 153, 171, 173, 176, 179, 180, 185, 187

Asherah – 23, 24, 26, 174

Assmann, J – 35, 36

Athanasian Creed – 112, 118, 129, 130, 138, 140, 141, 143, 150

Athanasius, Bishop of Alexandria – 75, 84, 98, 102, 115, 120, 121, 129, 173

Auerbach, Leo – 37, 38

Augsburg Confession – 139, 178

Augustine of Hippo, Saint – 4, 44, 118, 121-125, 132, 133, 163, 168, 177

Australian Constitution – 9

autobiography – 6

Autolycus – 55, 57, 80

Ayres, Lewis – 95, 99, 108, 111, 118, 123,176

Baal – 25, 26

Babylonian Talmud – 27, 37-40

Baptist – 4, 8, 139, 178,182

Barth, Karl - 133

bias – 7, 144

Bible – 1, 15-19, 22-24, 26, 30, 38, 147, 156, 157, 160

Biliniewicz, Marius – 9

Book of Common Prayer – 139

Book of Mormon – 154, 157, 159-163, 168

bronze serpent - 31

Brueggerman, Walter – 16

Bull, Bishop – 67, 79

Caiaphas – 49

Calvin, John – 133, 135, 136, 145-151, 153, 155, 156, 178

Canaanite religion – 15, 23-26

Cappadocians – 62, 65, 75

Caroli, Peter – 150, 151

Carroll, Warren H – 93

Catholic Church – 8, 10, 46, 72, 92, 128, 131, 135, 144, 145, 147, 148, 150, 151, 155, 157, 163, 178, 181, 182

Chalcedon Creed – 112

Channing, William Ellery – 156, 158, 159

Charlemagne - 132

Chazan, Robert – 48

Christology – 84, 94, 96, 156

Clark, Mary T – 118, 123, 124, 133

Cleary, John – 8

Clement of Alexandria – 44, 50, 55, 57-61,

203

71, 73, 79-81, 175

coercion – 8

Congregationalist – 4, 139, 178

conscience – 9, 10, 149, 156

Constantine, Emperor – 2, 5, 71, 83-103, 105-115, 117-120, 122, 123, 125, 126, 129, 131, 136, 149-151, 162, 164, 166-169, 171-173, 176, 177, 179, 180, 183, 185

Constantinople Creed – 111, 112, 122, 125, 140, 176, 177

Council of Constantinople (381 A.D.) – 71, 86, 112, 118, 123, 129, 172, 177

Council of Serdica (342 A.D.) – 198, 109, 121

Coxe, A. Cleveland – 60, 71, 77

Cranmer, Thomas – 4, 44, 133, 135-139, 143-145, 151, 152, 158, 163, 168, 172, 178, 180

Cross, Frank Moore Jr – 26

Cyrus – 32, 34

David, King – 14, 26, 29, 40

Davies, Philip R - 27

De Moor, Johannes – 24, 32, 33

Defender of the Faith - 137

De fide orthodoxa - 108

De Principiis – 72, 74

De Trinitate - 76, 123

deuteronomizers – 31

Dibb, Andrew MT - 148

Dickson, John – 8

Dionysius of Rome – 79, 81

Distinction personarum – 109, 121

Divine Council – 3, 14, 23-25, 27, 29, 30, 32, 33, 40, 71, 85, 174, 175

Doctrine and Covenants - 163

Easter – 83, 101

Economic Trinitarianism – 68, 73

Edelman, Diana – 27, 31-33, 35

Edict of Milan – 83, 86-88

Edward VI, King – 135-137, 151, 178

Eichrodt, Walter - 16

El – 24-26, 30, 42

Elizabeth I, Queen - 137

Elizabeth II, Queen - 54

Elohim – 14, 20, 22, 25, 30, 32, 174

Emery, Gilles – 125-128, 133, 147

Episcopal Church of America - 139

Eusebius, Bishop of Caesarea – 89, 95, 96, 100-102, 119, 120, 189

Eusebius, Bishop of Nicomedia – 89, 94, 95, 98, 101, 102

Eustathius, Bishop of Antioch – 92, 95, 101, 102

Eustathius, Bishop of Beroea – 89

Evangelical Christians - 155

Ezekiel – 17, 20

filioque clause – 3, 111, 118, 125, 130-133, 140, 141, 144, 153, 158, 169, 172, 178

Forty-Two Articles – 135-137, 151, 163, 178, 180

Gerstenberger, Erhard – 15

Gideon – 21, 32

Givens Terryl – 139, 156, 157, 159, 160, 162, 178

Grant, Robert M – 88-97, 99-103, 106, 107, 119

graven image – 30

Gregory of Elvira – 108, 117, 121, 177

Gregory of Thaumaturgus – 45, 78, 79, 81

Grudem, Wayne - 133

Hadrian, Pope - 132

Hagar - 53

Handy, Lowell K – 27

Hanson, RPC – 122, 176

Haran, Menahem – 17

Harvey, William - 146

Heiser, Michael S – 23-25, 30, 32
Hellenism – 23, 32, 69, 124
henotheism – 13, 173
Henry VIII, King – 133, 135-137, 151, 178
Hezekiah – 31
Hill, Edmund – 121, 124
Hippolytus – 45, 73-77
homoousios – 84, 96-100, 103, 105-109, 111, 113-115, 118-122, 149, 173, 176
hypostases – 81, 108, 109, 121, 125, 147
Incarnation – 17, 48, 55, 123, 142
interfaith cooperation – 8, 154, 158, 173
Iraeneus – 45
Isaac – 53, 59
Isaiah – 20, 26, 48
Jacob – 21, 22, 50, 54, 77
Jehovah – 26
Jehovah's Witnesses – 4, 153, 154, 157, 163-169, 180
Jerome – 72
Jerusalem Council (circa 50 A.D.) – 129
Jerusalem Talmud – 27, 38-41, 45, 55, 174
Jesus of Nazareth/Jesus Christ – 3, 7, 9, 12, 43-52, 54, 59, 60, 64, 65, 67, 68, 74, 76, 77, 79, 80, 82, 85, 100, 105, 110, 111-115, 128, 130, 140, 142-144, 148, 151, 154-156, 158, 159, 163-168, 171, 172, 175, 176, 180, 182, 183
John, Apostle – 11, 49, 51, 73, 96, 100, 113, 115, 159, 162
John of Damascus, Saint – 126
Joseph, in Egypt - 160
Joshua – 26, 32, 50, 54,
Judaism – 8, 13,15, 36, 43, 45, 46, 49, 58, 85, 172-174, 183
Julius, Bishop of Rome - 120
Justin Martyr – 44, 49-55, 57, 71, 72, 75, 80, 175

Kasher, Rimon – 17
Kaye, Bishop – 67
Kelly, JND – 111, 122
knowledge by revelation – 5, 62-68, 125-129
International Covenant on Civil and Political Rights (ICCPR) – 9
Latter-day Saints (see also, The Church of Jesus Christ of Latter-day Saints) – 4, 7, 153, 154, 157-160, 162, 163, 166-168, 180
Leo III, Pope - 132
Levenson, Jon – 14, 15, 18
Levering, Matthew – 126, 127, 133
Licinius – 83, 86-88, 90, 91, 93, 94, 102, 106
Luther, Martin - 147
Macarius, Bishop of Jerusalem - 92
Maimonides – 17, 18, 47
Maitland, Frederic William - 19
mal'akh – 14, 21, 22
Marcellus of Ancrya – 108-111, 117, 120, 121, 177
Marcion – 67, 69, 71, 88
Mary, mother of Jesus – 7, 141, 143, 155
Mary, Queen – 135, 137
Maxentius - 86
Mercury – 35
Messiah – 40, 43-45, 47-49, 52, 160, 172, 175
Mesopotamian religion –12, 15, 23
Methodism – 4, 8, 136, 139, 151, 178
Metrophanes, Bishop of Constantinople – 92
mia hypostasis – 108, 109, 121
monolatry – 13, 173
monotheism – 6, 13, 14, 23, 26, 30-34, 36, 39, 42, 43, 46, 48, 49, 83, 85, 172, 173, 183

Mormons (see also The Church of Jesus Christ of Latter-day Saints) – 9, 152, 154, 157

Morris, Paul – 7, 10

Moses – 21, 26, 30-32, 43, 45, 46, 52, 54, 160, 174, 175

Muller, Richard – 146-148

Narcissus of Neronias - 120

Nathan, NA – 72-75

Nebridius - 123

Needham, Nick - 132

Nicaea, council of – 1-5, 50, 61, 70, 74, 77, 81-87, 89, 90, 92, 93, 96-99, 101, 102, 106-111, 114, 117-123, 129, 136, 144, 149, 151, 152, 164, 168, 169, 171-173, 176, 177, 179, 183

Nicene creed – 2-4, 9, 59, 67, 71, 75, 97, 98, 100, 103, 105, 106, 108-113, 115, 117-123, 125-128, 133, 136, 138, 140, 143, 145, 147, 149-151, 153-155, 157-160, 162-164, 166-169, 171-173, 180, 182, 183

Novatian – 45, 76, 77, 126

Ochs, Christoph – 47, 48

Okolie, Andrew - 181

one substance – 44, 45, 64, 66, 82, 107, 108, 110-115, 122, 126, 138, 140, 142, 163, 166-168, 172, 175, 176

Onesimus - 179

Origen – 44, 61, 71-75, 78, 81, 82, 108, 109, 175

Ormerod, Neil – 123-125

Ossius, Bishop of Cordoba – 84, 88-93, 96-101, 105-107, 114, 118-120, 171, 173, 176, 179

passibility of God - 139

Pate C. Marvin – 49, 53

Paul, Apostle – 11, 12, 45, 49, 51, 78, 96, 100, 160, 179

pantheon – 30, 33, 36, 85, 174

Petavius - 67

Peter, Apostle – 11, 45, 47, 51, 129

Peterson, Daniel C – 26

Philemon – 179

Philo – 36

Plato – 57, 58, 72, 73, 81

Plucknett, Theodore – 19

Pollock, Sir Frederick – 19

polytheism – 3, 19, 22-24, 26, 27, 31, 32, 35, 42-44, 46, 47, 49, 50, 52, 69, 71, 80, 81, 85, 114, 153, 157, 175

physiomorphic – 30, 174

Praxeas, against - 63, 65, 68, 69

Presbyterianism – 136, 139, 151

Prodicus – 67, 69, 71

Puritans - 139

Quinlan, Michael – 7, 10

Rabbi Akiba – 39

Rabbi Bar-Kapara – 39

Rabbi Isaac - 41

Rabbi Samlai – 40, 41, 55

Rees, LaBouff, Rowatt, Johnson and Finkle - 182

resurrection – 11, 12, 15, 44, 113, 138, 141, 143, 164

resurrected body – 10-12, 43, 144, 151, 163, 166, 168, 174

Richard of Saint Vector - 126

Roberts, Robert E – 62-65, 67, 68

Romney, Mitt – 8

Rufinius - 72

Rule of Faith – 62, 63, 65, 73

Sabellius – 76, 78, 79-81, 109, 121, 148

Sarah - 53

Scarry, Elaine – 16

Schaff, Philip – 105, 111, 112, 176

schism – 4, 77, 93, 94, 131-133, 153, 172, 177-179, 187, 188

Schmidt, Brian B – 27, 30-32

scriptural understanding – 9, 10, 20, 68, 96, 113, 123, 124, 136, 144, 145, 148, 156, 159, 167, 177

SEIROS – 8

Sermon on the Mount – 46

Servetus, Michael – 132, 135, 136, 145-152, 155, 178

Shook, John – 181, 182

Six Articles of Faith – 136, 137

Smith, J Warren - 123

Smith, Mark S – 35

social trinitarianism – 126, 127

Socrates - 51

sola scriptura – 136, 14, 147, 150, 152, 154, 155

Solomon, King – 14, 29, 31

Sommer, Benjamin – 14-27, 30, 32, 37, 174

Stark, Rodney - 153

Stead, Christopher - 98

Stephen – 45

subordination of the Son – 50, 68, 75, 99, 112, 157, 158, 168, 175

Tacitus – 35

Tarasios, Eastern Patriarch - 132

Tatian – 64, 71

Tertullian – 9, 44, 50, 61-74, 81, 82, 96, 108-110, 113-115,, 118, 121, 149, 168, 172, 175

The Church of Jesus Christ of Latter-day Saints – 4, 7, 153, 158

Theodosius, Emperor – 118, 122, 177

Theophilus – 44, 50, 55-57, 80, 175

theriomorphic – 30, 174

Thirty-Nine Articles – 135, 136, 178

Thomas, Apostle – 11, 12, 174

Thompson, Thomas L – 27, 33-35

Three Witnesses to the Book of Mormon - 162

Titus - 51

Torah – 17, 38

Transcendentalism - 156

Trinity – 1-5, 7, 8, 43-45, 49, 50, 55-58, 60, 61, 63, 65-82, 84, 96, 100, 112, 117, 118, 120, 121, 123-133, 135, 136, 138, 140-142, 144-147, 149-153, 155-159, 164, 166, 167, 172, 175, 183

Trinity, a mystery – 66, 68, 127, 157

Trypho, Dialogue with – 49, 50, 52-55, 80, 175

Tuggy, Dale – 156, 157

Ulrich, Jorg – 96, 98, 107-109, 119-121

una substantia – 73, 109, 121

Unitarians – 4, 136, 148, 150, 153-159, 163, 167, 180

University of Notre Dame Australia – 7, 8

upper room – 11, 12

Valentinus – 76, 69, 71, 97

Vicentia, presbyter representing the Bishop of Rome - 119

Victor, presbyter representing the Bishop of Rome - 119

virgin – 48, 54, 60, 63-65, 138, 141, 143

Von Harnack, Adolf – 68

Voss, Gerard – 129

Warfield, Benjmain Breckenridge – 150

Welch, Sikkink and Loveland - 181

Wesley, John - 139

Westminster Confession of Faith – 4, 135, 136, 139, 144, 151, 154, 163, 178

Whyshogrod, Michael – 48

Wilbur, Earl Morse – 132, 135, 148-150

without body, parts or passions – 4, 138, 139, 143, 151, 168

Yahweh – 12, 14, 24-26, 29-34, 42, 174

Zeezrom – 161

Zevallos, Z, 181

www.ingramcontent.com/pod-product-compliance
Ingram Content Group UK Ltd.
Pitfield, Milton Keynes, MK11 3LW, UK
UKHW041305180426
11947UKWH00009B/697